A Taste
of the Wild

A.J. McClane

A Taste of the Wild

A Compendium of Modern American Game Cookery

PHOTOGRAPHY BY DONNA TURNER

TRUMAN TALLEY BOOKS

DUTTON

NEW YORK

DUTTON
Published by the Penguin Group
Penguin Books USA Inc., 375 Hudson Street,
New York, New York, 10014, U.S.A.
Penguin Books Ltd, 27 Wrights Lane,
London W8 5TZ, England
Penguin Books Australia Ltd, Ringwood,
Victoria, Australia
Penguin Books Canada Ltd, 10 Alcorn Avenue,
Toronto, Ontario, Canada M4V 3B2
Penguin Books (N.Z.) Ltd, 182–190 Wairau Road,
Auckland 10, New Zealand

Penguin Books Ltd, Registered Offices:
Harmondsworth, Middlesex, England

First published by Truman Talley Books • Dutton, an imprint of New American Library,
a division of Penguin Books USA Inc.
Distributed in Canada by McClelland & Stewart Inc.

First printing, December, 1991
10 9 8 7 6 5 4 3 2 1

LIBRARY OF CONGRESS CATALOGING-IN-PUBLICATION DATA
McClane, A. J. (Albert Jules), 1922—
A taste of the wild : a compendium of modern American game cookery
/ A.J. McClane.
p.   cm.
"Truman Talley books."
Includes bibliographical references and index.
ISBN 0-525-93346-8
1. Cookery (Game)   I. Title.
TX751.M43   1991   91-8005
641.6'91—dc20   CIP

Printed in the United States of America
Produced by Blaze International Productions, Inc.
Designed by Robert Reed

For Diane
and the good days past and future from
Maine to Montana

Masters of the Game

Nobody understands game cookery better than the chef who has spent years afield hunting the foods that represent this discipline. The majority of recipes in this book were created by friends who not only are professionally skilled in the culinary arts but, equally important, are by avocation sportsmen. Although game has long been a menu favorite with our family, especially when entertaining guests, most of the dishes we enjoy are not the author's inventions. Few of the recipes in this book, however, have ever been published or even reduced to notes. In most cases they had to be worked out in the chef's various restaurant kitchens or in our own kitchen at home.

In no particular order of gratitude I have to thank Alain Jorand, who started his career in Reims, France, and then moved to Germany and Africa before returning to La Chaumière as sous-chef. He eventually arrived in Palm Beach Gardens, where he now presides at St. Honoré, one of the most outstanding restaurants in Florida.

Cyrille Wendling began in the famed restaurant Auberge de I'll in Alsace (one of the traditional hunting provinces of France), then went on to Restaurant Paul Bocuse before an award-winning career in Canada and eventually becoming executive chef at La Vielle Maison in Boca Raton, at present the only five-star restaurant in the southeastern U.S.

Another great kitchen talent, Norman Van Aken, rose to stardom as executive chef at Sinclair's American Grill, then later honchoed Louie's Backyard in Key West, Florida.

A member of the Master Chefs Institute, his book *Norman Van Aken's Feast of Sunlight* (Ballantine Books, 1988) is as much a philosophy about cuisine as it is a cookbook.

Jeff Summerour has won many awards since his appointment as executive chef at the Sheraton Hotel in Charleston, South Carolina; however, his current role of managing six kitchens and three restaurants as executive chef for the PGA National Resort in Palm Beach Gardens seems like a mind-boggling next step. His signature restaurant, The Explorers, is a game-oriented oasis.

Looking west, we have J. Alex Jaramillo from New Mexico by way of the Hyatt Regency of Dallas, Texas, and presently executive chef at the Tamarron Resort near Durango, Colorado. Chef Jaramillo also supervises three restaurants, and the signature room is Le Canyon, where venison and buffalo dishes are among his many award-winning originals.

Another master of the game with whom I've spent many days afield and in the kitchen, Jay Bentley, now operates the Continental Divide Restaurant in Ennis, Montana. Chef Bentley first wore his toque at Louis XVI in New Orleans, then migrated to Cafe Lafitte in Miami before the call of Montana's wild inspired a solo enterprise that has been a phenomenal success. In the deep snows of winter, Bentley is a corporate cooking consultant who lectures throughout the United States.

New England is not without some great game chefs such as George Carone and Francis Clogston, who preside at Hemingway's Restaurant in Killington, Vermont. Hemingway's is a 130-year-old renovated farmhouse owned by Ted and Linda Fondulas, where dining is an ultimate experience. Older still is The Inn at Sawmill Farm in West Dover, Vermont. It dates back two centuries. Owners Rodney Williams, wife Ione, and son Brill combine their talents to make it "one of the twelve most perfect hideaways in the world" according to *Travel and Leisure* magazine. Chef Brill's offering for a November game dinner encompassed sautéed quail, breast of woodcock, braised rabbit, sliced pheasant, and roast venison—an incredible parlay right to the winning *tarte tatin*.

The fact that people actually drive a hundred miles or more to dine with Georgia Miller at the Elk Lake Guest Ranch in the middle of the Red Rock Lakes National Wildlife Refuge in Montana would qualify her for Mobil's four stars (which all of the mentioned chefs have earned), if any investigator could survive the last forty miles of bad road. An avid sportswoman and former television talk show host, executive chef Miller does wondrous things with game of all kinds.

Also on the distaff side, Romi Perkins, whose husband, Leigh, owns the Orvis Company in Manchester, Vermont, is no amateur in the field or the kitchen. Romi has journeyed around the globe with rod and gun, and her book *Game in Season* (Nick Lyons Books, 1986) is based on years of devotion to properly cooked fish and game.

I also want to thank some of my gourmet hunting friends who contributed suggestions, criticisms, and even game birds when our freezer was bare: Leonce Picot, Lou Gainey, Jim Kimberly, Marilyn Watkins, Russel Thornberry, Arthur Oglesby, Sam Clements, Dan Kleiser, Henri Bealem, Francis Cheong, John Phillips, Peter Verstappen, Jeffrey Vandow, and Tom McNally.

Contents

A Taste
of the Wild

INTRODUCTON

A TASTE OF THE WILD

When the first wave of Dutch settlers arrived in New Netherlands in 1620, the island of Manhattan was literally an Eden of game birds and animals. Passenger pigeons created a feathered eclipse in their earth-darkening flights; ducks, geese, and brant rafted in quacking and honking legions along what is now Pearl Street (the original waterfront) to the Battery; heath hens scampered in the meadows around what would become Washington Square; snipe, plover, and curlews rose in speckled clouds from the Kips Bay and Turtle Bay marshes; whitetail deer, bobcats, wolves, black bears, and wild turkeys roamed the oak and chestnut forests north of Fifty-Fifth Street, and mountain lions stalked the elk from granite ledges along the Hudson shore east to Harlem. Fat cabbage-patch rabbits, soon to be triggered northward by the agrarian advance of man, were so abundant on one island to the east that it was identified by the cottontail's Dutch name, *coney.* Manhattan was then bisected from south to north by a moccasin-rutted trail called the Broad Way Indian Path. This path was crossed by crystalline trout streams with "divers remarkable waterfalls tumbling down from lofty rocks"—on a modern numerical grid they would be found at Seventeenth, Twentieth, Forty-Second, and Fifty-First streets. Here brilliantly crowned wood ducks took their baths like portly Persian satraps, while grouse and woodcock ghosted through nearby alders. Although the Dutch had little previous experience with game as a food, one settler, David de Vries, observed: "Nothing is wanted but good marksmen with powder and shot."

On the opposite side of the Hudson, Mahlon Stacy wrote (*The History of New Jersey*, 1680), "As for venison and fowls, we have plenty; we have brought home to our houses

Overleaf: A flock of snow geese in flight.

by the Indians, seven or eight fat bucks of a day and ten or twelve turkeys." In Stacy's kitchen, cooking of any kind was a restricted art form; the wood-burning cooking stove was still more than a century away, and meals were prepared on indoor fireplaces using iron pots attached to cranes by S-shaped hooks or trammels that could regulate their height over the coals. Hearty game "stewes" and roasted meats were common fare in hearthside cookery. And nobody went by a book.

During the three centuries following the first printed cookbook (*Platina's De Honesta Voluptate*, published in 1475), writing about food encompassed such disparate topics as how bears cohabitate, how to draw an arrowhead out of a wound (good to know if the chef burned the venison chops), the temptations of the master in dallying with servant maids, or "distemper got by an ill husband" (apparently a hangover) and health warnings, such as that dining on sparrows stimulates lust. (This did nothing to discourage the popularity of roasted sparrows.) Hannah Glasse's *The Art of Cooking Made Plain and Simple*, published in 1747, was to some extent a diatribe on the immorality of French domestics of the female sex, rather than the virtues of their cuisine. Although game cookery appeared in hand-drafted manuscripts by the ancient Greeks and Romans, these "recipes" continued to be truncated well into the eighteenth century, without any clue as to quantities of ingredients—or the chef's intent. The reader might be instructed to stew a partridge with "copious herbs and spices," then told to add a touch of mace to help prevent colic and body fluxes, or ginger to prevent heartburn. In the pharmacopoeia of the day, a belief that sassafras cured syphilis may have inspired a wide use of filé powder; still, the popularity of these aromatic leaves in making gumbos has never diminished. When the first American cookbook—Amelia Simmons's *American Cookery* (earlier books were English in origin though they carried American imprints)—was published in 1796, there were not enough actual recipes in circulation to suggest the scope of the settler's groaning board.

The appetites of the colonists are better reflected in the Schuylkill Fishing Company of Pennsylvania, established in 1732, the oldest gourmet society in existence. (Although some European clubs predate it, none has survived 259 consecutive years.) Sending an "official warrant" to its members, Thomas Streech, the company's governor in 1744, directed: "WHEREAS, great quantities of rabbits, squirrels, pheasants, partridges, and others of the game kind, have presumed to infest the coasts and territories of Schuylkill [a tributary of the Delaware River] in a wild, bold and ingovernable manner; THESE are therefore to authorize and require you, or any of you, to make diligent search for the said rabbits, squirrels, pheasants, partridges and others of the game kind, in all suspected places where they may be found, and bring the respective bodies of so many as you shall find. . . ." Gourmet society aside, game remained a subsistence food for the early settlers as they trekked northward in the Appalachians. For example, the Pennsylvania of Philip Tome in 1786 was both an idyllic and a savage land. The Tome family ventured ninety miles up the Susquehannah River by keel boat from where Harrisburg is now located and remained at Farris Creek for about four months, "when the Six Nations of

Indians began to trouble the inhabitants." After prudently moving south again and being "distressed" by the Indians for eighteen months, the Tomes finally returned upriver near the mouth of Pine Creek and built a home in the wilderness. Elk, bears, whitetail deer, and wild turkeys were plentiful, as were wolves and mountain lions, and for thirty years the family lived off the land (*Pioneer Life or Thirty Years a Hunter*, published by Philip Tome in 1854). Elk were so abundant along Kettle Creek, Young Woman's Creek, Trout Run, and Pine Creek that Philip often found herds of forty or more feeding on river mosses—stags that stood "sixteen hands high at 500 to 600 pounds." Tome left no record of food preparation beyond the making of "jerky," but in the tradition of Platina he described various remedies for rattlesnake bite, evidently a very common problem at that time, including a poultice of red onions, salt, and gunpowder.

Never in American history was the consumption of game more fashionable (or closer to its nadir) than in the late nineteenth century, when "lobster palace" society ruled New York's kitchens. The ubiquitous lobster was the titular antecedent of what was to become known as café society. Seafood of all kinds at Delmonico's, Rector's, the Waldorf, Sherry's, the Savoy, and Holland House was merely a prelude to the triadic form of a medieval banquet when fish, fowl, and game were presented in endless sequence. This became a contest when a *gross bonnet* like Charles Ranhofer of Delmonico's (Ranhofer's work, *The Epicurean*, published in 1893, is the best of various Delmonico books and offers a view into the past in providing recipes for such a legendary food as the passenger pigeon) or Oscar Tschirky of the Waldorf came under the influence of gold-plated nabobs—J. Pierpont Morgan, Henry Frick, Jay Gould, Stanford White, John "Bet-a-Million" Gates, Randolph Guggenheimer, and James Buchanan "Diamond Jim" Brady—who dictated mind-boggling menus for 200 or 300 guests. A $10,000 game dinner with the garde-manger standing on a stanchion like a traffic cop, directing fifty chefs as they sautéed 600 snipe in 93-score butter with the team precision of the Harlem Globe Trotters—before turning a hand to the next nine courses—was a culinary assault without parallel. The prerequisite caviar (it was a give-away item in the sawdust-floored beer halls of New York when free lunches were in flower and frequently oversalted to inspire a greater thirst) was often followed by smoked brook trout, Maryland terrapin, a casserole of plover, robins, curlew, rail, and pigeon, then a rabbit *gibelotte* before the roast of canvasback duck, which primed the palate for a saddle of mountain sheep with chestnut puree. Between porcine grunts, a torrent of vintage Champagnes and grand cru Burgundies dispelled any guests' vapors or collywobbles. But the skein of this wild tapestry unraveled for many reasons—for which we are all permitted a grateful burp.

By the mid–twentieth century, because of man's anthropomorphic tendency to see birds and animals as having human characteristics (but blind to the four billion factory-farmed creatures annually killed by the livestock industry to support our American protein requirements), the hunting of game became a volatile social issue in both the Old World and the New. The protracted maundering of the anti group has no factual basis in terms of modern conservation policies and practices. The tremendous increase in big-game herds and in many game birds during the last sixty years is due largely to the American sportsman, whose hunting license fees and various special taxes reaping billions of dollars go to support wildlife management programs. However, this book is not a morality tale—although ignorance and greed are part of the record. Today game can be bought at local supermarkets, from specialty butchers, or simply by stalking it with a credit card in the growing field of mail order. It may not always be a true taste of the wild, but that's another story . . .

The use in this volume of scientific names for various animals and fowl may seem out of place in a cookbook, but for accurate reference it is the only reliable nomenclature we have, as market names and common names in different languages can sometimes be misleading. The relationships of various game by family and genera can also be better understood (as, for example, the similarity between the Scotch grouse and our willow ptarmigan, or the European or New Zealand red deer being identical with our American elk). Some game distributors now include scientific names in their client's literature, which is valuable information, as an increasing number of exotics are being imported from Europe, such as the recent marketing of the capercaillie, hazel grouse, black grouse, and wood pigeon. Scientific names are universally recognized, and this greatly simplifies kitchen research for the serious chef with an adequate library.

The Meat Thermicator: Internal temperature is the key to cooking game successfully.

1. THE SECRET OF GAME COOKERY

Each year some nineteen million Americans blow the moths out of their gun barrels and sally forth to harvest a bounty of wild game for the table. This invariably opens a floodgate of recipes for quadruped and fowl that, while often succulent in concept, usually lack the most important instruction—the ultimate temperature of the meat. Those cryptic phrases "cook for 45 minutes or 1 hour at 350°F" and, parenthetically, that wondrous disclaimer "until the meat is fork-tender" have been the downfall of many amateur chefs. For that matter, there is a plethora of expense account restaurants with game specialties where the *toque blanche* should be drummed from his kitchen in a square-wheeled tumbril.

Wild game of any kind is a very lean meat. It offers a galaxy of superlative flavors, from the mildly nutlike ruffed grouse to the pungent woodcock—so aromatic that in the old days real devotees wore huge napkins over their head and plate to savor the escaping steam. Do not confuse game flavor with "gamy," that deplorable condition that comes from improper field dressing—or from prolonged aging. All game is lower in cholesterol than domestic meats, higher in protein and calcium, lower in calories, and free of chemicals and additives. Its great virtue, that it's not buffered by excess fats, poses one culinary problem, and the presence of highly contractile muscle and sinew another. A teal that wings over the marshes at forty-five miles per hour does not equate to a fattened barnyard muscovy that couldn't flap a tail feather, and a whitetail deer that leaps over eight-foot-high deadfalls has little in common with a factory-farmed veal that will never walk a step in its brief life. For these reasons you cannot be casual about what is rare, medium, or well-done. Anybody with minimal experience can eyeball a beefsteak on the grill and be reasonably confident, even have enough time to finish a martini, but a wild duck breast or a saddle of venison cooks from rosy perfection to overdone quicker than you can singe a quizzical eyebrow.

The most critical factor in game cookery is arriving at the correct internal temperatures. For my palate, dark-meated birds such as woodcock, snipe, dove, ptarmigan, blue grouse, sharptail grouse, Hungarian partridge, prairie chicken, and any wild goose or duck should be pink in the center of the breast—a tender and juicy state at 140 to 145°F on a meat thermometer. In white-meated birds, notably quail, ruffed grouse, pheasant, chukar partridge, and wild turkey, the juice will run clear at 145 to 150°F, and the meat will be firm, moist, and at peak flavor. Transposing the tests for doneness in domestic birds, which is common in a panicked kitchen when our nimrod arrives home clutching a Canada goose, is disastrous. At the standards in modern cookbooks—180 to 185°F for chicken or turkey and 190°F for goose or duck—any comparable game bird is virtually incinerated.

The legs and wings of most wild fowl are tough and stringy. Finger-testing an old tom gobbler, brant, or mountain quail for doneness by domestic instruction (when its legs can be moved up and down easily) is an exercise in frustration. You may find pen-reared birds from game farms that will wiggle their limbs, but I long ago decided that these hyperactive parts are merely decorative at table. It is the breast, with which game birds are liberally endowed, that provides 90 percent or more of the edible meat. However, when the legs and wings are excised along with the neck, giblets, and remaining portions of the carcass, you have the basis of a unique stock that can be turned into an ambrosial gravy, a velvety Sauce Veneur or Sauce Bordelaise. Don't hesitate to combine venison bones and goose legs or grouse carcasses with wild turkey wings—they all marry into a fragrant nectar that in days of plenty can be stored in pint-size plastic freezer containers.

With venison, which collectively includes the most popular big-game antlered animals such as moose, caribou, whitetail and blacktail deer, mule deer, and elk, the secret lies in some work with a knife. Except for that choice cut, the saddle, you must remove as many of the visible tendons as possible. These elastic sinews contract under heat and toughen the meat. They can be excised with a sharp pointed blade. I find venison most enjoyable at 135 to 140°F, while it is still pink at the center; it is blood-rare at 130°F, medium at 150°F, and well-done (for my taste, beyond repair) at 160°F. Wild boar and feral hogs are safely cooked at 137°F, the standard for domestic pork, at which point it is medium-rare, but at 145°F it is moist and tender.

If you depend on time and temperature cycles when cooking game, remember that oven dial settings are subject to error; thermostats are often 50 to 100 degrees off, even at some professional test kitchens I've worked in. An oven thermometer helps, but chambers do have "hot spots," and the only direct answer is a meat thermometer. The ordinary kind with its short, spikelike insert has limitations; a cheap one may not give you an accurate reading, or may give no reading at all in small birds, and it is tricky to use when pan sautéing or charcoal broiling or when making a quick check on a casserole.

I use a hand-held Meat Thermicator, a somewhat expensive thermocouple with a long retractable needle that gives instant readouts in targets as minuscule as the golf-ball-size breast of rail or an inch cube of venison. For the serious kitchen, game or otherwise, it's well worth the investment.

A pair of felled snow geese on the ice.

2. AGING AND FREEZING GAME

There is no question that all game meats are improved by being stored for a short period of time in a controlled environment at low temperatures to become more tender and flavorsome. However, the ancient tradition of hanging game, or the practice of *faisander*, as once described by that French gourmet Grimod de la Reynière, would discourage most diners; indeed, it would send them reeling from the table: "A pheasant should be suspended by its tail, and eaten when it detaches itself from this incumbrance. It is thus that a pheasant hung on Shrove Tuesday is susceptible of being spitted on Easter Day." Personally, I have no taste for a pheasant after three weeks of mortification at room temperature, when it plops to the floor by its own weight. In feather, I would keep a bird in the refrigerator no more than one week, and when plucked, no more than four days. Admittedly, intense flavors in products of any kind can be immensely satisfying, whether a heady Limburger cheese, or that ultimately sweet wine, Chateau D'Yquem, or even the Swedish version of fermented fish, *surströmming*, which after four months has been known to blow the lid off a barrel. But prolonged aging is out of character for game, particularly when in a state of near rot. The very thing that sets wild meats apart from the domestic kind is their unique flavors, which are lost in overaging and never developed in underaging. This is not a question solely of elapsed time from the killing to the cooking but of *how* the product is aged. As a general rule for all plucked game birds, three days in the refrigerator is enough aging before cooking or freezing. I freeze quail, dove, grouse, duck—any bird up to the size of a pheasant—in tightly lidded plastic containers filled with water. Sealed in ice, there is no chance of freezer burn, no loss of flavor, and their shelf life can be up to one year at a constant temperature. However, for the average hunter, the game that presents the most controversy and also the most spoilage is the deer.

I had my first taste of venison when I was a youngster working on a dairy farm in the Catskill Mountains, back in the 1930s. During those years of the Great Depression, rabbits, squirrels, and woodchucks were an almost monotonous diet for many farm families, especially woodchucks during the spring season when they consumed our cauliflower—an important cash crop—about as fast as we planted it. My employer, Evan Todd, killed a fine whitetail deer that fall, which he hung in the barn. I don't know what Evan knew about aging venison, but it seemed to me that the buck, field-dressed in hide, was becoming a permanent ceiling fixture. Typically, at that time of the year the weather was reasonably warm by day but cold at night, with ambient temperatures dropping to the low twenties before dawn. It's probable that the meat was alternately freezing solid, then thawing, and being in hide just added to the problem. By the time Evan got around to skinning the deer, and his wife cooked it, I decided it was the worst food I had ever tasted.

Since then I have sampled numerous barn- and garage-aged venisons (there are not many places you can safely hang a 200- or 300-pound animal) from Maine to British Columbia and have come to the conclusion that the sooner a deer is completely dressed and delivered to the freezer, the better the quality of the meat. Hanging venison for more than twenty-four hours, or sufficient time for the meat to cool and be butchered, is unnecessary. Portions to be soon eaten, other than those to be frozen, can be held under refrigeration (ideally at 36°F) for a week to ten days. If you have access to a commercial meat locker, and these are scattered across the country in rural areas, where the deer can be butchered, quick-frozen, and properly wrapped, it is well worth the cost. Much of the dogma about aging game originated in the era before refrigerators and freezers were common household appliances. The fact that venison slowly tenderizes to perfection while in a frozen state was once demonstrated by the Meatcutters Institute in a comparison tasting with venison that had been hung under the most ideal conditions for up to thirty days.

3. Marinades
and Sauces

Many years ago there was a restaurant on Fifty-Second Street in New York, just a short distance from our old *Field & Stream* office, that was totally dedicated to a game menu. However, the establishment had a short career. At one visit I had an authentic venison ragout, and at a subsequent dinner, listed under the same name, apparently mutton that had been marinated in red wine and gin with crushed juniper berries. This is an ancient ploy. The cubes of "venison" were striated with fat, which no animal of the deer kind is able to develop. I suppose the chef also faked it as bear meat, as that uncommon item was listed frequently, and I'm sure it was often in short supply. The point is that when aged long enough in a marinade any meat will taste so strongly of the liquid ingredients that the integrity of the product is completely lost.

A good marinade should enhance flavor, not overpower it. Bear in mind that marination is not generally an essential procedure. Doves and quail, for example, certainly don't require it; but when they are held overnight in a bath of Chablis, then sautéed in butter and the pan deglazed with the marinade, which is reduced to a third, you have a sauce that fairly sparkles of dove or quail flavor and a bird that is all the more succulent. Only certain game meats need marination, such as an antelope roast, the meat of a pronghorn, which becomes very dry in cooking, or the ham of a wild boar that has gone to tusk (old boars have an overly porcine flavor). However, even prime cuts of other game can be made all the more tender and tasty with the judicious use of a liquid or dry marinade. In my experience, the best liquid recipes contain either salt or soy sauce, plus an acidic ingredient such as lemon, lime, or orange juice, vinegar, or wine, or a com-

The delicate nutlike flavor of pheasant is enhanced by a variety of well-made sauces.

bination of these acids to penetrate and tenderize the meat. They also require an oil of some kind to lubricate and prevent the meat from drying out. The use of aromatics in the marinade, such as chopped vegetables, herbs, mustard, ginger, paprika, garlic, juniper berries, or citrus skins, presents many rewarding options. A dry marinade consists of salt, herbs, and spices such as powdered ginger or paprika, which can be rubbed into the meat—which is particularly applicable when doing stews and casseroles.

Some old European cookbooks suggest marinating game for as long as ten days, at which point it must be predigested. Generally speaking, six hours at room temperature or overnight in the refrigerator is sufficient for small cuts or delicately flavored meats. Longer periods, from four to seven days, may be required to tenderize and flavor large roasts, particularly from old animals. It is not necessary to completely cover the meat with marinade, provided it is rotated often enough so that the entire surface can absorb the liquid. However, it is essential to use a glass or ceramic container, as metal of any kind reacts to acids and produces a very unpleasant flavor. For very large roasts, or whole animals such as a wild pig, I use a big plastic kitchen garbage bag; the meat can be turned easily when the bag is tied off. Remember, many marinades may also be used for basting during the cooking process or incorporated into a sauce or gravy.

As with marinades, sauces are not essential to the enjoyment of the natural goodness of game meats. I have often broiled wild birds and chops in a hinged grill basket over hardwood coals, getting them crusty and smoky, and eaten them out of hand (which somehow benefits the ambience of a pine-scented forest) with no other seasoning than a sprinkle of salt and pepper. However, a plain duck breast or venison chop is one experience, but at a candlelit dinner party, the former served with a silky Sauce Framboise and the latter with a spicy Sauce Poivrade is quite another. I think part of the reason that some backwoods iconoclasts object to sauces is the "sauce" itself. The common practice of many sporting camps of adding flour and milk to oily pan drippings is at best a mucilaginous gravy and at worst indigestible. Yet it would be sinful to waste the rich juices from an elk or moose roast when they can be added to a brown sauce, alias Sauce Espagnole—probably the most versatile of all sauces in the game kitchen.

The quality of the wines used in making sauces and marinades will definitely influence the end product. When wines are used in cooking, with the application of heat the volatile alcohol becomes evanescent and only the flavor remains. The finer the wine, the better the flavor. It is self-defeating to use so-called "cooking wines" or wines that have turned to vinegar just to save a dollar. Obviously a classic label is not required, but you should cook with a wine that you would enjoy drinking, and it need not be expensive. A good California jug wine under the generic Burgundy, or the Pinot Noir, cabernet sauvignon, and zinfandel varietals are eminently suitable when a red wine is required. The same is true of Chablis, which is accepted as a generic in America (the true French Chablis is a varietal made from the Pinot Chardonnay grape), whenever a dry white wine is required. In my opinion, the best of the French reds for sauces and marinades are the robust and spicy wines of the southern Rhône, under the appellations of Gigondas and Côtes-du-Rhône (I will eliminate Châteauneuf-du-Pape from that region as it is too pricey to cook). There are hundreds of labels on the market from various Rhône vineyards that are consistently inexpensive yet very drinkable. If Madeira is called for in a recipe, avoid the sweet ones. Madeira, like sherry and port, is a fortified wine that ranges from very dry in the form of Sercial (less than 2 percent sugar) to very sweet Malmsey (6 to 9 percent sugar). These brown wines begin life as light red wines or *vinho claro*, but through a long process of ''baking'' and aging they change color and develop that unique burnt caramel flavor that enhances sauces. Madeira is sweetened according to its label designation, and for purposes of cooking I prefer Verdelho, a medium-dry wine such as the popular Rainwater Madeira. Among sherries I avoid the sweet *oloroso* category, although they are delightful by the glass, and use a nutty and dry *amontillado* such as Pedro Domecq's La Ina.

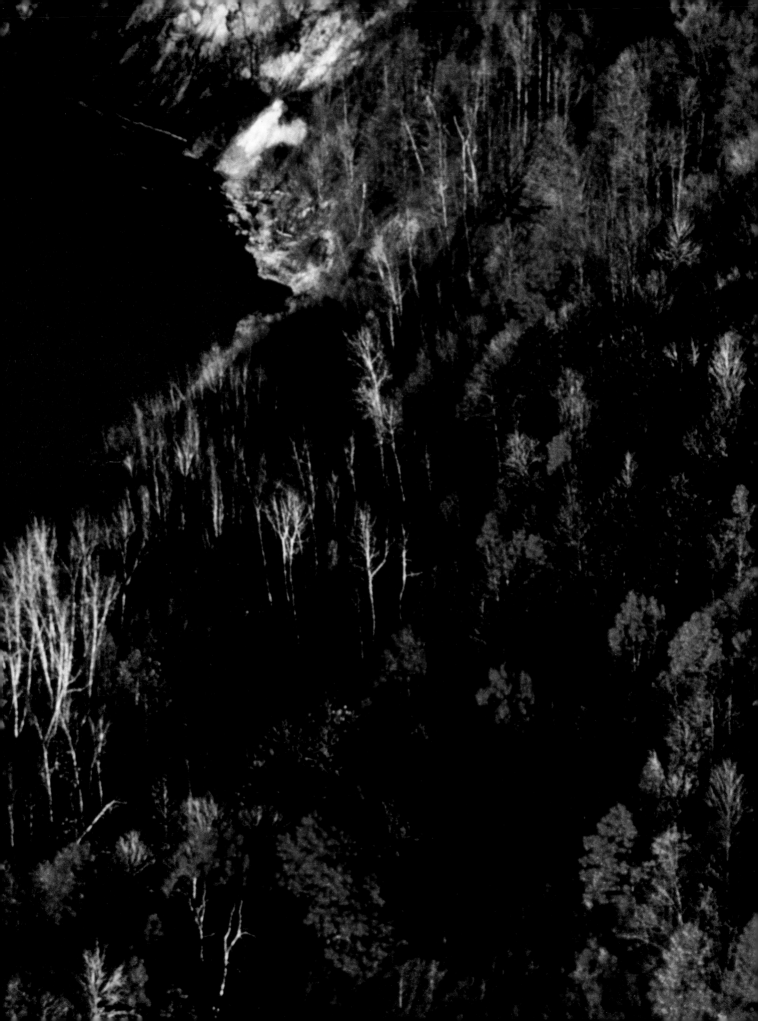

MIREPOIX BORDELAISE

Prepare this mirepoix just before you need it for flavoring sauces or braises. For some recipes, especially for braising, 2 tablespoons chopped ham, salt pork, bacon, or fresh pork rind may be added to impart more flavor. The fresh pork rind will add some gelatin.

2 carrots, 6 to 7 ounces
      total
2 onions, 6 to 7 ounces
      total

2 tender celery ribs
3 fresh parsley sprigs
1 fresh thyme sprig *or* ½
      teaspoon dried
1 small bay leaf
2 to 3 tablespoons butter or
      oil

Scrub and scrape the carrots, peel the onions, and wash and dry the celery, parsley, and fresh thyme. Chop the fresh ingredients into pieces no larger than ¼ inch; this may be done in a food processor fitted with the steel blade. Crumble the bay leaf and dried thyme (if you use it) into the mixture. Heat 2 tablespoons of the butter in a heavy saucepan. Stir in the vegetable mixture and simmer over moderate heat for 15 to 20 minutes. Shake the pan or stir with a wooden spatula to prevent sticking or burning. If necessary, add the remaining tablespoon of butter or oil. If the vegetables are browning too fast, reduce the heat to low.

SAUCE ESPAGNOLE

(CLASSIC BROWN SAUCE)

MAKES 2 QUARTS

This rich, flavorful sauce requires some time to prepare. However, it can be frozen in 1-cup and 2-cup containers, so it is worthwhile to make a large amount.

ingredients for double recipe of Mirepoix Bordelaise (see Index)

2   leeks
½   cup (¼ pound) butter, clarified
1   cup all-purpose flour, sifted
4   quarts strong clear Game Stock (see Index) or veal stock
1   bouquet garni
1   pound very ripe tomatoes
2   cups dry white wine

Prepare a double recipe of the mirepoix vegetables, but omit the bay leaf and thyme. Add the leeks, carefully washed and chopped. Melt the butter for the mirepoix in a heavy pan and simmer the vegetables, stirring occasionally, for 15 minutes, until tender and golden.

In a separate pan, melt the clarified butter. Sprinkle in the flour and stir. Set the saucepan over low heat and cook, stirring, until the mixture forms a brown roux. Pour in 3 quarts of the stock, whisking well, and add the mirepoix. Stir over moderate heat until the mixture comes to a boil. Add the bouquet garni. Reduce the heat to a low simmer and cook the sauce for at least 1 hour (2 hours is better), skimming often. The sauce should be reduced, and the process of skimming should have removed most of the fat globules and any scum.

Meanwhile, blanch, peel, and seed the tomatoes and chop them. After the sauce has been cooked and skimmed, add the tomatoes and the white wine. Let the sauce simmer for another hour, skimming when necessary.

Strain the sauce into a wide shallow container and stir it until it is cool. Store in the refrigerator overnight.

The next day, lift off any fat that remains. Scrape the sauce into a large saucepan and pour in the remaining quart of stock. Simmer the sauce for another hour, skimming often. The sauce should be reduced to about 2 quarts. Serve the sauce or again pour it into a wide shallow container and stir until cool. Refrigerate or freeze.

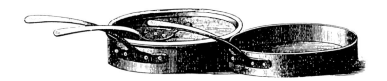

SAUCE POIVRADE
(FOR GAME)

The characteristic of this sauce is the peppery taste blending with that of the various aromatics and made piquant by the vinegar. It is important, however, not to use excess pepper. It must be added to the sauce only at the last minute. Allowed to cook for a long time, pepper develops an acrid taste. A small amount, added at the end of the preparation of a dish, produces a better result than a large quantity put in at the beginning.

ingredients for ½ recipe
Mirepoix Bordelaise
(see Index)
½   **cup mushroom peelings**
       (optional)
game trimmings
½   **cup white wine vinegar**
½   **cup dry white wine**

2   **cups Sauce Espagnole**
       (see Index)
2½   **cups Game Stock (see**
       Index)
5   **peppercorns, crushed**
2   **tablespoons unsalted**
       butter

Prepare the ingredients for the mirepoix. If you wish, add the mushroom peelings. Cook the mixture in butter or oil as directed in the mirepoix recipe. Chop the game trimmings into ¼-inch pieces. When the vegetables are soft, add the game trimmings and continue to simmer the mixture until everything is cooked and golden brown. Pour in the vinegar and wine, stir well, and bring the mixture to a boil. Reduce to a simmer and cook for about 1 hour or until the liquid

is reduced by half. Stir in the Sauce Espagnole and 2 cups of the stock. Bring the mixture to a boil, then simmer for 1 to 1½ hours. Stir occasionally and skim as needed. Add the crushed peppercorns and simmer for 5 minutes longer.

Pour the sauce through a fine strainer into a clean saucepan, pressing well on the solids to release all the juices into the sauce. Add the remaining ½ cup stock. Simmer for about 10 minutes longer, then strain again.

Return the sauce to the pan and bring it to serving temperature. Cut the butter into small pieces and add them, one at a time, to the sauce, swirling in each piece by gently moving the pan. As soon as the last piece of butter is melted, serve the sauce. The butter thickens the sauce slightly and makes it glossy.

GAME STOCK

MAKES 4 QUARTS

4 to 5 pounds deer, elk, moose, or other animal bones, sawed or cracked into 2- to 3-inch pieces, and/or 1 or more game bird carcasses to make up the total weight (see Note)
2 large onions, unpeeled and halved
2 large carrots, cut into chunks
½ cup vegetable oil
6 quarts water
1 bay leaf
2 teaspoons salt
1 teaspoon black peppercorns
2 celery ribs, including tops
1 teaspoon dried thyme *or* 3 fresh sprigs
4 fresh parsley sprigs
2 leeks (white part only)

In a large stockpot, place the bones, onions, and carrots in the oil and cook over medium heat. Let the bones brown and the onions and carrots blacken. Do not burn the bones. The burned onions and carrots will give an amber color to the stock. Add the water and remaining ingredients. Bring to a boil, then lower the heat and skim any scum that forms on the surface. Simmer for about 3 hours, uncovered, until about 4 quarts of liquid are left. Strain through a fine sieve and let cool. Remove any fat from the top. May be kept frozen in small plastic containers and used as needed.

Note:

If no game animal bones are available and you are using bird carcasses only, substitute veal or beef bones.

SAUCE DEMI-GLACE

MAKES ABOUT 3 1/2 CUPS

This rich sauce is used as a basis for many brown sauces, such as bordelaise, chasseur, and madère.

1   quart Sauce Espagnole
     (see Index)

1   quart strong clear Game
     Stock (see Index) or
     veal stock
½   cup dry Madeira

Mix the sauce and stock together in a heavy saucepan and simmer over low heat for at least 1½ hours, skimming often. Pour the mixture through a fine sieve into a clean saucepan. Bring to serving temperature and stir in the Madeira. The sauce should be reduced by half and should be smooth and shiny. It will give a glossy coating to foods.

SAUCE MADÈRE I

(MADEIRA SAUCE)

MAKES ABOUT 2 CUPS

2   cups Sauce Demi-Glace
     (see Index)
¼   cup dry Madeira
2   tablespoons unsalted
     butter

Bring the sauce to serving temperature and stir in the Madeira. Cut the butter into small pieces and add them, one by one, to the sauce, letting each piece melt before adding the next. Shake the pan to blend, but do not stir.

Sauce Madère II
(Madeira Sauce)

MAKES ABOUT 3 CUPS

½ pound mushrooms
2 shallots
¼ cup butter
salt and pepper to taste
1 quart Sauce Espagnole
    (see Index)
¾ cup dry Madeira
2 teaspoons minced fresh
    parsley

Wipe the mushrooms with a damp cloth and trim the base of the stems. Chop the mushrooms. Peel and mince the shallots. Melt the butter in a heavy saucepan and sauté the mushrooms and shallots until tender and golden brown. Season with salt and pepper. Stir in the sauce and simmer the mixture over low heat until reduced by a third. Pour the mixture through a fine sieve into a clean saucepan, pressing on the mushrooms to release all the juices. Bring the sauce to serving temperature; stir in the Madeira and the parsley.

GLACE DE VIANDE
(MEAT GLAZE)

MAKES ABOUT 1 QUART

3   carrots, ½ pound total
3   onions, ½ pound total
1½ cups chopped celery ribs
      and leaves
8   pounds game and veal
      bones with some meat
1   bouquet garni

Preheat the oven to 450°F.

Scrape the carrots and peel the onions. Cut 1 carrot and 1 onion into thick slices. Chop the remaining carrots and onions and combine with the chopped celery. Put the game and veal bones in a large roasting pan with the sliced carrot and onion. Brown them in the oven, stirring occasionally. When the bones are well browned and the vegetables almost caramelized, turn the whole mixture into a large heavy stockpot and add the chopped vegetables. Deglaze the roasting pan with water and add the deglazing to the stockpot. Pour in enough water to fill the pot—5 to 6 quarts. Bring to a boil, reduce to a simmer, and let the liquid cook for about 20 hours.

Ladle the mixture through a colander into a clean kettle. Discard all the solids in the colander. Return the liquid to low heat, add the bouquet garni, and continue to simmer, stirring and skimming often. When the liquid is reduced by half, pour it through a fine sieve lined with a triple layer of moistened cheesecloth. Transfer the liquid, which will be syrupy, to a clean heavy saucepan and set it over an asbestos pad to prevent scorching. Continue to simmer, skimming as needed and stirring often with a wooden spatula, until the glaze is very thick, like a jam. Pour the glaze into small containers or into a shallow cake pan. The glaze will become firm as it cools. If you have poured it into a cake pan, turn it out when cold and firm and cut into small cubes. Pack them individually in plastic bags and store in the refrigerator or freezer.

TRUFFLE SAUCE

MAKES ABOUT 1 CUP

¼ cup butter
4 shallots, minced
⅛ teaspoon black pepper
⅔ cup dry red wine
⅓ cup Sauce Demi-Glace
(see Index)
¼ teaspoon dried thyme
¼ teaspoon dried chervil

¼ cup cognac
salt and pepper to taste
3 tablespoons minced
truffles

In a skillet, melt the butter and sauté the shallots until transparent. Add the ⅛ teaspoon pepper, wine, Sauce Demi-Glace, thyme, and chervil. Simmer until the liquid is reduced by a quarter. Add the cognac, salt, and pepper. Stir and continue cooking until slightly thickened. Add the truffles and heat for about 1 minute. Serve with any game bird or meat of your choice.

SAUCE FRAMBOISE

MAKES 2 1/2 TO 3 CUPS

Sauce Framboise is ideal with the breast meats of ducks, geese, doves, and woodcock that are to be broiled or pan sautéed. For this purpose, marinate the breasts in raspberry vinegar for 6 to 8 hours and add the marinade to the broth; any loss in volume (½ cup) can be compensated for with additional vinegar.

1   tablespoon butter
1   tablespoon finely
      chopped shallots
1½ tablespoons arrowroot
½   cup raspberry vinegar
1   cup chicken broth
1   8-ounce box frozen
      raspberries (with
      sugar), thawed

In a saucepan, melt the butter. Add the shallots and sauté until soft, then sprinkle with arrowroot. Add the vinegar and broth and simmer until thickened. Add the raspberries to the sauce and continue simmering until warmed. Sauces thickened with arrowroot reach their maximum density at 160 to 175°F, and further heating causes thinning, so do not overheat.

GRAPE SAUCE

MAKES ABOUT 1 CUP

This sauce is especially good with white-meated birds such as quail and pheasant and rich, dark-meated birds such as woodcock, dove, and ptarmigan.

½ cup sugar
1½ cups water
2½ pounds white, green, or
     red seedless grapes

1 teaspoon chopped
    shallots
1 cup dry red wine
1 teaspoon cognac
1 tablespoon heavy cream

Dissolve the sugar in the water in a saucepan to make simple syrup. Poach ½ pound of the grapes in the syrup for 5 minutes or until the grapes are plump and tender; reserve. Squeeze or process the remaining grapes to make 1 cup strained juice.

In a saucepan, combine the shallots, red wine, and extracted grape juice and simmer over low heat until the liquid is reduced by half. Stir in the cognac and cream and simmer for about 2 minutes.

To serve, sprinkle the game bird with poached grapes and reheated sauce.

4. WOODCOCK

In praising the woodcock, Brillat-Savarin, who obviously devoted most of his life to dining at hallowed tables, observed that "the mouth waters in anticipation of delight." That is an understatement. I drool over my L. L. Bean boots. It has few peers in the game kitchen. Presumably the author of *La Physiologie du goût* (*The Physiology of Taste*) was including both his native *bécasse* and the smaller American woodcock, because he spent several years on our shores, during which period he hunted for and cooked everything from squirrel to wild turkey.[1] It is unfortunate that woodcock, unlike quail and pheasant, are not amenable to pen rearing. There is a sporadic and minor source of supply in American markets originating from Sweden, but ordinarily they must be collected in the wild. You can take to the woods anywhere from the Maritime Provinces of Canada to Louisiana and all over the eastern half of the United States and hunt in coverts that make a Marine boot camp obstacle course look like an infant's playpen. Typically these dense stands of birch and alder, booby-trapped with bogs and briers, are so thick that a flushed bird must spiral upward before going full throttle into a twisting flight. Aside from their sprained ankles, ripped underwear, and dogs that go back to the car in disgust, woodcock hunters are notorious for shooting down treetops. This annual ritual, which I have attended since my first springer spaniel trusted me with a loaded

---

[1] Not a professional chef but a lawyer from the French Alps, Jean-Anthelme Brillat-Savarin (1755–1826) spent most of his life in Paris. His book, published shortly before he died, is still the bible of epicures. Among his aphorisms: "Tell me what you eat: I will tell you what you are."

A golden retriever waiting patiently for the hunt to begin.

gun, occurs from October through January as the migratory birds travel from north to south. On the British Isles the best shooting is found in Ireland. Birds from all of Scandinavia migrate via Denmark and Great Britain and concentrate on the Emerald Isle in tremendous numbers during the month of October.

The woodcock is a member of the family Scolopacidae, belonging to one of the three subfamilies, which includes the snipe. There are six woodcock species, the American woodcock (*Scolopax minor*), the European woodcock (*S. rusticola*), and four others of remote culinary interest on the islands of Southeast Asia, Sumatra, Java, New Guinea, the Celebes, the Moluccas, the Japanese Ryukyu Islands, and the southern Kuril Islands. Woodcock are normally migratory within their own continental limits, but European stragglers have been found as far west as Ohio and as far south as Alabama after a long period of westerly winds. Both the American and European woodcock are important game birds, with a harvest of 1.7 million annually in North America and in excess of three million in Europe; only a few European countries compile harvest data, but the first accurate survey in France (1976), where the total had previously been estimated at 200,000 birds, revealed a kill of 1.5 million in that country alone.

Although the woodcock was seemingly little appreciated in ancient Greece and Rome (at least not on the level with flamingos' tongues and ostriches' brains), it was considered a great delicacy during the medieval period, when migrating birds were netted in their evening flights, providing the synonym for twilight, "cockshut" time. The earliest description of woodcock shooting in the New World appears in *The Sportsman's Companion* (anonymous, 1783), which was the first American publication on hunting game birds. According to William G. Sheldon in his definitive work *The Book of the American Woodcock* (The University of Massachusetts Press, 1971), "The woodcock came into its own as a game bird a decade or two before the Civil War, and the shooting records of the sportsmen and market hunters of that time indicate an abundance of birds unknown to modern hunters." A number of technical books have been written about the life history and hunting of woodcock, but few reflect the joys of eating them, and none to the extent of Guy de la Valdene's *Making Game* (Willow Creek Press, Oshkosh, Wisconsin, 1985). Valdene's 202-page essay is not a cookbook, as "making" is used in a sporting sense, yet his detailed descriptions of dining on woodcock are in the best tradition of Brillat-Savarin.

The woodcock is a strange bird. For one thing, its ears are located ahead of its eyes, probably to listen for earthworms, which it digs out with its long bill. Its throat passage terminates in a rudimentary stomach; some cookbooks tell you to remove the gizzard, but the bird doesn't have one, so don't bother looking. (It does have an unusually long, coiled intestine, which innocent chefs throw away; but in European kitchens this is a delicacy known as the *trail*. It's finely chopped and seasoned with salt, pepper, grated nutmeg, and lemon juice, then sautéed in butter and spooned onto toast points.) And to confound ornithological order, the breast meat of a woodcock is dark and the leg meat is white.

In his *Larousse Gastronomique*, Prosper Montagné outlines thirty-three recipes for woodcock. Not to demean Holy Writ, some of these instructions strike me as being professional exercises, such as the *Bécasse aux Huitres à l'Ancienne*, wherein the bird is stuffed with oysters in a thick velouté sauce based on a concentrated fish stock. Despite my passion for both fish and game, I can't relate the wonderfully robust flavor of a woodcock to oysters *à la crème*. It reads like a misalliance looking for a cause. Over the years I've noticed that in European restaurants (which are legally supplied with woodcock by syndicate shooters) most recipes are basically simple: the birds are roasted, grilled, or served in a casserole. Père Bise[2] in Talloires, France, does an incredibly good *pâté froid de bécasse*, but a true lover of woodcock asks only that the bird be tender and juicy.

In the American kitchen one must be very careful in using recommended cooking times given in European recipes. The American woodcock is often only half the size of its Old World relative. The average weight of our native bird is six to seven ounces, while the average in Europe is about twelve ounces with individual woodcock exceeding eighteen ounces. So bear in mind that the number of birds suggested in my recipes can be reduced by half if you are buying imported woodcock at the market. Before I ever saw the European species, it was with subsequent embarrassment that I ordered three *morkulla* at the Stads Hotell in Karlshamn, Sweden. Although the waiter looked puzzled, he probably assumed that I had an infinite stomach capacity (after a day of pike fishing on the cold Baltic my appetite *was* honed), but what arrived after the prerequisite gravlax was a sufficiency suitable for that infamous Louis—birds that weighed about ten ounces each. Court diarists tell us that Louis XIV would have considered this a mere appetizer as the Sun King, who employed both François Pierre de la Varenne as his chef and the Marquis de Béchamel as his steward, thought nothing of devouring over a hundred oysters before commencing on the *bécasse*.[3]

---

[2] Under Marius Bise, the Auberge carried a three-star rating with the *Michelin Red Guide* for thirty-three years. Demoted to two stars after his death, it was again promoted to three stars in 1985. Marius was a hunter, and to what extent traditional game dishes will appear is unknown at this time.

---

[3] In the naturopathic practice of that era, to relieve the royal gout, Louis XIV soaked his legs in hot Burgundy, presumably a grand cru.

COOKING NOTES

The woodcock is one of the few game birds that can be served rare. Some enthusiasts believe that the only way to cook one is to fly it through a warm kitchen. I am not that dedicated, but a split woodcock wrapped with slices of bacon and cooked on glowing briquettes until the bacon chars and the meat turns pink at the center—that is to say medium-rare or a 140°F thermometer reading in the breast—is an ambrosial dish. I also enjoy woodcock done in a casserole; this moist method is foolproof for other small game birds as well, such as quail, dove, and snipe. For best results, I prepare the dish a day or two in advance and let it sit in the refrigerator; this permits the game flavor to blossom, and it reheats beautifully.

Woodcock can be eaten the same day they are shot; however, three days of refrigerator aging in feather will find them much more tender. Most hunters skin their birds, which is a deplorable practice as those specks of fat in the skin add greatly to the flavor and it takes only a few minutes to dry-pluck a woodcock. If the bird is to be drawn, make a small cut above the vent to remove the entrails; a common European practice is to leave the birds undrawn for cooking, with the head turned under a wing. Personally, I have never found the virtue of cooking a whole undrawn bird as the interior trail still requires further cooking if the breast meat is to be on the rare side, and it's far easier to remove the plumbing of a cold bird. The head of a European woodcock provides a small brain dividend relished by Old World epicures, but its flavor escapes me. I draw my birds but reserve the heart, liver, and intestine, which can be finely chopped, then sautéed in butter and mixed with truffled foie gras, to be served separately on toast points. Roast woodcock should be cooked in a very hot oven (475°F) for ten to twelve minutes; the larger European birds require fourteen to sixteen minutes, but in either case the bird is rare at an internal breast temperature of 130°F, medium-rare at 140°F, and medium at 150°F, beyond which it loses identity.

WOODCOCK WITH COGNAC

SERVES 4

4   woodcock
½   cup (¼ pound) butter,
       approximately
½   cup cognac
salt and cayenne pepper to
       taste
lemon juice to taste

Preheat the oven to 475°F.

Clean and truss the wood-cock, stuffed with their gib-lets. Coat generously with butter and roast until still quite rare, so that when carved, the juice runs pink. Carve and set aside the breasts and thighs on a warm plate. The rest, includ-ing skin and giblets, should be chopped fine. Add to the pan. Flame with the cognac and cook over high heat until the liquid is reduced by half. Add any juice from the birds from the platter. Season and pass through a large sieve, pressing hard on the meat. Add a few drops of lemon juice to taste; heat the sauce without boiling and serve with the woodcock.

CREAMED WOODCOCK SEVILLE

SERVES 3

3   woodcock
salt and pepper to taste
½   cup (¼ pound) butter
2   cups heavy cream

Clean and truss the wood-cock. Season with salt and pepper. Place the butter in a skillet and, when hot, braise the birds well. When done to taste, drain off the juices from the skillet and reserve. Unbind the birds and keep them warm. Remove any fat left in the pan and return it to the heat. Add the cream and re-duce by half. Add 2 or 3 table-spoons of the reserved juices. Pass the sauce through a cheesecloth-lined strainer and pour it over the woodcock.

Serve immediately.

WOODCOCK STEW

½   cup vegetable oil
4   woodcock, plucked and dressed
1   cup diced lean bacon
2   medium onions, sliced thin
2   medium carrots, diced
2   medium turnips, diced
1   veal knuckle or shank bone, cracked
hot water
1   bay leaf
½   teaspoon crushed dried thyme
5   peppercorns
1   teaspoon salt
2   celery ribs with leaves, diced
2   tablespoons minced fresh parsley

½   teaspoon Worcestershire sauce
1   tablespoon tomato paste
½   cup cooked wild rice
dry sherry
4   slices French bread, toasted and buttered

In a large stew kettle, heat the oil over high heat and brown the birds on all sides. Add the bacon, onions, carrots, and turnips and cook over medium heat until all are browned. Add the veal knuckle and hot water to cover. Add the herbs and seasonings. Cover and simmer for about 1½ hours or until the birds are tender.

Remove the birds and reserve. Simmer the stew for 30 minutes more. Remove the bone. Add the celery, parsley, Worcestershire sauce, and tomato paste. Simmer until the celery is tender. Return the birds to the pot. Taste and add salt and pepper as needed. Stir in the wild rice, heat through, and serve in bowls with a dash of sherry and the toasted French bread floating on top.

Note:

Partridges, doves, or quail may be substituted, or a mixture of birds may be used.

CASSEROLE OF WOODCOCK
WITH LINGUINE VERDE

SERVES 6

I serve this casserole with buttered fiddlehead ferns. Fresh ones can be found only in the spring, but the frozen kind can be quickly heated with virtually no flavor loss.

salt and pepper to taste
12   woodcock, plucked and dressed
all-purpose flour as needed
½   cup peanut oil
1   medium onion, chopped fine
2   tablespoons butter
¼   cup dry sherry
3   tablespoons orange juice
1   tablespoon grated orange zest
1   tablespoon fresh tarragon *or* 1 teaspoon dried
3   cups Glace de Viande (see Index)
1   pound linguine verde
chopped fresh parsley for garnish

Salt and pepper the birds, then roll each one lightly in flour. Quickly brown the birds in oil over medium to high heat, preferably in a cast-iron skillet. Remove the birds from the pan and set them side by side in an ovenproof casserole. Drain the residual oil from the skillet and wipe it clean.

Preheat the oven to 300°F.

Sauté the onion in the butter until golden, then add the sherry, orange juice, orange zest, tarragon, and Glace de Viande. Stir until well blended and pour over the birds. Cover the casserole and simmer in the oven for about 50 minutes. Meanwhile, cook the linguine until al dente and drain.

To serve, place 2 woodcock in the center of each of 6 warmed plates and surround them with a ring of linguine verde. Pour the sauce over the woodcock and sprinkle with chopped parsley.

Shooting pheasant with two guns and a loader, Norfolk, England

5. PHEASANT

The pheasant that fly past the windows of my mind plane swiftly across midwestern cornfields, with the big roosters shining gold in the autumn sun, and those driven in towering flight come jinking downwind over a Scottish moor or trade low across the river at Beauly Castle and instantly disappear in the larch. In another view there are old apple orchards and vineyards dusted with a powder of snow in the hills around Ithaca, New York, where in college days I first hunted pheasant; any curriculum for a fall semester included a daily ration of pheasant broth. My roommate and I would keep a bird simmering for hours on our hot plate until the water was reduced to a wild essence. But in another window, where bright flowers fade not, I always see Gabrielle, a Hungarian Dior model of cut-crystal beauty; electric to the touch, she didn't walk, she slithered like a trout in purling currents. In those fleeting days between a war and reality, I was writing for a Paris-based fishing magazine, *Au Bord de l'Eau*, earning just enough francs to stay in an apartment whose lobby smelled like ammonia and a thousand dead Gauloises. Too young to be prudent, on our first date I decided to blow the bankroll and take her to dinner at Maxim's. I ordered that house specialty, a truffled and roasted pheasant with fresh fig stuffing, and by the time a Grand Marnier soufflé arrived, a casual flirtation seemingly blossomed into a mad romance. Hungarians must have a thing about pheasant, as even that scholarly food writer, George Lang, devotes three pages to one marathon pheasant recipe in his wonderful book *The Foods of Hungary*. The trouble was, of course, that Gabrielle soon discovered that Maxim's was not my inherited playpen, and my publisher, Tony Burnand, was not about to underwrite her passion for that glorious bird.

Overleaf: A line of guns for a pheasant shoot, Yorkshire, England.

Presumably, Gabrielle found her true love with a pheasant farmer on the gypsy plains of Hortobagy.

For over a thousand years, long before wild populations became established in the New and Old Worlds, domesticated pheasant graced baronial tables and is probably one of the sybaritic foods that St. Thomas of Aquinas had in mind when speaking of lust in his *Summa theologica*: "consupisence is desire of the delectable." Delectable is certainly an operable word. The pheasant is a chickenlike or gallinaceous fowl of the family Phasianidae. There are about fifty different species on a world basis, but the one common to North America and our cuisine is the Chinese ring-necked pheasant (*Phasianus colchicus*). Actually, our modern American bird is not a pure strain, as it has some English and Japanese genes in its ancestry, but that in no way detracts from its edibility.

George Washington is generally credited as being the first to attempt establishing this nonnative fowl in Virginia (1786), the pheasant being a gift from the Marquis de Lafayette; however, at least one stocking had been made some fifty years earlier on Governor's Island in New York. These and subsequent introductions, including one made by Benjamin Franklin's son-in-law, were unsuccessful until the birds were released in the Willamette Valley of Oregon by Judge Owen Denny, who served as U.S. consul to China in 1882.

According to Greek legend, the pheasant (*phaisianos*) had been delivered to Europe by Jason's Argonauts from the Phaisis River valley in Asia Minor. To the sound of trumpets and transported in cages composed of precious woods, live pheasants adorned the triumphal march of Ptolemy Philadelphus at his entry into Alexandria. It was the Romans who brought the bird to England at about the time of Christ; this was not the same bird as the Chinese ring-necked, but over the centuries wild Asiatic strains, including the ring-necked, were interbred, and thus the English pheasant evolved throughout Great Britain. If there is a practical difference between the wild English and American pheasants, it's only that when shooting I miss the former with greater frequency, which is not saying much, as these wily birds can seemingly fly through my shot pattern, on either side of the ocean.

In America, wild pheasants abound in seventeen states, with Iowa, Kansas, and South Dakota presently the major producers, harvesting seven million birds per season. And even in those other states with only marginal or submarginal natural habitat, there is a tremendous annual kill on private game preserves. There are about 1,700 preserves in forty-five states and six Canadian provinces, operating on a membership basis or open to paid hunting. The greatest number are located in rural areas of New York, New Jersey, Pennsylvania, Illinois, Wisconsin, and California. Preserves usually offer a common triad of pheasant, quail, and chukar partridge, and in many areas wild turkey and mallard duck shooting as well. Some of these preserves are available strictly on a day basis, but others are in the resort category, with elegant lodges and fine meals for overnight guests. The birds are not truly wild as they are reared in pens and planted in the fields—a rotating crop, replenished as frequently as the harvest demands. In addition to non-shooting game farms many preserves supply the commercial market and are as automated as the chicken industry. In Europe there is very little public bird shooting; most of it is done on estates, controlled either by a syndicate that leases the land or by individual owners who offer formal and organized hunting, especially for pheasant and grouse. While daily bag limits will measure in the hundreds, to keep perspective, all the birds go directly to market, as without that income few of the great landholdings would survive. Pheasant hunting can be a very costly experience in Europe, but amenities such as those found at Tulchan Lodge, a 21,000-acre Scottish playground, Falsed Kro on the island of Fyn in Denmark (the ultimate country inn, with superb French cuisine), Stanage Castle in Wales, or Zidochovice Castle in Czechoslovakia, formerly the hunting grounds of Archduke Frederick, are provided in the tradition and splendor of centuries past.

COOKING NOTES

Domesticated pheasant are usually younger, more tender birds than those taken in the wild; age and the wild pheasant's tendency to do a lot of running as well as flying often produce something resembling an old barnyard rooster. For the marketplace broilers or "baby" pheasant are killed when eight weeks old and the roasters or adult birds at twenty weeks. Some suppliers will even hang your pheasant in the European fashion if a stronger game flavor is desired. Among wild birds, a young cock can be recognized by its short spurs and the hen by its soft, pliable feet and light tan plumage (this darkens to a ruddy brown on an adult).

Freshly killed pheasant should be stored in the refrigerator for four days before being cooked, which is sufficient aging for a sweet bird. If it wears spurs like a Hollywood cowboy, six days of aging are recommended. Although the skin is fragile and therefore time-consuming to dry-pluck, it's worth the effort as it and attendant specks of fat add greatly to the flavor. Skinning a pheasant makes no more kitchen sense than skinning a chicken, yet that is a practice among innocent nimrods.

The breast meat of pheasant is white, the leg meat is dark, and the bird's flavor delicately nutlike. But the meat is easily dried to a cardboard texture if overcooked—which is a very common state, even in professional kitchens. The bird can't be popped in the oven like a fat chicken and left uncovered through its full cooking cycle. A good rule of thumb when roasting a whole pheasant (presumably with a stuffing of some kind) is to preheat the oven to 450°F and bake the bird, breast up and uncovered, for twelve minutes, basting frequently with melted butter. Then reduce the temperature to 350°F, cover the pan, and continue baking for fifty minutes. Remove the cover and roast the bird for an additional forty-five minutes, continuing the basting, at which point the pheasant should be golden brown and moist.

To broil a split or halved pheasant over charcoal at a high heat, or in the oven at 450°F, it will take about sixteen minutes, allowing eight minutes for each side, at which point it should be tender and juicy. The exact time will vary slightly according to the size and age of the bird, but by any cooking method the internal temperature of the breast should be 140°F.

PHEASANT CURRY

SERVES 4 TO 6

3   pounds pheasant, cut
    into serving pieces
salt to taste
1   teaspoon sugar
2   teaspoons ground
    turmeric
2   cups plain yogurt
½   cup safflower oil
4   garlic cloves, peeled and
    sliced
3   pieces of cinnamon
    stick, crushed
5   cardamom pods, crushed
2   star anise seeds, crushed
1   large onion, sliced
1   large onion, grated
1   tablespoon ginger juice

4   teaspoons ground dried
    chili (see Note)
2   teaspoons ground cumin
5   bay leaves

Sprinkle the pheasant pieces with salt, sugar, and turmeric. Pour the yogurt over the pheasant and marinate for 30 minutes.

Heat the oil in a large skillet and sauté the garlic, crushed spices, and sliced onion until the mixture is fragrant. Add the grated onion, ginger juice, ground chili, cumin, and bay leaves. Mix thoroughly. Add the pheasant pieces with the yogurt marinade and turn the pieces over so they are completely covered with the spice mixture. Cover the skillet and simmer until the pheasant is tender. Remove and discard bay leaves and any large pieces of whole spices. Serve with boiled rice.

Note:

Use pure ground Asian chili, not American chili powder, since the latter includes other ingredients.

PHEASANT PIE

3   whole pheasant, dressed
2   large onions, quartered
1   large celery rib, chopped
      coarsely
salt and freshly ground
      pepper to taste
1   cup (½ pound) butter
2   onions, sliced thin
2   celery ribs, diced
¼   cup finely chopped fresh
      parsley
1   pound fresh mushrooms,
      sliced
1   pound wild rice, cooked
      and drained
1   pound sweet sausage,
      cooked and cut into ½-
      inch rounds
3   tablespoons currant jelly
1   teaspoon grated orange
      zest
1   cup dry sherry
1   tablespoon cornstarch
¼   cup water
¼-inch-thick piecrust
      (homemade or store-
      bought)

1   egg white

In a large pot, cover the pheasant with water. Add the quartered onions, coarsely chopped celery, and salt and pepper. Bring to a boil and boil until just tender; do not overcook. Remove the birds from the broth; strain the broth and reserve 1 quart of it. Let the birds cool, then remove the skin and bones and cut the meat into chunks.

Melt the butter in a large skillet and sauté the sliced onions, diced celery, parsley, and mushrooms until the onions are transparent; do not brown. Add the cooked wild rice. Add the sausage and stir.

In a small pan, bring the reserved pheasant broth to a boil. Add the jelly, orange zest, and sherry, then bring to a simmer. Dissolve the cornstarch in the water and stir it into the sauce until thickened.

In an 8- by 12- by 3-inch casserole, alternately layer the rice mixture, then the pheasant meat, making at least 2 layers. Refrigerate until well chilled.

Preheat the oven to 450°F.

Place the piecrust on top and brush with a lightly beaten egg white to which a pinch of salt has been added. Make steam vents in the crust with a fork. Bake the pie for 15 minutes to brown the crust.

Reduce the oven temperature to 350°F.

Bake for 30 to 35 minutes and serve.

ROAST PHEASANT WITH RED CABBAGE

SERVES 6

The red cabbage can be cooked well in advance. It keeps well for a few days in the refrigerator or longer in the freezer. Proceed as for roast pheasant (page 48) and serve with the red cabbage as described below.

RED CABBAGE

Red cabbage takes a long time to cook but requires little effort. It freezes well.

2 pounds red cabbage, shredded fine
2 medium onions, sliced fine
2 teaspoons light brown sugar
1 tablespoon sultanas
3 apples, such as Cortland or Delicious, cored and chopped but not peeled
pinch of dry mustard
¾ cup red wine vinegar
¾ cup water
salt and black pepper to taste

Put all the ingredients into a heavy-bottomed saucepan that has a tight-fitting lid. Make sure the mixture is well seasoned with plenty of black pepper but not too much salt. Set over very gentle heat or in a coolish oven and stew gently, giving the pan a shake every now and again to prevent the cabbage from sticking to the bottom. After 2 to 3 hours the cabbage should be reduced to a soft, slightly thick mixture with just enough moisture remaining to coat the leaves nicely. If too much liquid remains, remove the lid and boil rapidly, stirring occasionally until the right consistency is obtained.

SOUFFLÉ OF SMOKED PHEASANT

SERVES 6

2 cups ground smoked pheasant meat
2 cups very hot béchamel sauce
4 eggs, separated
pinch of cream of tartar

Preheat the oven to 375°F.

Stir 1½ cups of the pheasant into the béchamel sauce. Stir in the egg yolks. Beat the egg whites with the cream of tartar until stiff, then fold them gently into the béchamel, being careful that they do not fall.

Spoon the mixture into 6 buttered 3-inch porcelain soufflé dishes. Sprinkle the rest of the pheasant on top of the mixture. Bake for 20 minutes and serve immediately.

PHEASANT WITH PICKLED CABBAGE AND SAUSAGES

SERVES 5 TO 6

2 young pheasant
8 to 10 juniper berries, crushed
6 slices streaky bacon
¾ cup sweet red wine or ruby port
8 breakfast-size pork sausages
butter
1 1-pound can sauerkraut
freshly ground black pepper
1 tablespoon all-purpose flour
1 cup Game Stock (see Index) or chicken stock
salt and pepper to taste

Roast the pheasant as described for Roast Grouse with Cranberries (see Index), putting the crushed juniper berries inside the bird in place of the cranberries, using the bacon to cover the breasts, and pouring the wine into the roasting pan. The pheasant will take 40 minutes for rare birds and 55 for well-done. When they are cooked, remove them from the pan and keep warm.

While the pheasant are roasting, fry the sausages in a little butter to brown them evenly all over. Heat the sauerkraut, drain it well, and spread it on a warmed flat serving dish. Brush it with butter and grind black pepper all over it. Shake the juniper berries out of the pheasant into the roasting pan and put the pheasant on top of the sauerkraut. Surround with the fried sausages and keep warm while you make the sauce.

Put the pan with the roasting juices and the juniper berries over the heat and whisk in the flour. Add the stock and bring to a boil, stirring steadily. Simmer for 2 or 3 minutes and season with salt and pepper. Pass the sauce separately or pour it over the pheasant and sausages.

PHEASANT PAPRIKASH

SERVES 4

2   pheasant, dressed and
        quartered
coarse salt and freshly
        ground pepper to taste
1   teaspoon garlic powder
2   tablespoons sweet
        Hungarian paprika
        plus additional as
        needed
10   tablespoons (5 ounces)
        unsalted butter
½   pound (about 2 medium)
        onions, sliced thin

3   garlic cloves, peeled and
        minced
boiling water
½   pound mushrooms,
        sliced

Coat the pheasant with salt, pepper, garlic powder, and paprika. Let the pheasant stand in this dry marinade for 12 hours in the refrigerator.

In a large skillet, melt ½ cup of the butter and sauté the onions and garlic until lightly browned. Add the pheasant pieces and cover with boiling water. Tightly cover the skillet and simmer over low heat for 1 to 1½ hours, until tender. During this period, add additional paprika, 1 tablespoon at a time, until a red color is achieved.

In a small skillet, sauté the mushrooms in the remaining butter until tender and add to the pheasant just before serving.

Serve with broad noodles garnished with parsley.

SAUTÉED PHEASANT
A LA JULIE WILSON

SERVES 2

1   3-pound pheasant,
      dressed
salt and pepper to taste
¼   cup clarified butter
2   tablespoons cognac
¼   cup dry white wine
1   quart light cream
2   fresh pineapple slices
1   cup brewed coffee
2   tablespoons butter

Cut the bird into 8 serving pieces. Season with salt and pepper. Heat 3 tablespoons of the clarified butter in a skillet and sauté the pheasant pieces on both sides until browned. Continue cooking over low heat, until done, then remove from the pan. Pour off the fat and deglaze the pan with the cognac and wine. Add the cream and reduce the mixture until the sauce is thick.

Meanwhile, cut the pineapple slices into ⅓-inch dice and sauté the dice in the remaining tablespoon of clarified butter without letting them color. Finish the sauce by adding the coffee and whipping the mixture with a balloon whip or a rotary egg beater. Whip in the 2 tablespoons butter, bit by bit, to fluff up the sauce. Taste and adjust the seasoning.

Arrange the pheasant pieces on a platter and nap them with the sauce. Sprinkle the pineapple dice over all.

PHEASANT A LA SOUVAROV

1   pheasant, 2½ to 3
      pounds, dressed
2   ounces foie gras
1   ½-ounce whole black
      truffle
1   thin sheet of fresh pork
      fat, 6 by 6 inches
2   tablespoons butter
1   tablespoon cognac
5   tablespoons dry Madeira
1   cup Game Stock (see
      Index)
½   cup all-purpose flour
⅓   cup water

Preheat the oven to 425°F.

Stuff the pheasant with the foie gras and the truffle, cut into small cubes. Truss the bird and bard it with the fresh pork fat. Melt the butter in a roasting pan. Place the pheasant in the pan, resting it on one side. Roast for 10 minutes, turn it onto its other side, and roast for 10 minutes. Then turn it breast side up and continue to roast for 5 minutes. Lift the pheasant from the pan and remove the barding fat and trussing strings.

Reduce the oven temperature to 400°F.

Skim the fat from the roasting pan. Deglaze the pan with the cognac and Madeira, stirring to scrape up all the brown bits. Reduce the mixture slightly, then add the stock.

Put the pheasant in an oval earthenware *cocotte* (casserole), put the cover in place, and seal it hermetically with a paste made of the flour and water, leaving a small unsealed area for steam to escape. Place the *cocotte* in the oven and bake for 10 to 15 minutes to complete the cooking. Pass the sauce through a very fine sieve and serve it around the pheasant.

BREAST OF PHEASANT WITH FRESH SAGE

SERVES 4

¼ cup butter
2 cups all-purpose flour
salt and white pepper to
    taste
4 pheasant breasts, boned
10 fresh sage leaves *or* 1
    teaspoon dried
2 tablespoons tomato paste
2 tablespoons brandy
1 cup heavy cream

Melt the butter in a sauté pan over moderate heat. Pour the flour into a plastic bag and season it with salt and white pepper; shake well to mix. Shake the pheasant pieces, one at a time, in the seasoned flour. Gently sauté the pieces in the butter; do not over-brown them. Remove the pieces to a warmed serving dish or individual plates as they are done.

Increase the heat under the sauté pan and add the sage leaves and tomato paste. Deglaze the pan with the brandy. Add the cream and stir briskly, mixing all the ingredients with the cooking residue from the pheasant. Reduce the sauce until thickened; add salt and pepper to taste. Pour the sauce over the birds and serve with a good sauvignon blanc.

La Marguerite de Faisan

SERVES 8

4 young pheasant, dressed
salt and pepper to taste
2 bay leaves
leaves from 2 fresh thyme
     sprigs *or* 2 teaspoons
     dried
1 head of garlic, peeled
     and separated into
     cloves
4 onions
¾ cup (6 ounces) unsalted
     butter, approximately
¼ cup grenadine
5 tablespoons red wine
     vinegar
4 carrots
4 turnips
¼ pound snow peas
¼ cup tomato *concassée*

One day ahead, cut the birds into 4 pieces. Bone the breast portions, but keep the last bone in the legs. Save all the fat, bones, and skin. Melt the fat and set aside to use later.

Put the legs in a glass or enameled container and sprinkle them with some salt and pepper, the bay leaves, thyme, and garlic. Marinate the legs in this dry marinade overnight.

The next day, preheat the oven to 200°F.

Add the melted fat to the legs and roast them for 3 to 4 hours.

To prepare the onions, peel them and cut them into julienne strips. Sauté them in 2 tablespoons of the butter over moderate heat for about 10 minutes; do not let them color. Pour in the grenadine and ¼ cup of the vinegar; season with salt and pepper. Put the onions in the 200°F oven and bake them until all the liquid has evaporated; the onions will be translucent and have a nice red color.

Make a pheasant stock with the reserved bones and skin. Reduce it until it is well flavored, then strain. There should be about ½ cup. Scrub and peel the carrots and turnips. Cut both vegetables into even shapes, such as ovals or olive shapes. Cook them in boiling salted water until just tender. Cook the snow peas in boiling salted water for a few minutes only; they should still be green and a little crisp. Rinse them in very cold water and drain well.

About 10 minutes before serving, cut breast meat into thin slices and cook slices in about 3 tablespoons of unsalted butter for about 10 minutes; meat should still be pink. Transfer the slices to a warm plate. Deglaze the pan with the remaining tablespoon of vinegar and add a little of the garlic roasted with the legs. Simmer for a minute to reduce the liquid. Add pheasant stock, bring the sauce to a boil, then finish it with the remaining tablespoon of butter, cut into bits. Add the bits one at a time and whisk to blend in each piece before adding the next. Reheat vegetables and legs. Arrange the meats on a platter and garnish with onions, tomatoes *concassée*, carrots, and turnips. Spoon sauce over all.

SMOKED PHEASANT WITH SALAD OF GREENS AND WILD MUSHROOMS

SERVES 6 TO 8

1   head of oak leaf lettuce
1   head of curly chicory
1   head of radicchio
2   bunches of arugula
juice of 2 lemons
½   cup virgin olive oil
salt and pepper to taste
1   whole smoked pheasant,
      about 3 pounds
½   cup Mustard
      Mayonnaise (recipe
      follows)
½   cup Cumberland Sauce
      (recipe follows)
3   fresh chanterelles or
      morels
¼   cup butter

Trim and wash all the salad greens and dry them in a towel. Mix all together in a large bowl. Make a dressing of the lemon juice, olive oil, and salt and pepper. Set the dressing aside; keep the greens cool.

Debone the pheasant. Cut the leg meat into julienne strips and mix with the Mustard Mayonnaise. Cut the breast meat into thin slices and dip them into the Cumberland Sauce before setting them on a platter, arranging them in an attractive fashion. Place the leg meat strips on the platter as well.

Wash and trim the wild mushrooms, cut into julienne strips, and sauté them in the butter over moderate heat. When they release juices, cook for a minute longer. Dress the greens with the dressing, then pour the mushrooms and the butter, still hot, over all; toss to mix. Serve the salad in a glass bowl to accompany the pheasant.

MUSTARD MAYONNAISE

MAKES 2 CUPS

3   tablespoons prepared
      hot French mustard

2   cups mayonnaise

Add the mustard to the mayonnaise and stir gently to combine well.

Smoked Pheasant with Salad of Greens and Wild Mushrooms.

CUMBERLAND SAUCE

MAKES 1/4 CUP

1   orange
1   lemon
¼   cup currant jelly
2   tablespoons port
1½   teaspoons minced
        shallots
1   teaspoon prepared
        mustard
pinch of cayenne pepper
pinch of ground ginger

With a citrus zester or very fine paring knife, cut julienne strips of zest from the orange and lemon until you have 1 tablespoon of each. Drop the strips into a small saucepan of boiling water and allow to boil for 2 minutes. Drain, plunge into cold water, and drain again. Extract the juice of the orange and the juice of half the lemon.

Put the currant jelly into a saucepan and set over low heat until the jelly is melted. Add the port, shallots, orange and lemon zest, orange and lemon juices, mustard, cayenne pepper, and ginger. Mix all ingredients together. Use as a sauce for cold venison or any game.

TERRINE OF PHEASANT AND WILD DUCK WITH CIDER CHUTNEY

SERVES 12 TO 14

4 pheasant, 2½-pound hens
2 wild or muscovy ducks, 4-pound hens
¼ pound duck liver
4 teaspoons olive oil
6 medium shallots, chopped
4 garlic cloves, peeled and chopped
3 tablespoons fresh thyme leaves
2 tablespoons chopped fresh rosemary
1 tablespoon chopped fresh sage leaves
1 tablespoon chopped fresh parsley
2 teaspoons ground allspice
8 juniper berries
2 tablespoons cracked black peppercorns
4 teaspoons salt
½ teaspoon fresh lemon juice
¼ cup brandy
¼ cup dry Madeira
2 tablespoons dark rum
1 cup dry white wine
½ cup fresh lemon juice
1 teaspoon ground nutmeg
1 teaspoon salt
1 teaspoon ground white pepper

2 tablespoons unsalted butter
½ cup diced carrot
½ cup diced zucchini
1 pound thin bacon strips
Cider Chutney (recipe follows)
fresh thyme sprigs for garnish

Skin the birds and separate the meat from the bones. Set aside 2 duck breasts and 2 pheasant breasts. Chop the rest of the meat. Sauté the duck liver in 2 teaspoons of the olive oil and cook until medium-rare. When cool, add to the chopped meat along with shallots, garlic, herbs, spices, black peppercorns, and 4 teaspoons salt. Then add the ½ teaspoon lemon juice, brandy, Madeira, and rum. Marinate for 24 hours in the refrigerator.

Cut the reserved duck and pheasant breasts into strips. Put them in a bowl with the white wine, ½ cup lemon juice, nutmeg, 1 teaspoon salt, white pepper, and the remaining 2 teaspoons olive oil. Marinate in the refrigerator for 24 hours.

Process the chopped meat along with its marinade through a sausage grinder using a medium-size die.

Heat the butter in a skillet and lightly sauté the carrot and zucchini. Let the vegetables cool and then fold them into the ground mixture.

Preheat the oven to 325°F.

Line an 8-cup terrine mold with some of the bacon strips. Spread a layer of ground meat mixture on the bottom. Place a layer of duck and pheasant strips over the layer of ground meat. Continue to alternate layers until the terrine is full, making sure you finish with a layer of ground meat. Cover with bacon strips.

Bake in a bain-marie in the oven for 1 to 1½ hours. Place a weight on the terrine, let it cool, and then refrigerate it for 1 to 2 days.

Unmold and remove excess fat. Cut into ½-inch slices and serve with Cider Chutney. Garnish with fresh thyme.

CIDER CHUTNEY

SERVES 12 TO 14

3 pounds large McIntosh apples, peeled, cored, and chopped
10 shallots, chopped
2 ounces fresh gingerroot, peeled and cut in half
1¼ cups light brown sugar
⅔ cup dried currants
1 teaspoon whole coriander seed
2 teaspoons dry mustard
1 cup honey
pinch of cayenne pepper
1 quart apple cider
Spiced Vinegar (recipe follows)
3 tablespoons granular gelatin *or* 10 gelatin leaves

In a saucepan, mix all ingredients except for the gelatin leaves. Bring to a boil and simmer for 10 to 15 minutes, until the apples are tender. Remove the gingerroot. Add the gelatin leaves and dissolve. Chill for 2 days.

SPICED VINEGAR

2   cups cider vinegar
1   tablespoon black
       peppercorns
1   teaspoon ground mace
1   teaspoon whole cloves
6   bay leaves
1   teaspoon chopped
       peeled fresh
       gingerroot

2½   teaspoons mustard seeds
1   teaspoon whole allspice
       berries
3   cinnamon sticks
2   teaspoons celery seeds
1½   teaspoons salt

Bring all ingredients to a boil in a saucepan and simmer for 5 minutes. Cool and strain out the spices.

A South American **perdiz** *(partridge), Argenti*

6. PARTRIDGE

In a "Key West Letter" (*Esquire*, February 1935) Ernest Hemingway described a perfect partridge dinner in one—albeit long—sentence. "There were lots of partridges outside of Constantinople and we used to have them roasted and start the meal with a bowl of caviar, the kind you will never be able to afford again, pale grey, the grains big as buck shot and a little vodka with it, and then the partridges, not overdone, so that when you cut them there was the juice, drinking Caucasus burgundy, and serving french fried potatoes with them and then a salad with roquefort dressing and another bottle of what was the number of that wine?"

The name *partridge* is often erroneously applied to our native ruffed grouse in New England and to the bobwhite quail in the southern United States, as early settlers saw physical similarities in these birds. There are only two true partridges on the North American continent: the Eurasian, or gray, partridge (*Perdix perdix*), commonly known here as the Hungarian partridge because of the source of its original brood stock, and the chukar partridge (*Alectoris graeca*) of India, both of which are established in our West. Hungarian partridge were first released in the United States in 1899, but successful plantings were not established until a decade later on the prairies and wheatlands of central Canada; viable populations of chukar partridge have existed since 1935. The gray partridge is a popular game bird at table in Europe (*perniici* in Italy, *perdreau* or *perdrix* in France, *perdiz* in Spain, *fogoly* in Hungary), as is the somewhat larger red-legged partridge (*Alectoris rufa*), which does not occur in North America.

Pen-reared chukar partridge is the important commercial species in the American market. Ordering a brace by phone is simple, but collecting one in the wild is something else. Chukar are found in rugged terrain on steep mountain slopes, where they habitually run *uphill* in thick sagebrush before flushing. One must be of sound wind and limb, as well as a competent marksman, to collect the makings for a Hemingway dinner. It is well to note also that in our Rocky Mountain habitats these birds often gorge on the bulbs of wild onion, which is no dividend to partridge flavor if the crops are left in for too long a period, particularly in hot canyon country; they should be dressed in the field by the end of the hunt if not sooner. The meat of the chukar is comparatively light in color as opposed to that of the smaller Hungarian partridge, which is dark with a more pronounced game flavor. The Hungarian is most abundant in the stubble fields of Alberta, Manitoba, and Saskatchewan and is undoubtedly the bird described in that "Key West Letter" as it ranges into the eastern Mediterranean.

The red-legged partridge is not widely distributed in Europe; it is indigenous to Spain, Portugal, and southwestern France. This is the "French partridge" that the Marquis de Lafayette gifted to General George Washington along with a half dozen pheasant in 1786, although why he sent a simple bird (that died aboard ship somewhere around Baltimore) instead of a reproductive pair is something of a mystery. Redlegs from France were brought to Great Britain at the end of the eighteenth century, but the pure wild strain is now everywhere rare in Europe, as it is not an easy bird to propagate. As a result, the modern redleg is mainly a hybrid cross with the chukar partridge; it is better adapted to farming and widely used for release shooting. Today this hybrid occurs along the entire eastern seaboard of the United Kingdom and has been extending its range each year. Imported to Scandinavia in 1983, it now flourishes in Denmark, which is the fowl called "red partridge" in the import American market.

The redleg and its hybrid are supernal birds at table, and nowhere do they find greater popularity than in Spain, particularly around La Mancha and Toledo. In Toledo, that ancient city on the Tagus River, red-legged partridge, or *perdia roja*, is a specialty of many restaurants, the classic dish bearing its name—*salmorejo de perdiz a la toledana*—and one house that does it especially well is Venta de Aires in Tembleque (Circo Romano 25). Shooting redlegs is not only a challenging sport, but in its season, from mid-October through December, it is a pricey social event comparable to Scotland's red grouse season.

Perhaps the most exotic partridge to enter some American kitchens is Erkel's francolin (*Francolinus erckelii*) as the U.S. distribution of this African bird is limited to the islands of Hawaii, Lanai, Oahu, and Kauai. A large partridge weighing from 2½ to 3½ pounds, it is comparable to the chukar in flavor and in having light-colored meat. Actually, there are thirty-odd species of francolins in Africa and Eurasia, and while Hawaii also supports introduced populations of the gray francolin (*F. pondicerianus*) and black francolin or "black partridge" (*F. francolinus*), both from India, the Erkel's is much the better bird at table.

CHEF BRANDENBERGER'S
PARTRIDGE BREAST SAUTÉ

SERVES 2

3   slices bacon, cut into ¼-
inch strips
5   tablespoons butter
1   small onion, cut into
rings
10 mushrooms, sliced
1   medium unwaxed
cucumber, unpeeled,
cut into strips
2   quarters of peeled
tomato
1   teaspoon dry mustard
2   tablespoons vodka
2   tablespoons
Worcestershire sauce
1   cup sour cream
1   boned partridge breast,
cut into ½-inch strips

black pepper to taste
all-purpose flour as needed
¼   cup chopped fresh dill
or 1 tablespoon dried
¼   cup chopped fresh
parsley

In a frying pan, sauté the bacon strips in 2 tablespoons of the butter until they begin to crisp. Add the onion, mushrooms, cucumber, and tomato and continue sautéing until brown. Remove from the pan and keep warm in a low oven.

In a small saucepan, mix the dry mustard, vodka, and Worcestershire sauce. Add the sour cream and simmer for 4 minutes. Set aside.

Pepper and flour the partridge strips and sauté in the remaining butter in a skillet for 3 to 4 minutes, until tender. (Partridge, like veal, cooks quickly.) Add the cooked vegetables, half of the dill, and half of the chopped parsley; mix in the sour cream sauce. Reheat and transfer to a deep serving dish. Sprinkle with the remaining parsley and dill. Serve with noodles or rice.

PARTRIDGE BREAST
WITH LOBSTER FARCE

SERVES 4

2   partridge breasts,
        skinned and boned
white pepper to taste
Lobster Farce (recipe
        follows)
3   cups strong chicken
        stock, or more as
        needed
2   egg yolks
¼   cup butter, melted and
        cooled
Sauce Périgourdine (recipe
        follows)

Separate each whole breast into halves. Gently pound each piece flat between sheets of waxed paper until it is of even thickness. Season each

piece with white pepper and spread with an equal amount of the lobster mixture. Roll up each piece with the farce inside and wrap in aluminum foil. Bring the chicken stock to a bare simmer and in it poach the rolled breast pieces for about 10 minutes or until tender. Insert a thin skewer through the foil to test; the skewer should pierce the meat easily. Let the breasts cool in the stock.

Preheat the oven to 350°F.

Meanwhile, combine the egg yolks with the butter and beat well to mix. When the partridge breasts are cool, remove the foil and place the rolls in a buttered ovenproof dish heated to sizzling. Place the dish in the oven. Brush the rolls with the mixture of egg yolk and butter and continue to brush them often as they bake. Bake the rolls until they are golden.

Serve with Sauce Périgourdine and accompany with a buttered vegetable mixture such as Brussels sprouts, sweet chestnuts, morels, and carrots.

LOBSTER FARCE

1   raw ½-pound lobster
        tail, shelled
1½   teaspoons snipped fresh
        dill *or* 3 teaspoons
        dried
pinch of sugar

1¼   teaspoons sturgeon
        caviar
1½   teaspoons salmon caviar

Cut the raw lobster into

chunks and put them in the bowl of a food processor fitted with the steel blade. Chop the lobster to a paste. Add the remaining ingredients and process until well mixed.

SAUCE PÉRIGOURDINE

1 cup Sauce Espagnole (see Index)	1 ounce truffle essence (available at specialty food stores)	1 ounce truffle, chopped
	¼ cup dry Madeira	Heat the sauce and add the truffle essence, Madeira, and chopped truffle.

WILD PARTRIDGE WITH BLACK TEA AND GINGER SAUCE

SERVES 3

3   partridge or squab
salt and pepper to taste
6   tablespoons unsalted butter
½   cup dry sherry
1   tablespoon soy sauce
1   tablespoon Earl Grey tea leaves
1   small piece (about 2 inches) of fresh gingerroot, peeled, blanched, and julienned
2   cups light cream
½   pound mung bean sprouts for garnish

Preheat the oven to 425°F.

Cut the birds in half and sprinkle them with salt and pepper. Place in a roasting pan with 2 tablespoons of the butter and roast for 20 minutes. Remove the birds from the oven and pour excess grease out of the pan. Deglaze the pan with the sherry and soy sauce. Add the tea leaves and simmer on top of the stove for 2 minutes. Pour the liquid through a strainer into a saucepan. Add the ginger and cream. Allow the sauce to reduce until thickened. Keep the sauce hot while you sauté the bean sprouts in 2 tablespoons of the butter over high heat. Reheat the partridge just to warm before serving. Swirl the remaining 2 tablespoons of butter into the sauce to finish it.

Arrange the birds on a heated platter and spoon the sauce around them. Garnish the birds with the sautéed sprouts and serve with rice cooked with saffron and wrapped in a blanched cabbage leaf.

Overleaf: Wild Partridge with Black Tea and Ginger Sauce.

Pâté of Partridge

4	partridge
5	tablespoons vegetable oil
1	carrot
1	large onion
6	cups cold water
1	bouquet garni: white portion of 1 leek, 1 celery rib, ½ parsley root, 1 bay leaf
1	teaspoon salt
20	juniper berries
2½	garlic cloves, peeled
6	white peppercorns
¼	pound boneless pork
½	pound bacon
2	teaspoons seasoning salt, such as Spice Islands

grated zest of ½ orange
freshly ground white pepper to taste

1	tablespoon butter
2	shallots, minced
2	tablespoons cognac

grated zest of ¼ lemon
5 to 6 ounces goose liver, marinated in port

1¾	ounces shelled pistachios
1	ounce truffle, cut into small dice
1¾	ounces pickled tongue, cut into small dice

butter for the mold

1¼	pounds pastry dough for pâtés
1	egg yolk
2	tablespoons heavy cream

Preheat the oven to 400°F.

Skin the partridge and set the breast meat aside. The leg meat and other bits should weigh about ½ pound. Put all bones, tendons, and skins in 3 tablespoons of the oil in a roasting pan and roast for 10 minutes. Scrub the carrot and peel the onion; cut both into large pieces. Add these to the roasting pan and stir the bones and vegetables together. Continue to brown, stirring occasionally, for about 30 minutes longer. Deglaze the pan with a little of the cold water. Put the bones, vegetables, and deglazing in a stockpot, add the rest of the cold water, and bring to a boil. Reduce to a simmer. Let the stock cook for 3 hours, skimming it often. At the start of the last hour, add the bouquet garni, salt, 8 of the juniper berries, 1 garlic clove, and the whole white peppercorns. Strain the finished stock through a cheesecloth-lined sieve, return it to the heat, and reduce it to 1 cup. Reserve.

Cut the boned and skinned partridge (other than the breast meat), pork, and bacon into strips; keep the bacon separate. Scatter 1½ tea-spoons of the spiced salt, 8 of the remaining juniper berries, crushed, 1 garlic clove, crushed, and half of the grated orange zest over the strips. Sprinkle with ground white pepper. Refrigerate. Put the meats twice through the finest blade of a meat grinder; put the bacon once through the same blade. Put the ground meat in a bowl set over a larger bowl of ice and work the ground bacon into the mixture. Finally force this mixture (forcemeat) through a sieve.

Rub the reserved breast meat with the remaining spiced salt and some ground white pepper. Brown the pieces quickly in the remaining 2 tablespoons oil; remove them from the pan and discard the oil. Melt the butter in the same pan and cook the shallots in it until translucent. Deglaze the pan with the cognac and add ⅓ cup of the stock. Bring to a boil and skim carefully. Pour the mixture over the breast pieces and add the rest of the grated orange zest, the grated lemon zest, remaining ½ garlic clove, and 4 juniper berries, crushed. Cut the marinated goose liver into dice and work this, the pistachios, the truffles, and the diced tongue into the forcemeat.

Butter a 6-cup pâté mold and line it with the prepared dough; leave excess dough hanging over the sides of the mold. Arrange a third of the forcemeat in the dough-lined mold. Cut off the ends of the breast pieces. Arrange half of the breasts on the forcemeat, cut ends together. Sprinkle with some of the cognac and stock mixture used for marinating the breasts. Cover with another third of the forcemeat. Arrange the rest of the breast pieces on top, sprinkle with the remaining cognac and stock mixture, and finish with the remaining forcemeat. Press down several times with a wet cloth to make the mixture firm and to release any air bubbles.

Preheat the oven to 425°F.

Fold the overhanging dough over the forcemeat, cut off any excess dough, and decorate with the rest of the dough, cut into decorative shapes. Mix the egg yolk and cream together and brush this mixture over the top of the dough and the decorations. Make a small hole for steam to escape and insert a chimney made of foil. Bake the pâté for 15 minutes.

Reduce the oven temperature to 350°F.

Bake for 30 minutes longer or until the fat that rises in the chimney is completely clear.

Let the pâté cool completely; then, if you wish, pour liquid port wine aspic through the chimney to fill the spaces left through shrinkage in baking.

Serve with honeydew melon, and mint jelly flavored with Armagnac.

Pâté of Partridge.

Hunting on the moors of Scotland

7. GROUSE AND PTARMIGAN

Because August for me is an important month for angling in North America, I have never attended "The Glorious Twelfth" of August, that opening day of red grouse shooting in Great Britain, notably on Scotland's heather-clad moors. I have, however, often made the trip in September and October, when I can still enjoy the grouse and other shooting and catch the last runs of salmon in the fall season on Highland rivers. People come from all over the world for this traditional event, as much to socialize as to bag grouse; depending on the success of the year's crop, a total of 250,000 to 800,000 are harvested throughout the United Kingdom. The luxurious sporting lodges and castles that cater to road-company royalty are worth a detour; indeed some are veritable fiefdoms, and the demand for bookings often exceeds the supply. Such pristine settings as Invercauld Castle on the River Dee in Aberdeenshire, the Farleyer Manor House on the River Tay in Perthshire, and Bolton Abbey in Yorkshire maintain their centuries-old facade of obsolescent gentility. The cuisine, of course, is superb. Obviously, though, one doesn't have to venture farther than London restaurants such as Leith's, the Rue St. Jacques, Langan's, or the Connaught dining rooms to enjoy perfect roast grouse. For that matter, the whole panoply of available British game can be viewed at Harrods world-famous Food Halls (Randall & Aubin, 16 Brewer Street), which is worth a visit. However, as in all hunting, it is less the eating than the total experience of having been afield that makes dining not an essential act but a joyous rite, with an entirely different flavor.

Grouse hunting in America is more demanding. Here there are no organized shoots orchestrated by professional gamekeepers, nor opulent dining with candlelight sparkling in the bubbles of a Moët & Chandon. Our sport is basically in the public domain (although you have to get permission to trespass on private lands), and the only accommodation may be a strategically located motel or country inn. However, the splendors of hiking the fall woods, especially in riotously colored New England, through old winy-smelling apple orchards, mysterious alder swamps, and tangles of fox grapes with a staunch pointing dog, have thrilled generations of Americans. I have been at it for a half-century. And what we hunt under the name *grouse* is not the same bird that thrives in the crags of Scotland. Given my choice at table, I would select our ruffed grouse above all others, but in a way it's like comparing apples to oranges, as either one is a taste treat in its own right.

Eighteen species of grouse (family Tetraonidae, which includes the ptarmigans) are distributed in North America, Europe, and Asia. Nonhunting chefs tend to speak of grouse in a collective sense, treating them in recipes as one bird (which is often self-defeating). Actually, these birds display an extreme variation in flavor and size, from the very mild, nutlike white meat of our North American ruffed grouse (*Bonasa umbellus*), weighing about 1½ to two pounds, to the dark and possibly inferior meat of our western sage grouse (*Centrocercus urophasianus*), weighing from three to seven pounds; because of their sagebrush diet, they must be drawn immediately after being killed, or the sweet flesh can become permeated with bitter sage oil. (Sagebrush is not to be confused with sage, that delightfully pungent herb common to stuffing in fowl cookery.) Other native grouse include the blue grouse (*Dendragopus obscurus*), which commonly weighs 2½ to three pounds, and the much smaller spruce grouse (*Canachites canadensis*); both of these can be rather strongly flavored late in the season, when they move to higher altitudes and feed heavily on conifer needles (this is especially true of the spruce grouse, but I've had very good luck in the kitchen with the blue of Montana, only once getting an off-flavored bird). In addition we have the sharptail grouse (*Pedioecetes phasianellus*) and the greater and lesser prairie chickens (*Tympanuchus cupido* and *T. pallidicinctus*). The prairie chicken, or pinnated grouse, once occurred by the tens of millions in the United States, wherever there was undisturbed grassland, but that pristine habitat has long gone under the plow. The now extinct heath hen, an eastern seaboard race of the chicken, furnished the prelude. The last survivor was recorded at Martha's Vineyard in 1931. The only viable populations left today are in Kansas, Nebraska, Oklahoma, and the Dakotas. The sharptail grouse is more abundant, however, especially in stubble fields of the Prairie Provinces of Canada. Both the chicken and the sharptail are heavy consumers of cultivated crops such as sorghum, oats, and corn, which produce birds of excellent flavor. None of the aforementioned grouse species enter the commercial American market, yet they represent a very significant harvest on the sportsman's table. Personally, I feel our ruffed grouse of the Appalachians, fattened on clover, berries, beechnuts, and acorns, is clearly the winner for the most delicate of flavors, and the spruce grouse is too pine-oriented to be worth hunting.

There are three species of the dark-meated ptarmigan in the grouse family that occur in North America: the willow ptarmigan (*Lagopus lagopus*), the whitetailed ptarmigan (*L. leucurus*), and the rock ptarmigan (*L. mutus*). The red grouse that made Scotch moors famous is actually a race of the circumpolar willow ptarmigan (*L. l. scoticus*), which is common to western and northern Canada and Alaska. Except for the red grouse, these birds have three distinct color phases—spring, summer, and autumn. For camouflage, beginning in autumn, the ptarmigan molts and adapts a white plumage (in western Norway, where the weather is influenced by the Gulf Stream and snow is unusual, it molts into a skewbald coloration with patches of white) and becomes what is known in the American restaurant trade as the "snow grouse." The only difference among ptarmigan from a kitchen standpoint is one of size; a male willow will weigh about 1½ pounds, the rock slightly over one pound, and the whitetailed about three-quarters of a pound. I have hunted ptarmigan in the Brooks Range of Alaska, the alpine areas of British Columbia, and on a month-long trip around Iceland years ago, before resorts of any kind existed, practically lived on *rupa* and salmon. Ptarmigan have an assertive game flavor, which I greatly enjoy, and when served with the traditional bread sauce and a fruit preserve, preferably cloudberry or lingonberry, they make a memorable meal.

Aside from the ptarmigan, three other members of the grouse family are presently (1991) being exported to the American market. The least interesting of these from a table standpoint is the capercaillie. The name derives from Gaelic, meaning "cock of the woods." The largest of the Old World grouse (*Tetrao urogallus*), the capercaillie is widely distributed but not numerous in the pine forests of Europe. It is most abundant in Austria and the Black Forest region of Germany, where it is known as the *Auerhan*. A mature cock bird may weigh in excess of twelve pounds, or twice the size of our largest North American grouse, the sage grouse. However, the elusive capercaillie is more of a hunting trophy than a gourmet delicacy. Young birds that have been summering on plants and berries are edible, but during winter, when the snow covers the ground, capercaillie feed almost exclusively on pine needles, which give their flesh a turpentine flavor. Several attempts were made to establish capercaillie in the United States beginning in 1904 at Grand Island, Michigan, and later in New York, but these introductions were unsuccessful. Perhaps this failure was gastronomically justified as satirical German recipes for the *Auerhan* always conclude with the admonition to "throw the bird away and eat the pot." In my several dining experiences with elderly capercaillie, it would appear to be good advice.

Another newcomer to our market is the black grouse (*Lyrurus tetrix*), also known as black game in the Scottish Highlands and *coq de Bruyère* in France. The glossy black cock bird is fairly large, reaching a weight of four pounds, while the gray or brown hens scale at about two pounds. The meat of this grouse is medium-dark in color and is inclined to be dry in texture; it requires a reasonable period of aging to become tender and achieve flavor.

By contrast, the third grouse of recent introduction to the American market is an epicure's delight; the hazel grouse (*Bonasa betulina*) is a diminutive generic counterpart of our ruffed grouse in a dressed weight of six to seven ounces. I count the hazel grouse, with its finely textured, moist white breast meat, as one of the finest game birds available. In designing our menu for a recent dinner at the Breakers Hotel in Palm Beach for the *Chevaliers du Tastevin*, I introduced the hazel grouse, which chef Karl Ronaszeki prepared as *suprême de gelinotte*, with the breast meats boned and flattened and gently sautéed in butter, then laced with the pan juices after deglazing with a dash of Madeira. The leg meats were cooked a few minutes longer until crisp and well done, a delicious dividend just big enough for a few bites. This was accompanied by fresh chanterelle mushrooms and gooseberries.

ROAST GROUSE WITH CRANBERRIES

SERVES 4

Leith's restaurant on Kensington Park Road is a name synonymous with game cookery in London. It is the domain of food columnist Prue Leith, who also operates Leith's School of Food and Wine. Her roast grouse recipe is a cranberry classic, optionally done with bread sauce and fried crumbs. Ms. Leith observed that "In autumn I'm certain that my favourite food is grouse, just as in winter it is parsnips, in spring it is sea trout, and in July it is raspberries. I have a distinct prejudice about out-of-season food. Grouse is a dreadful price but it does repay the expense in pure gastronomic pleasure. They may be served either with a conventional gravy flavoured with cranberries, or in the traditional way with bread sauce, redcurrant jelly, the juices from the roasting pan, and with fried buttered breadcrumbs."

4   young grouse
butter
freshly ground black pepper
    to taste
¼   pound fresh or frozen
    cranberries

4   slices fatty bacon
¾   cup ruby port or strong
    sweet red wine
¼   teaspoon salt plus
    additional to taste
4   slices white bread,
    toasted
1   teaspoon all-purpose
    flour
⅔   cup Game Stock (see
    Index) or chicken
    stock
sugar to taste
1   bunch watercress for
    garnish
Bread Sauce (optional; recipe
    follows)
Fried Crumbs for Game and
    Poultry (optional;
    recipe follows)

Preheat the oven to 400°F.

Set the grouse livers aside. Wipe the grouse inside and out with a clean damp cloth, then put them into a small roasting pan. Spread them with a little butter and grind pepper fairly generously all over them. Fill the cavities of the grouse with the cranberries and put the bacon over the top of the breast. Pour the wine into the roasting pan and add ¼ teaspoon salt to the pan. Roast the birds for 30 minutes for rare or for 40 minutes for well-done, basting once or twice and removing the bacon from the breasts 10 minutes before the end of the cooking time to allow the birds to brown nicely.

While the grouse are cooking, fry the livers quickly in butter, then mash them to a paste with a little more butter. Season the paste with salt and pepper. Cut off the crusts of the pieces of toast and spread with the liver mixture. Put the toast on a heated serving dish. Tip the cranberries out of the grouse into the roasting pan and lay the grouse on top of the toast. Keep warm. Put the flour in the roasting pan with the cranberries. Add the stock and heat on top of the stove, stirring steadily, until boiling. Season with salt and, if sour, a little sugar. Serve the sauce separately. Garnish the grouse with sprigs of watercress.

BREAD SAUCE

4   cloves

a few slices onion

a good pinch of ground
        nutmeg

1   bay leaf

1   cup milk

2   slices white bread, crusts
        removed

¼   cup butter

salt and white pepper to
        taste

Put the cloves, onion, nutmeg, bay leaf, and milk into a saucepan and bring slowly to a boil. Once it is boiled, set aside to infuse for 10 minutes or so. Strain the warm milk over the bread. Break up with a fork and mix well. Return the mixture to the saucepan and stir while bringing to a boil. Once hot, beat in the butter and season with salt and pepper.

If the sauce is allowed to stand, it may separate. In that case, add a little cream or milk and beat well. Bread sauce should have a thick but creamy consistency—more a cream than a paste. Serve the sauce with the grouse as an alternative to cranberry sauce.

FRIED CRUMBS FOR
GAME AND POULTRY

6 to 8 tablespoons butter

1   cup slightly stale white
        bread crumbs

Heat the butter in a skillet until foaming and add the bread crumbs. Fry over moderate heat, stirring constantly with a wooden spoon. If the crumbs promptly absorb all the butter, add a little more. Keep frying until the crumbs are browned, crisp, and very buttery. Bread crumbs are frequently underfried so that they are a soggy paste. It is important to keep the crumbs moving, or some of them will burn while others are still soft and pasty. Put the hot crumbs in a warm serving dish and pass around with a deep spoon or ladle.

ROAST HAZEL GROUSE

SERVES 2

2   hazel grouse
salt and white pepper to
        taste
2   thin slices fatback
2   teaspoons butter or
        margarine
2   cups Game Stock (see
        Index)
½   to 1 cup heavy cream
2   teaspoons all-purpose
        flour
6   tablespoons currant jelly

Dress the birds, rinse them thoroughly, dry them, and rub them with salt and white pepper. Truss the birds. Bard them with fatback and tie it in place with white string.

Preheat the oven to 400°F.

On the stove, brown the butter in an ovenproof pan large enough to hold the birds. Arrange the birds breast down in the pan and brown them on all sides. Add the stock, cover the pan, and roast the birds for about 20 minutes. Baste with the pan juices as needed or add more stock if the juices reduce too much.

Transfer the birds to a platter. Skim and strain the pan juices; there should be 1 to 1½ cups; if not, add more stock. Mix a few tablespoons of the cream with the flour to make a paste. Add the rest of the cream as needed to the pan juices. Over low heat, stir in the paste. Bring the sauce to a boil and let it simmer for 3 to 5 minutes, until reduced and thickened. Stir in the currant jelly until melted. Season the sauce to taste.

Remove the fatback and trussing strings from the birds and split them. Serve them with the sauce.

Quail with white grapes in a pastry

8. QUAIL

Hunting quail—for that matter, eating them—can be a lifetime dedication. I recall hunting at Hobcaw Barony, the South Carolina plantation of Bernard M. Baruch, the millionaire confidant of presidents whose prowess with the gun was phenomenal. Together with my old friend Bob McCahon, who started his movie-directing career with that World War II documentary *The Fighting Lady* and who was no slouch with a .20-gauge, we rode forth by horse and put up covey after covey. Mr. Baruch, then age eighty-two and deaf as a fence post, made us look like we were shooting blanks. Of course Mr. Baruch had over sixty years of practice on those rocketing targets, and with a frequent score of twelve birds for fifteen shots the fact that he couldn't hear the muffled thunder of wings going left and right was obviously no handicap. The only other gentleman who could match that elder statesman was Paul Butler, whose dynasty included the Oakbrook Polo Club, the Sun Ranch, and Butler Aviation, just to mention a few diversions that occasionally interfered with his quail hunting. Paul's candlelit quail dinners in his Palm Beach mansion were a weekly event until his passing at the age of ninety. Although that classic *caille à la périgourdine*, quail stuffed with foie gras and served with truffle sauce, has almost become an institutional dish in today's fashionable restaurants, the Butler kitchen, like the Baruch kitchen, allowed that only the quail flavor would do—bathed in butter and broiled, then served on toast points. The delicate white breast meat of a bobwhite is a traditional sufficiency of riches.

When my wife and I moved to Palm Beach, Florida, in 1952, there was still plenty of quail hunting available not far from town. Today the palmetto and pine cover we once hunted is under giant shopping malls or condominium complexes, and a wild quail dinner is far afield. But even in less settled areas of the Southeast mechanical "clean" farming practices that began early in the 1950s eliminated much of what once was the greatest bobwhite habitat in the United States. There are still some old plantations, particularly in Georgia and the Low Country of South Carolina, where wild coveys are plentiful and hunters can be accommodated at a price, as well as a number where released birds provide good shooting, but most of the quail that now enter our kitchen are flushed at the local market or at Bonnette's Hunting Preserve. Although the plump little semi-domesticated kind are every bit as good to eat (for that matter, you don't have to grope with your teeth for bird shot), the thrill of working with good pointing dogs to an exploding covey rise certainly adds to their flavor. There is some fine bobwhite hunting in Missouri, Nebraska, Kansas, Oklahoma, and Texas, with open seasons in at least twenty-five other states providing an annual harvest of some twenty million birds.

Quail are small chickenlike birds of the family Phasianidae. About thirty species are found in the Western Hemisphere, mainly in South America, but six are native to the United States. These birds vary in size from four to ten ounces (in feather) according to species and sex, and all are under twelve inches in length. The most widely distributed is the bobwhite (*Colinus virginianus*), which occurs from Mexico to Canada and is the only species found in the eastern half of the United States. In our South, bobwhite are often and erroneously called "partridge," which originated with early European settlers who saw a feathered resemblance between the species; even one of the bird's favorite foods is known as partridgeberries. The bobwhite is one of two quails in our commercial market. The other five species—the California or valley quail (*Lophortyx californica*), scaled or blue quail (*Callipepla squamata*), Mearn's or Montezuma quail (*Cyntronyx montezumae*), mountain or plumed quail (*Oreortyx pictus*), and Gambel's or desert quail (*Lophortyx gambelii*)—have a more limited distribution. These are all western species taken by hunters and do not enter the commercial trade. Other than the bobwhite, our dominant market bird is the introduced pharaoh quail (*Coturnix coturnix*), which is native to Europe in the Mediterranean countries and to the Middle East. Farmed in both Canada and the United States, it is fast becoming our most important commercial species. Manchester Farms alone in Dalzell, South Carolina, delivers 5½ million pharoah quail to the marketplace annually. The pharoah, unlike American quails, is a migratory bird with a very ancient history.

According to the Holy Bible, when Moses led the starving Israelites from Egypt and across the Desert of Sin, "The Lord spoke to Moses and said, 'I have heard the grumbling of the Israelites. Tell them: In the evening twilight you shall eat flesh, and in the morning you shall have your fill of bread, so that you may know that I, the Lord am your God.' In the evening quail covered the camp, and in the morning 'manna' [which the Bible compares in appearance to a coriander seed] covered the ground like hoarfrost."[1] Al-

---

[1]Exodus, 16: 11–13. *The Quail and Manna*, The New American Bible, St. Joseph's Edition.

though one tends to see allegory in biblical stories, the fact remains that the pharaoh make tremendous migrations from Europe in the fall to winter in the Sudan and back again in the spring. After crossing the Mediterranean, the birds are flying so low that they come aground in exhausted flocks and are easily netted. The Desert of Sin is in the quail's flight path, so the story is probably less a parable than an actual migratory phenomenon. In Egypt today, especially in the seaside city of Alexandria, where the birds make first landfall, restaurants do a thriving business in spiced and grilled quail from September to early November—undeniably a heaven-sent food.

COOKING NOTES

As with all small game birds, quail are easily overcooked. A whole dressed bird weighs from two to six ounces, depending on the species. Our largest native quail is the mountain quail, which can weigh ten ounces in feather, and the smallest, the Mearn's quail, may weigh no more than three ounces in feather. Among bobwhites, northern populations are somewhat larger, weighing up to 8½ ounces, than southern birds, which seldom exceed six ounces in feather. Thus cooking times vary considerably, but the internal temperature of a perfect quail should be from 140 to 145°F. The less reliable eyeball test for doneness is when the breast meat is punctured nearest the wing bone (use a food pick, not a fork) and the juice runs clear. In direct heat methods such as roasting, pan frying, and deep frying, one minute of overcooking can make the difference between a moist bird and a tough, dried-out quail. The safe time periods usually given for an average 3½- to four-ounce bird are eight to ten minutes in a preheated 475°F oven for roast quail, ten to fourteen minutes for pan frying in half an inch of cooking oil (skillet covered for the first five minutes), and seven minutes for deep frying in oil at 350°F. For braising, the quail should be sautéed as quickly as possible over high heat, or the birds will be cooked through before being added to the casserole dish; once in a liquid environment, quail retain moisture and can tolerate longer cooking times.

Quail can be eaten the same day they are killed; however, aging for three to four days in feather under refrigeration beautifully defines the wild flavor—as does plucking rather than skinning the birds. The neck and wings should be completely snipped off and the legs snipped at the joint above the foot. At market, quail are sold in feather and drawn, plucked whole and deboned (but with leg and wing bones), and deboned and split. Quail hearts and livers are a delicacy when sautéed and served on buttered toast, but it requires at least twenty birds to provide a significant hors d'oeuvre for two diners.

Quail dinners as done below the Mason-Dixon line are not something you will find in Egypt or poolside at the Four Seasons. As an invited guest at the John Harrisons' Fife Plantation in Bluffton, South Carolina (which has its roots as a 1735 land grant from the king of England), you would experience a dinner format that is inviolate. The feast begins with local oysters, shrimp, or crabmeat from the May River, followed by the roasted quail (or dove or snipe, depending on the day's bag) accompanied by either rice, grits, baked hominy, or candied sweet potatoes. The vegetables will be butter beans, broccoli, okra, and baked tomatoes. Either corn bread or homemade biscuits must be at hand, as well as the essential fig or blackberry preserves. This is hearty and simple fare, but after a long day afield traditionalists will have it no other way.

Like other small game birds, quail are often served on toast points to collect their juices. Optionally, when a sauce or gravy is featured they can be mounted on trenchers—either a halved large hard roll or two-inch-thick slices of French bread with the centers scooped out to hold the bird. The trenchers are buttered and toasted, and the sauce or gravy is poured over all.

BRAISED QUAIL WEATHERVANE

SERVES 4

4   slices bacon, diced
8   quail, split
salt and freshly ground
        pepper to taste
½   cup all-purpose flour
¼   cup finely chopped
        onion
1   teaspoon finely chopped
        garlic
½   cup dry red wine
½   cup beef bouillon
1   tablespoon tomato paste
½   cup heavy cream

Brown the bacon bits in a flameproof casserole until crisp. Transfer to paper towels to drain. Season the quail with salt and pepper and dredge lightly with flour. Brown the quail, skin side down, in the bacon fat over moderately high heat. Transfer the quail to a warm platter as they brown.

Lower the heat and add the onion and garlic to the casserole. Cook until transparent, then add the wine, bouillon, and tomato paste. Return the quail to the casserole, cover, and simmer for 15 to 20 minutes. Add the cream and bacon bits and heat through. Serve on wild rice.

KIMBERLY'S PAN-FRIED CURRIED QUAIL

SERVES 2 TO 4

1   cup all-purpose flour
1   tablespoon curry powder
½   teaspoon ground ginger
1   teaspoon salt
1   teaspoon pepper
1   egg
½   cup milk
8   quail, dressed
vegetable oil
Mango Chutney (recipe follows)

In a bowl, combine the flour, curry powder, ginger, salt, and pepper. Mix thoroughly with a whisk. In a second bowl, combine the egg and milk and mix thoroughly with a whisk.

Dip each quail in the egg and milk mixture and then in the flour mixture, giving the birds a complete coating.

Pour oil to a depth of about ½ inch into a large frying pan (preferably cast iron). Heat the oil to the point where a small piece of bread will brown quickly when dropped into the pan. Place the quail in the pan breast side down and cover tightly. Fry for 5 minutes, remove the cover, and turn the quail over with tongs so they are spine side down. Continue turning so the birds brown evenly, frying until the internal temperature of the breast is 140°F—13 to 18 minutes, depending on the size of the quail. Remove the quail and drain for 1 minute on paper towels before serving. Mango Chutney (recipe follows) makes a delightful accompaniment.

MANGO CHUTNEY

MAKES 12 1-CUP JARS

Mangoes are a summer fruit, so to have a supply of chutney on hand for the fall and winter quail season, home canning is necessary. This chutney complements many other game bird dishes.

2 cups white vinegar
2 pounds dark brown
  sugar
1½ tablespoons mustard
  seed
1 tablespoon ground
  ginger
¼ pound crystallized
  ginger, diced
1 teaspoon hot red pepper
  flakes
1 teaspoon ground cloves
1 teaspoon celery seed
1 teaspoon ground
  cinnamon
1 tablespoon salt
1 pound raisins
7 cups peeled, pitted, and
  chopped mangoes
juice of 4 small limes

Bring the vinegar and brown sugar to a boil. Add all the spices and simmer for 5 minutes. Add the raisins, then the mangoes and lime juice. Stir well. Cook, uncovered, for 1 hour at a low simmer. Seal in sterilized 1-cup mason jars.

Chef Norman Van Aken flambés qu

STUFFED QUAIL WITH MORELS IN PUFF PASTRY

SERVES 8 AS A FIRST COURSE OR 4 AS A MAIN COURSE

8 tomatoes, about 2½ pounds
4 shallots
10 tablespoons (5 ounces) unsalted butter
salt and pepper to taste
4 pounds fresh spinach
2 pounds fresh morels or other seasonal wild mushrooms (see Note)
2 garlic cloves, peeled
12 fresh parsley sprigs
½ cup dry white wine
2 cups quail stock or veal stock
8 quail
1 pound puff pastry
2 egg yolks
2 tablespoons water

To make the tomato *concassée*: blanch and peel the tomatoes, halve them, and remove all seeds. Chop the pulp and let it drain in a strainer for 1 hour. Peel and chop half of the shallots. In a saucepan, melt ¼ cup of the butter. Add the shallots and tomato pulp to the butter and cook over low heat until soft but not reduced to a puree; they should still have texture. Season with salt and pepper. Set aside.

To cook the spinach, cut off any roots and pull off the stems. Wash the leaves in 3 or 4 changes of room temperature water and drain. Plunge the spinach into boiling salted water in a large kettle and leave for 2 minutes. Lift out to a colander, then put into ice-cold water. Drain and press out all the water. Set the spinach aside.

Wash and trim the mushrooms and cut them into small pieces. Peel and chop the remaining shallots and the garlic cloves. Wash, dry, and chop the parsley. Melt ¼ cup of the remaining butter in a large skillet and in it cook the mushrooms, shallots, and garlic. At the end, when the vegetables are brown, add the parsley and cook for another minute. Set the mixture aside to cool.

To make the sauce, pour the wine into a saucepan and reduce by half. Add the stock and several ladles of the sautéed mushrooms. Simmer the sauce to reduce it slightly. Set aside.

Preheat the oven to 350°F.

Debone the quail. Place them on a work surface and spread them open. Season the inside with salt and pepper. Stuff the birds with the remaining cooled sautéed mushrooms and fold together. Roll out the pastry to a thin sheet and cut it into 8 pieces, each large enough to wrap a quail. Wrap each quail, trying to give the pastry package the shape of the quail. Beat the egg yolks with the water and brush this glaze on the pastry-covered birds. Set the quails on a baking sheet and bake for 15 minutes, until the pastry is cooked through and golden brown.

Cut the remaining 2 tablespoons of butter into bits. Reheat the sauce, then remove the pan from the heat and whisk in the butter. Season with salt and pepper to taste. Arrange each quail on a plate along with some spinach and some of the tomatoes as side dishes. Serve the sauce separately or put some sauce on each plate and some in a sauceboat.

Note:

Since morels are costly and available for only a short time of the year, you may substitute other flavorful mushrooms that are available.

Squab garnished with parsley and tomato

9. PIGEONS AND DOVES

In 1956, while doing some exploratory fishing for the Venezuelan government, we set out from Robelicito by jeep to cross that heat-hazed plain known as the Llanos, which stretches for hundreds of miles from the foothills of the Andes to the Orinoco. There were no roads in those days; in the rainy season the Llanos is a sea of mud, but in the dry season it is as hard as a concrete highway. Much of the land is grassy and flat, spotted with acacia trees and giant ant hills similar to those of the African veld, but where water exists there is jungle and game of all kinds. The sun can be brutal in that part of the world, and on the third day out, it was a shimmering red disk like the eye of a madman blinking in the gray smoke of a brush fire that almost encompassed the horizon. Possibly it was the fire that triggered the flight, but for hours the sky was filled with blue stone pigeons passing overhead. The migration certainly wasn't of the magnitude of the now extinct passenger pigeon described by Audubon in the Ohio River valley of 1813, when "the sun was obscured as if by an eclipse, and their dung fell like melting flakes of snow," but it was awesome nevertheless. Dependent as we were on living off the land, we shot enough pigeons for an evening meal, splitting and then whacking the birds flat with the blade of a machete so they would cook evenly over an open fire. I simply rubbed each half with olive oil, salt, and pepper and placed them over the coals in a hinged grill, basting with a dollop of oil now and then to spark a flame and get the birds crusty. I made a pot of brown rice and peas, then sliced some fresh sweet pineapple that was stowed in our trailer, and by the time dusk gave way to the Southern Cross we had a meal fit for that legendary chef Taillevent (real name

Guillaume Tirel, author of the oldest of French cookbooks, *Le Viandier*) who was flattening pigeons for Charles V in the year 1375.

On a world basis there are more than 280 species of doves and pigeons in the family Columbidae, occurring in both temperate and tropical zones. Taxonomically there is no difference between the two, except that doves are generally smaller than pigeons. The rock dove, or feral pigeon, was first domesticated in Egypt in about 3000 B.C. and has since evolved into hundreds of strains, most of which are found flocking in the parks of cities (true wild pigeons bear no relation to the feral rock dove as they are not only wary of man but swift in flight, providing a target about the size of a billiard ball traveling at forty miles per hour). Some strains are bred in captivity for the production of squab, with the farms located mainly in South Carolina, Maryland, Pennsylvania, and New York. However, domestic squab differ from the wild dove and pigeon species that are harvested by hunters in being gamier in flavor and often chewier, if not rubbery, in texture as the shooter cannot selectively target young as opposed to adult birds. Among the wild doves and pigeons in our sphere of kitchen influence are the white-winged dove (*Zenaida asiatica*) of the Southwest and Mexico, the bandtailed pigeon (*Columba fasciata*) of the far West, the white crowned pigeon (*Columba leucocephala*) of the Bahamas and West Indies, and the ubiquitous mourning dove (*Zenaida macroura*).

The mourning dove is the most widely distributed and abundant game bird in North America. It occurs in every state in the Union, including Hawaii and southeastern Alaska. With an annual harvest of forty-nine to fifty million birds in the thirty-three states where it is legally hunted, it is the most popular wild fowl at table, particularly in the South. On the old plantations, especially in the Low Country of South Carolina, dove is as traditional at table as spoon bread, country ham, grits, and collard greens. Beginning in September, organized dove shoots are as much a social event as the grouse season is in Scotland, when antebellum manor houses trade invitations for a day in the field and an evening at the groaning board. Unlike its relative the passenger pigeon, which had a highly specialized mast diet and nested but once a year, the mourning dove eats any seed or grain available and may nest as often as four or five times annually. And while the passenger pigeon was almost reclusive by colonizing in once abundant deciduous forests, the mourning dove thrives best where man has burned over, chopped, and plowed the woods into open farmland. In more recent years, with the widespread decline of quail habitat, where the bobwhite was once our number-one game bird, the popularity of dove hunting has increased tremendously, yet with no measurable effect on its standing population.

The white-winged dove is found in the southwestern United States, notably in Texas, and its range extends down through Mexico, Central America, and as far south as Chile. It also occurs in small numbers along our gulf states and in south Florida. In Latin America it is known as the *paloma blanca* and appears by the millions over the grain fields of Mexico and Colombia. The citadel of whitewing shooting today is the Hacienda Alta Vista, a hunting and fishing lodge on the shore of Lake Vicente Guerron in Mexico.

Little more than a century ago in the eastern half of the United States, passenger pigeons occurred in uncounted billions. Except for our bison herds, no other wildlife was as important as a source of food and income for farmers and professional hunters. When railroads penetrated critical nesting areas, the pigeons were shot and delivered to city-bound trains by wagonloads. The fledgling squabs, which commanded a much higher price (fifty cents a dozen as opposed to thirty cents for the adults), were simply shaken from the trees. The post–Civil War Fulton Market processed 18,000 pigeons per day, and 1,800,000 birds were taken from one nesting site near Plattsburg, New York.

As table fare, I would rate the mourning dove as superior among the wild species. The meat is dark and rich, similar to that of the woodcock but milder in flavor and always uniquely tender. A dressed bird weighs only about three to four ounces, and while two are generally considered a portion, three doves are suggested for hearty appetites. There are two schools of thought on dressing doves; the quick method is to "shuck the bird out" by holding the dove breast up in both hands and, with thumbs on opposite sides of the keel bone, pressing down and apart. The delicate skin will separate, and you can easily pry the breast meat out. Admittedly there is little meat elsewhere on a dove, but I think the skin adds a dollop of flavor with its infinitesimal fat, so I pluck my birds. Doves are easy to defeather if plucked promptly after the shoot. As with all small game birds, you have to be careful about timing the cooking process as they come to a peak in texture rather quickly. As with other dark-meated birds, they can be served rare (red at breast center) when the internal temperature is 130°F, medium (light pink at breast center) at 140°F, which is my preference, or well-done (cooked through but still moist) at 150°F.

In medieval times every royal household in Europe had its "dovecote" for squabbing pigeons to ensure a regular supply of young birds. The squab was considered such a delicacy that in both England and France only wealthy landowners were permitted by law to erect a pigeon loft. However, because of the low reproduction rate among pigeons, squab could never compete with other poultry on a commercial basis, and even today, when compared to the 4.2-billion-bird chicken industry, it remains a somewhat exotic, or ethnic, food, primarily in the realm of Chinese and French restaurants. But in the past two years the bird has become a very trendy dish in *nouvelle* kitchens, usually served in a puddle of raspberry sauce. Nevertheless, ample supplies of squab are regularly stocked in supermarkets and specialty meat shops throughout the country. Squab are medium-dark-meated (not as dark as the mourning dove), plump-breasted birds with a pale game flavor. The meat is somewhat firmer in texture than that of chicken, but it can be cooked in a variety of ways, provided it is truly a squab. Some notable restaurants fail to make a distinction between squab and the adult pigeon, which quickly toughens with age. A squab should be no more than four weeks old at maximum, preferably three weeks, and weigh no more than twelve ounces and preferably less; anything heavier qualifies as a pigeon, yet birds weighing fifteen to eighteen ounces are sometimes marked as "squab."

If you have a choice between fresh and frozen squab, fresh is definitely best. The birds can be roasted, baked, stewed *en casserole*, deep-fried, minced and stir-fried, split and grilled over charcoal, or made into a mousse (the most ethereal of that genre is done by the Lion d'Or in Washington, D.C.). Essentially they can be treated in any manner by which you would prepare a chicken. However, they will toughen and dry out if overcooked. The ideal internal temperature is 140°F at the breast center, when the juice is bloodless and runs clear. The usual cooking time is about 45 to 55 minutes at 400°F, depending on the size of the bird.

In the following recipes, which call for light soy sauce and dark soy sauce, the distinction is not one of color, which is a deep brown in either case. What Chinese chefs refer to as light and dark is really the viscosity of the sauce, the dark being a denser or thicker fluid and less salty than the light. I use Pearl River brand Mushroom Soy Sauce for the dark and Pearl River brand Superior Soy for the light.

SQUAB SOONG

SERVES 2

In Cantonese, *soong* means loose; the ingredients are intended to be mixed, but not bound together, as in an omelet or crêpe.

2 tablespoons soybean oil
1 squab breast, deboned and diced
2 tablespoons diced water chestnuts
¼ cup diced mushrooms
¼ cup diced bamboo shoots
1 garlic clove, peeled and minced
dash of dry sherry
dash of white vinegar
dash of dark sesame oil
½ teaspoon dark soy sauce
½ teaspoon cayenne pepper (optional)
salt and pepper to taste
2 large Boston lettuce leaves

In a wok, heat the soybean oil to 350°F. Stir-fry the squab, water chestnuts, mushrooms, and bamboo shoots for about 30 seconds. Add the garlic and stir for another 20 seconds. Mix in the sherry, vinegar, sesame oil, soy sauce, cayenne if desired, and salt and pepper.

Divide the mixture in half and mound neatly on the lettuce leaves. Wrap the lettuce around the squab mixture and eat as a finger food.

COLD WHOLE SQUAB

SERVES 2

This squab preparation is traditionally a finger food and is usually served as an appetizer.

5 quarts chicken stock
½ teaspoon five-spice powder
2 scallions, diced
2 thin 1-inch slices fresh gingerroot
1 teaspoon dried orange peel
1 tablespoon dry sherry
¼ cup dark soy sauce
pinch of sugar
salt and pepper to taste
2 whole squab, dressed

Combine all ingredients except the squab in a stockpot. Bring to a boil, then simmer for at least 10 minutes to mingle the flavors. Add the squab, bring back to a boil, reduce the heat, and simmer for 5 minutes. Remove the pot from the heat, let it cool, then chill in the refrigerator. Serve cold, either whole or cut into joints.

DEEP-FRIED SQUAB

SERVES 2

¼   cup light soy sauce
¼   cup dark soy sauce
2   tablespoons dry sherry
pinch of sugar
pepper to taste
2   whole squab, dressed
soybean oil for deep frying
lemon wedges for serving

Combine the soy sauces, sherry, sugar, and pepper in a small bowl. Brush this marinade inside and outside each bird. Allow the squab to rest for 30 minutes, drain any excess fluid from the body cavity, and let rest again until the birds are dry. Heat enough oil for deep frying to 325°F. Add the squab and fry for 8 to 10 minutes. This low temperature will crisp but not burn the skin. Serve whole or halved with lemon wedges.

SQUAB CHOPS WITH TRUFFLES AND FOIE GRAS

SERVES 6

6   squab
¼   cup port
2   tablespoons cognac
½   pound duck foie gras
1   large truffle
7   tablespoons unsalted
     butter
2   shallots, minced
1   egg yolk
½   teaspoon salt plus
     additional to taste
⅛   teaspoon ground allspice
1   tablespoon truffle juice
1   onion, chopped
1   carrot, chopped
1   cup dry white wine
1   cup veal stock
1   tomato, peeled and
     chopped
1   fresh thyme sprig
6   ounces pork caul
pepper to taste

Dress the squab, setting the livers and hearts aside for the stuffing. Debone the breast and legs. Set aside 6 leg bones to use as bones for the chops. Reserve all remaining bones for the stock. Split the breast and marinate in the port and cognac for 2 to 3 hours. Cut the foie gras to make 6 neat slices and set all scraps aside for the stuffing. Cut the truffle into 12 thin slices.

To make the stuffing, grind together the meat from the legs, the scraps from the foie gras, the livers, and the hearts. Melt 2 tablespoons of the butter in a skillet and sauté the minced shallots for 2 minutes; do not let them color. In a bowl, mix the ground meats, the shallots in the butter, the egg yolk, ½ teaspoon salt, the allspice, and the truffle juice. Set in the refrigerator until ready to use.

To make the squab stock, brown the reserved bones in a heavy saucepan over moderate heat. Add the onion and carrot and continue to cook for 10 minutes, stirring occasionally. Deglaze the pan with the white wine, scraping up all the brown bits from the pan. Pour in the veal stock and the marinade from the breast meat and add the tomato and thyme. Let the stock cook slowly for 1 hour. When done, it should have the consistency of a light syrup. Strain the stock through a fine strainer

into a clean container and keep in a cool place until ready to use it.

Preheat the oven to 350°F.

Spread the pork caul out on a work surface and cut it into 6 equal squares. Put a thin layer of stuffing on each square, using about half of the mixture altogether. Put one breast piece on the stuffing, then on top arrange one of the reserved leg bones so that it will look like a chop bone. Put a slice of foie gras on top, then 2 truffle slices. Place the second breast piece on top, then cover everything with another layer of the stuffing. Use the caul to wrap the package, forming a chop shape with the leg bone sticking out at one side. Melt 3 tablespoons of the remaining butter in a shallow roasting pan and place the chops in it in a single layer. Roast them for 10 minutes; the breast meat should remain pink.

When the breast meat is done, remove chops from the pan. Spoon off the fat from the pan and deglaze the pan with the strained stock, scraping the bottom of the roasting pan. Bring the liquid to a simmer. Cut the remaining 2 tablespoons of butter into small pieces and add them, one at a time, to the liquid, whisking each piece in before adding the next. Season the sauce with salt and pepper. Serve each chop on a dinner plate and spoon about 3 tablespoons of sauce on top. Serve with sautéed wild mushrooms, fresh green beans, and *noisette* potatoes.

Roast Stuffed Squab with Brown Rice and Caramel Sau

ROAST STUFFED SQUAB WITH
BROWN RICE AND CARAMEL SAUCE

SERVES 6

6 squab	2 tablespoons chopped celery	¼ cup chopped shelled walnuts
¾ cup brown rice	6 tablespoons butter	½ teaspoon crumbled dried thyme
½ medium onion, chopped	½ cup diced apples	½ teaspoon ground sage
		salt and pepper to taste

¼ cup butter
1 cup firmly packed dark brown sugar
2 tablespoons water
2 tablespoons maple syrup
½ cup dry vermouth
2 tablespoons Sauce Demi-Glace (see Index)

Debone the squab and reserve the bones for the sauce.

To prepare the stuffing, cook the rice according to the package directions until almost tender. In a skillet, sauté the onion and celery in 2 tablespoons of the butter for 2 minutes. Add ¼ cup of the apples, 2 tablespoons of the walnuts, the herbs, and salt and pepper. Mix with the brown rice. Season the inside of the squab with salt and pepper and stuff them with the rice mixture. Pat each squab into its natural shape and tie with butcher's twine.

Preheat the oven to 400°F.

CARAMEL SAUCE

To make the caramel sauce, melt the ¼ cup butter in a heavy skillet. Add the brown sugar, water, and maple syrup and stir to blend. Set aside off the heat. Roast the reserved bones in a shallow pan until browned. Deglaze the pan with the vermouth and add the Sauce Demi-Glace. Add the deglazing to the brown sugar mixture and simmer for 30 minutes to make a caramel sauce. Strain.

Reset the oven to 350°F.

Brush the birds with 2 tablespoons of the remaining butter. In a heavy skillet over high heat, sear the squab until pale golden on all sides. Transfer to a baking dish and roast until golden brown. Baste with caramel sauce while they are roasting.

Sauté the remaining walnuts and apples in the remaining 2 tablespoons butter until tender for garnish. When the squab are ready, place them on a round serving platter, pour the sauce over them, and sprinkle the garnish around them.

DOVE AND BROCCOLI CASSEROLE

SERVES 4 TO 6

2   pounds broccoli
salt
8 to 12 dove breasts
½   pound mushrooms
2   tablespoons butter
5   teaspoons minced onion
1   cup heavy cream
⅔   cup mayonnaise
½   cup milk
1   tablespoon curry powder
1   tablespoon lemon juice
2   ounces Cheddar cheese,
      shredded (½ cup)
white pepper to taste
1   cup cracker crumbs

Wash the broccoli, peel stems completely, and chop stems and flowerets into ⅓-inch pieces. There should be about 3 cups. Put broccoli in a stainless-steel saucepan, add ½ teaspoon salt, and cover with cold water. Bring to a boil and cook, uncovered, until broccoli is almost tender but still crunchy, about 5 minutes. Drain in a colander, rinse with cold water, and drain again. Set aside.

Poach the dove breasts in water with a pinch of salt until just tender, about 15 minutes. When cool enough to handle, remove meat from the bones and cut into slivers or cubes, keeping the pieces fairly large and approximately the same size. Lightly oil a 6-cup casserole. Arrange the drained broccoli with the pieces of dove meat in an even layer in the casserole.

Preheat the oven to 350°F.

Wipe the mushrooms with a damp cloth and trim base of stems. Chop the mushrooms. Melt the butter in a saucepan and sauté the minced onion until golden. Add the mushrooms and simmer, stirring often, until the mushrooms release their juices and begin to brown lightly. Slowly pour in the cream and continue to simmer until the mixture is well combined and begins to reduce. Remove the saucepan from the heat and stir in the mayonnaise, milk, curry powder, lemon juice, and cheese. Season with white pepper and add a little salt if needed. Mix well. Spoon the sauce mixture over the dove meat and broccoli. Sprinkle the cracker crumbs evenly on top. Bake for 30 minutes.

DOVE VÉRONIQUE CLARENDON PLANTATION

SERVES 4

8   doves, dressed
2   tablespoons chopped
    onion
6   tablespoons butter
salt and pepper to taste
1   cup Chablis
2   tablespoons chopped
    fresh parsley
2   tablespoons chopped
    fresh tarragon *or* 2
    teaspoons dried

1   cup seedless white
    grapes without stems,
    washed and dried
16   toast triangles

In a large skillet, brown the doves and the onion in the butter, turning them to color them evenly. Season with salt and pepper. Add ½ cup of the wine and simmer, covered, for 15 minutes, or until doves are tender. Add the remaining ½ cup wine, the parsley, and the tarragon. Simmer, uncovered, for 5 minutes. Before serving, add the grapes for just long enough to heat them through. Mount each bird on 2 toast points and spoon some of the sauce and grapes over it.

DOVE IN ORANGE AND WINE SAUCE

SERVES 4

8 dove breasts
6 tablespoons butter,
     melted
3 tablespoons all-purpose
     flour
1 cup orange juice
¼ cup Chablis, or more if
     needed
½ cup water, or more if
     needed
¼ cup light or dark brown
     sugar

2 tablespoons grated
     orange zest
salt and pepper to taste

In a skillet with a lid, sauté the dove breasts in half of the melted butter until browned. Meanwhile, in a saucepan, blend the remaining 3 tablespoons butter with the flour. Add the orange juice, wine, and water. Cook, stirring, until the mixture boils and thickens. Add the brown sugar and orange zest and season with salt and pepper. Pour the sauce over the browned doves in the skillet. Cover and simmer gently for about 1 hour and 20 minutes or until the doves are tender. Turn the doves and baste with the sauce occasionally. Add a little wine or water if the sauce becomes too thick.

Dove au Vin Rouge

SERVES 6

12 doves, dressed
salt and pepper to taste
all-purpose flour
6 tablespoons butter
1 cup finely chopped
      celery
1 cup finely chopped
      onion
1 small green bell pepper,
      seeded and chopped
      fine

1¼ cups chicken stock
½ cup dry red wine

Sprinkle the doves with salt and pepper and roll them in flour. Melt the butter in a skillet and brown the doves slowly on all sides.

Preheat the oven to 350°F.

Transfer the doves to a 2-quart casserole and add the celery, onion, bell pepper, and chicken stock. Cover the casserole and bake for 2 hours. Add the red wine for the last 30 minutes of baking time.

DOVE GRILLED OVER MESQUITE COALS

8   **white-winged or**
     mourning doves,
     dressed
4   **fresh jalapeño peppers**
onion salt to taste
8   **slices bacon**
soy sauce to taste

Wash the birds and blot dry with a paper towel. Insert one-half of a jalapeño pepper into the body cavity of each bird.

Sprinkle the doves lightly with onion salt. Wrap each bird in a strip of bacon and secure with toothpicks; then sprinkle generously with soy sauce.

In a charcoal grill, build a fire to one side using mesquite wood, mesquite charcoal, or regular charcoal with a few small chunks of mesquite added. Sear the birds directly over the coals, uncovered, for 2 minutes.

With barbecue tongs, move the birds, breast up, to the other side of the grill, off the fire, and cook with the lid on for 10 minutes. Turn the birds around so the opposite sides of the doves are facing the fire and cook for another 10 minutes. Remove the lid and again place the birds over the coals. Sprinkle liberally with soy sauce and cook, un-covered, for 1½ minutes on each side.

10. WILD TURKEY

The wild turkey is unquestionably the king of all game birds, not merely because of its size, which has been recorded at almost thirty pounds in modern times, but because of its delicate nutlike flavor. When roasted or smoked to a rich mahogany color, it becomes a memorable holiday feast. The velvety moist breast meat, with which our native bird is so richly endowed, inspired Benjamin Franklin (always the trencherman) to nominate the gobbler as our national emblem. The fact that it lost out to the bald eagle is hardly a culinary backlash. The ancient Maya people so revered the wild turkey that a potent drink called *balche* made of fermented honey and tree bark[1] was ceremonially given to the bird to cheer its spirits before going to the ax.

The wild turkey (*Meleagris gallopavo*) is a native North American member of the family Meleagrididae with an original range from southern Maine to South Dakota, including the lower portion of Ontario. It thrived south of this line, encompassing all of Mexico. While nearly extinct at the turn of the century, wild populations have increased dramatically to about two million birds in the United States due to various restoration projects. For example, Mississippi, with a population of more than 400,000 birds, and Alabama, with a population of 350,000, provide a combined harvest to hunters of more than 100,000 wild turkeys per year. While the initial efforts at restocking our forests with pen-reared wild turkeys were a dismal failure—the semidomesticated birds soon lost all

---

[1] Bark from *Lonchocarpus longistylus*, native to Quintana Roo, mixed with water; *balche* was also consumed by those attending ceremonial rituals—"if a person was not drunk, proper respect was not being shown to the gods" (*Relaciones de Yucatan*).

Jeff Summerour of The Explorers with his roulade of wild turkey and grilled pears.

sense of predator survival, becoming free lunch for bobcats and foxes (on our farm we had "wild" turkeys retreating to our barn)—the technique of capturing flocks of native birds with a cannon net and delivering them to unpopulated areas was a resounding success. These liberated birds reproduced in new habitats, and today the wild turkey is found in forty-five states.

There are four distinct subspecies differing mainly in details of plumage: the Eastern wild turkey (*Meleagris gallopavo silvestris*), Florida wild turkey (*Meleagris g. osceola*), Rio Grande wild turkey (*Meleagris g. intermedia*), and Merriman's wild turkey (*Meleagris g. merriami*). Distinct from these is a second species, the ocellated wild turkey (*Agriocharis ocellata*), which occurs only in the Yucatan, Guatemala, and Belize. There is little flavor difference in their individual excellence at table, except for the unique ocellated bird. According to Colonel Dave Harbour, who has spent a lifetime at the game and is the author of *Advanced Wild Turkey Hunting and World Records* (Winchester Press, 1983), the ocellated in its home range of rain forests is a "sweeter" bird due to an almost exclusive diet of berries. Dave told me that the ocellated "doesn't even speak the same language as other turkeys; instead of yelps and gobbles, it sounds like an old-fashioned sewing machine being cranked up."

There is no difference in flavor between a hen and a tom among wild turkeys. Prime birds are taken in the spring season. Due to the turkey's metabolism, a wild bird is lean at the end of summer and early fall and reaches its plumage stage about six months later. This is true throughout its range. The best birds at the table are those taken on spring hunts; an eighteen-pound fall gobbler will weigh twenty pounds the following March, and most of its weight goes to breast fat—poorly emulated by the commercial "self-basting" turkeys that are pumped full of alien vegetable oils. Southern turkeys are generally smaller in size than northern populations; in my home state of Florida, hens are usually six to eight pounds, the toms eleven to fourteen pounds. A gobbler over twenty pounds is a real trophy. Tame strains culled from many years of breeding, such as the domestic Broad-Breasted Bronze turkey, have been reared to over seventy pounds, at which point the gobbler practically collapses from sheer mechanical stress.

Turkeys were first domesticated in ancient times by the Aztec Indians of Mexico and were shipped to Spain in about 1520 by the conquistadores. From here the bird was sold to breeders throughout Europe. In the sixteenth century nobody made a distinction between them and the already popular guinea fowl, which came to Europe from Africa by way of the Turkish Empire, so they were both known as "turkie fowl." By the time our early colonists arrived at Plymouth in 1621, not only was the name *turkey* a historical conundrum, but ironically, some settlers brought along their tame breeding stock, which was like bringing coals to Newcastle since the virgin hardwood forests of North America were the ancestral home of every turkey in the world.

COOKING NOTES

Turkeys have more feathers than a Hollywood mattress. This quickly becomes apparent if you dry-pluck a bird in the field. The pinfeathers can be a real problem. Ideally the gobbler should be wetted down with scalding water in camp, plucked, then bled and chilled. At home the bird can be drawn and hung or aged in the refrigerator for a week at a temperature of 40 to 50°F. Like most game birds, wild turkey is easily overcooked, especially if the standard roasting recommendation for domestic birds—an internal temperature of 180 to 185°F—is followed. If you allow ten minutes per pound in a 350°F oven to arrive at an internal temperature of 145 to 150°F, the turkey will be firm yet moist and easily carved. The long legs of a wild turkey (longer and tougher than the domestic kind) are full of sinews and are virtually inedible unless these are carefully removed. Personally I reserve the legs for making game stock.

Traditionally a roast turkey is cooked with some kind of stuffing. In my opinion the best stuffing for all game birds should reflect the fowl's natural foods, including pecans, chestnuts, peanuts, walnuts, and pine nuts and fruits such as apples, cherries, grapes (or raisins), figs, and pears. Alien ingredients such as sausages, anchovies, and oysters do not complement delicately flavored birds such as quail, ruffed grouse, or wild turkey. The ubiquitous oyster dressing is to me a waste of bivalves. Oysters stuffed into a bird simply turn to rubbery pellets; they are better served on the half-shell as an introductory course—or, as done at formal colonial tables, presented in a casserole as a side dish.

CARVING BREAST MEAT

According to *The Boke of Kervynge* (Wynkn de Worde, 1508), the carving of game was done with great ceremony during the medieval period. One did not casually take a blade to bird or animal; in fact the various techniques required special knives, stylized hand positions, and predetermined strokes. Even the semantics differed: the skilled carver would *unlatch* a curlew, *alay* a pheasant, *display* a crane, *wing* a partridge, *break* an egret, or *unlace* a coney (rabbit). Specific and small portions were served in sequence, and at baronial dinners the better cuts separated noble guests from hungry commoners.

Although nobody is unlatching curlews or breaking egrets in this modern age, the simple procedure of carving a turkey breast defeats many home chefs. The breast meat is easily shredded if cut at an angle. After removing the leg and thigh, use a long, thin sharp knife to cut the breast meat *straight* down while holding the bird steady with a fork.

SMOKE-COOKED TURKEY

There are many variables in describing the procedures in smoke cooking, which depend on the type of unit used. Each manufacturer includes an instruction pamphlet that describes the essential details. However, the food preparation is simple and the flavor of the product delicious. For my part I prefer a water smoker, which slow-cooks meats in a moist heat. Although smoked turkey is ordinarily immersed in a brine solution before the smoking process begins, this is not necessary in smoke cooking; the introduction of salt provides a longer shelf life and doesn't contribute to the subtle flavor of a bird that is to be consumed within a few days. In a water smoker the grill that holds the bird is located directly over a water pan, and the heat source is below the pan. The water vaporizes slightly, providing moisture to the meat, while the charcoal and wood create an aromatic smoke. However, good results can also be obtained on any lidded charcoal grill of suitable size without the water pan.

To smoke-cook a wild turkey over dry heat I first roast the bird in a 350°F oven for about one-half the time that I would normally cook it; this should be done in a shallow roasting pan with the bird under a loose foil tent, basting occasionally with melted butter. The turkey is then transferred to the charcoal grill. Place an aluminum foil drip pan in the center of the grill and surround it with charcoal; there should be twenty-five to thirty briquets on each side of the pan, lengthwise. Burn the coals until gray and sprinkle with presoaked wood chips. Place the turkey on the rack over the drip pan and put the lid on the smoker, leaving the vents open. Add six to eight briquets and additional chips on each side of the pan every hour to maintain a heat of about 325°F. There is no absolute in timing a smoke-cooked turkey as the size of the bird, wind, air temperature, type of grill, and application of fuel will determine doneness. With the Meat Thermicator the internal temperature in the thickest part of the breast should read 155 to 160°F.

PAN-FRIED WILD TURKEY

SERVES 6

2 pounds turkey breast meat, cut into thin slices (about ¼ inch)
½ cup all-purpose flour
2 eggs
2 tablespoons water
¼ teaspoon ground nutmeg
1 cup cracker meal

1 cup vegetable oil
chopped parsley for garnish

Dust the turkey slices with the flour. Beat the eggs with the water and nutmeg. Dip the slices in the egg mixture and then in the cracker meal. According to the size of the pan and the number of slices, use a sufficient quantity of oil to sauté the turkey, adding more to the pan as necessary. The slices will cook quickly, about 2 minutes on each side. Garnish with chopped parsley.

Overleaf: Roast wild turkey with all the trimmings.

BRAISED WILD TURKEY

An old tom turkey will weigh about 18 to 20 pounds; this is especially true of the Eastern and Merriam varieties. The "beard" on a tom (which extends from the breast) may be 6 to 9 inches long, but as with the spurs above the feet (which are often eroded or broken) these don't indicate age. Experienced wild turkey hunters who have spent time in the kitchen favor braising an old bird over roasting, and optionally frying the thigh and breast meat.

1   large tom turkey, dressed
salt and pepper
2   large onions, peeled and quartered
3   celery ribs, cut into chunks

1   apple, peeled, cored, and cut into chunks
4   slices salt pork
4   cups turkey or chicken broth
1   large onion, peeled and chopped
2   celery ribs, sliced
1   large carrot, sliced
6   parsley sprigs
2   fresh rosemary sprigs
2   teaspoons fresh thyme leaves *or* 1 teaspoon dried
2   tablespoons cornstarch, mixed with enough warm water to make a paste

Preheat the oven to 450°F.

If the turkey is wet, dry thoroughly with paper towels.

Sprinkle inside and out with salt and pepper. Place the onion quarters, celery chunks, and apple in the bird's cavity. This is not a stuffing but maintains moisture and flavor. Tie the legs together with string, snubbing around the tail, and bind the pork slices to the breast area. Place in a roasting pan, uncovered, and roast until browned (about 20 minutes). Skim any fat from the pan and add the broth, chopped onion, sliced celery, carrot, parsley, rosemary, and thyme. Cover the pan tightly and cook on top of the stove over medium heat or in the oven at 350°F. Baste frequently with pan juices. Cook until the bird is tender (4 to 5 hours). Transfer the bird to a heated platter. Strain the pan juices, add the cornstarch mixture, and blend over medium heat until the sauce is thickened.

TURKEY SCALOPPINE WITH ZUCCHINI

SERVES 2

2   teaspoons butter or margarine
1   medium zucchini, cut lengthwise into 4 slices
¼   cup all-purpose flour
4   slices turkey breast meat, cut into thin medallions
1   teaspoon chopped fresh rosemary *or* ½ teaspoon dried
1   tablespoon lemon juice
2   tablespoons dry vermouth
12 capers
freshly ground black pepper

In a large skillet, melt 1 teaspoon of the butter over medium heat. Dust the zucchini slices with the flour and shake off the excess; reserve the flour. Cook the zucchini for about 2 minutes on each side or until lightly browned. Set aside on a warm platter.

Dredge the turkey slices in the reserved flour and shake off the excess. Add the remaining teaspoon of butter to the skillet and, when melted, sprinkle half of the rosemary into the pan and add the turkey slices. Cook for about 2 to 3 minutes, until lightly browned, then turn over, adding the balance of the rosemary so it adheres to both sides of the turkey. Cook for another 2 to 3 minutes, until the medallions are tender.

Arrange the turkey slices on a warm platter with the zucchini. To the skillet, add the lemon juice, vermouth, and capers. Bring to a boil and scrape any browned bits from the bottom of the pan. Pour the juices over the turkey and zucchini. Sprinkle with pepper to taste.

11. DUCKS AND GEESE

DUCKS

Of all the ancient cultures that extolled the virtues of duck cookery, none was more enthusiastic than the Egyptian. A golden shrine was found in the tomb of Tutankhamen (c. 1361 to 1352 B.C.) that depicts the pharaoh standing in a reed boat throwing a boomerang at a duck. In my latitudes, sitting muzzle to muzzle in a blind with a black Labrador whose steaming breath at zero degrees is fogging my glasses, downing a mallard with a bent stick seems ludicrous, yet the hieroglyphic reads, "it is a million that fall to the whistle of its wind." Indeed, the harvest was so great that Sebek-hotep, governor of Fayum Province, was given the title "Overseer of the Swamps of Enjoyment" and charged with conserving their flocks. What has transpired during the ensuing 3,000 years with the domestication of the duck, particularly in Europe and Asia, parallels the history of many game birds and animals that lost some culinary identity when farmed in captivity.

There are more than a hundred species of ducks on a world basis, and their relative table values in aroma, texture, and flavor—aside from the differences among species involved—is determined largely by the principal foods the birds have consumed. Technically there are seven tribes of ducks, and from a culinary point of view these can be divided into three broad groups: puddle ducks, diving ducks, and sea ducks. Puddle ducks can walk or run on land and are mainly herbivorous, eating either terrestrial plants and grains or aquatic vegetation when feeding in shallow water. The gourmet's classic puddle duck is a wild mallard that has been idling in corn and wheat fields or gorging on wild rice. Diving ducks, with their paddle-shaped feet located near the rear of the body (as opposed to the midpoint in puddle ducks), shun land but are able to swim great distances underwater in lakes and rivers, where their diet is primarily fish, mollusks, crustaceans, and aquatic plants. This diet may have a negative effect on duck flavor in some cases, but the canvasback, a diving duck that feeds principally on vegetation, is historically the bird of epicures. The third group, sea ducks, such as the scoters, which are also divers but essentially coastal inhabitants and disparagingly known as "fish ducks," are, except for the breast meat, strongly flavored. Fully 80 percent of their diet consists of mussels and clams, which concentrates a bivalve taste, especially in the oils of the skin. However, the completely skinned and carefully defatted breast, lightly brined to leech out the blood, then drained, is not only edible but comparable to that of more popular table species. Indeed, sea ducks have a faithful coterie of hypothermia-proof hunters who will face steaming whitecaps in New England's winter gales just to collect a "coot" stew. My old compatriot, Van Campen Heilner, the dean of peripatetic water-fowlers, once wrote, "if every state has a flag and a state flower, some of them should have symbolic ducks—a canvasback for Maryland and a coot for Massachusetts."

No game fish became more symbolic of opulent dining during the nineteenth century than roast canvasback duck, with its delicate and juicy flesh brought to peak on a diet of wild celery, then served with a black cherry and walnut stuffing. These birds once numbered in countless millions, but today the total population is probably fewer than 300,000, and a brace at table is an epicurean gift of galactic dimensions. In those days of plenty, stalking ducks at night with punt guns, jury-rigged in battery formation, and team shooting from sink boxes on the eastern shores of Maryland and Virginia and in the marshes of Long Island, took a critical toll. A two-man team of New York suppliers, who apparently melted their barrels in the spring of 1878, killed 640 ducks in a single day for a price of twenty-five cents a pair. In every bay and pothole, a greedy army of market hunters delivering to Chicago, Philadelphia, and Boston were bringing waterfowl and shorebirds to oblivion.

The canvasback suffered especially, not only from the gun; even nature conspired in the decline of the specialized breeding and feeding habitats these divers depend on. The colonists at James River reported a scarcity of canvasbacks as early as 1780 due to a winterkill of *Vallisneria* that destroyed the roots of this celerylike plant. Long before the age of herbicides, the duck that steamily graced every aristocratic table dove into troubled waters. For the nonhunting public, it disappeared when market shooting was abolished by the federal government in 1918. In recent years, due to our degrading aquatic habitat and the near extinction of *Vallisneria*, the canvasback duck often resorts to gorging on clams and fish, and the duck that once was called "feathered gold" is not always today of gourmet caliber.

But to anybody who has popped a pellet in the wind, a wild duck—be it mallard, redhead, wood duck, ringbill, black, teal, ad infinitum—is in a class by itself; the flesh of all wild ducks is lean with only specks of fat, a totally different product from heavily larded domestic breeds such as the white Peking, the Muscovy, and, at the height of obesity, the moulard. It was the arrival of the Peking (or Peckin among Yankee traders), brought from China to New York in 1873, that created what was for almost a century the world's largest duck industry in the tidewater creeks of Long Island's south shore.[1] When market hunting ceased, that Oriental import became our standard-bearer, but the only thing it had in common with a vintage canvasback was a quack.

To digress for a moment, in modern marketing there is a third category of duck (and other game) that is semidomesticated. The term *wild game* as applied to animals and fowl sold commercially is to some extent misleading.[2] It is illegal for hunters to sell wild game of any kind in America. Those products that enter the trade must by law be raised on preserves under semiwild or wild conditions and are subject to state meat inspection. To what degree the game is confined or consumes wild foods without supplemental feeding and the age at which it is harvested are variables that affect quality. Frequently, semidomestication will improve the product; the mallard duck, for example, retains its wild genetic characteristics, including the "home pond" instinct. Even though fed domestic fodder, when harvested at its tender best before it fledges (at six weeks), it is not as lean as a true wild duck or as fat as a domestic such as the Peking duck. Indeed the demand for mallard produced on some preserves, particularly among many embassies in Washington, D.C., where "wild" duck is the culinary fashion, is insatiable. And free-ranging mallard and black duck populations are declining because of the destruction of wetlands critical as winter feeding areas for waterfowl migrating from Canada; nine

---

[1]Soaring prices for waterfront property are a prime factor in the disappearance of duck farms. Since the 1960s Long Island production dropped from six million birds to the current 3.5 million per year, representing just 16 percent of the national market.

[2]It also follows that the Rock Cornish Game hen is not a game bird but a popular and tasty domestic chicken. This bird is derived from a White Cornish rooster crossed with a White Rockhen. The name *Cornish* indicates the origin of the breed in Cornwall, England. Historically, Cornish fowl were known as "Indian Games," as they are derived from Old English Game chickens crossed with Asells from India.

drake green-winged teal and a drake pintail.

million acres were destroyed in a recent twenty-year period due mainly to flood control projects and agricultural practices. As a result the quality of native birds is not everywhere reliable. The market wild mallard on the other hand, such as those fowl produced by Wildlife Nurseries in Oshkosh, Wisconsin, is consistently as flavorsome as a duck can be, by any cooking method.

COOKING NOTES

The great gap between cooking a genuine wild duck, one collected by a hunter over a set of decoys, and a domestic bird is in elapsed time. They are two different kitchen disciplines. Wild ducks are best prepared at high heat (475°F) with a roasting time of fourteen to fifteen minutes for small birds such as teal and bufflehead to about twenty minutes for the larger black, mallard, or canvasback. The duck will arrive at an internal temperature of 140°F, which finds the meat a medium pink, firm, and tender. However, it must be butter- or oil-basted to crisp the skin during cooking. The lean musculature of a bird that flies at speeds of forty miles per hour is vastly different from one that is reared in a pen. Domestic ducks, many of which thrive in a totally sedentary environment, never learning to swim, much less fly, require slow cooking for 1½ to two hours at low heat (325°F) for their fat to liquefy and drip away. Different methods are used to achieve a crisp finish. When making tea duck, for example, the Chinese first steam the bird, then smoke it, and then quickly brown it in a deep-fryer. Personally, I get good results on a barbecue grill by placing the birds on a rack over a large drip pan, which I surround with glowing briquets—cooking with the cover on. About an inch of water in the pan prevents the residual oil from igniting. This is a slow process with very fat domestic ducks but worthwhile if time is not of the essence. A ''crisp duck'' cannot be produced quickly; in fact the term has become a restaurant cliché. Some kitchens give a roasted bird a final few minutes under a broiler flame, which usually results in a still fatty, scorched, and overcooked fowl.

GEESE

The domestic goose is now only of minor importance in the American culinary scene. These large, fatty birds still appear on festive occasions, particularly among European ethnic groups, but our modern preoccupation with healthy fat-free diets doesn't enhance the popularity of this fowl. In the Old World, especially in France, where *pâté de foie gras* is an industry (and the dead goose a byproduct) a steaming dish of *cassoulet* nourishes winter spirits like no other stew. But the domestic goose can't be compared to the lean wild species that grace hunters' tables. Four species of wild geese are harvested in North America, the principal one being the Canada goose (*Branta canadensis*). The widely distributed Canada consists of seven races, all similar in appearance but differing greatly in size, with the smallest weighing no more than three pounds and the largest up to twenty pounds. In addition we have the white-fronted goose (*Anser albifrons*), commonly known as "specklebelly," which grows to about six pounds, and the snow goose (*Chen caerulescens*), which in a dark plumage phase is called the "blue goose" and attains a similar size. The fourth species, the brant (*Branta bernicla*), is more ducklike in appearance; it has a short neck and an average size of three to four pounds.

In common with wild ducks, the kitchen quality of geese is a reflection of their good resources. The Atlantic brant, for example, which my grandfather hunted in Great South Bay, Long Island, was considered a delicious bird before the disappearance of eelgrass (*Zostera marina*) beginning in about 1930. This mysterious epizootic occurred as far south as North Carolina, and neither the plant nor the bird has ever recovered. Eelgrass was the brant's principal forage, and it produced a succulent bird. Today, Atlantic brant feed chiefly on sea lettuce (*Ulva lactuca*), a barely life-sustaining alga, and as a result this goose is not worth cooking when it is legal to hunt—and there have been few open seasons in recent years. The Pacific or "black" brant, on the other hand, finds a variety of marine plants along its flyway and waxes fat from Alaska to Baja California. Brant are essentially coastal birds with a selective saltwater diet. Canada geese, once considered "mud flat" feeders and inferior to brant, benefited by the agricultural growth in America, particularly in corn, wheat, and rice; although never far from water, the Canada takes full advantage of farm crops. Perhaps the most important goose shooting area in the United States today is in the Texas rice country from Port Lavaca to the Louisiana border.

COOKING NOTES

Wild geese, like wild ducks, are very lean, dark-meated fowl and cannot be cooked properly in the time frames given for fat domestic birds. A wild goose is tender, pink, and juicy at an internal temperature of 130°F. At 150°F it is well-done, and at the 190°F recommended for domestic varieties it is totally inedible. As a rule of thumb, roasting time should be about twelve minutes to the pound in a 350°F oven. Medium-rare is by far the most popular presentation among veteran waterfowlers, at which point goose breast meat (in common with duck) resembles filet mignon in both texture and flavor. However, the legs and thighs will be undercooked; these can be excised beforehand and saved for the stockpot (my preference) or turned into a soup, salad, or casserole or cooked separately for an additional time period. I seldom roast small geese; birds of 2½ to four pounds can be skinned out as described for ducks (page 135) and the breast meat sautéed or charcoal-broiled. This is a good method when entertaining a large number of guests who may have different preferences—from very rare to medium-rare.

PRESSED DUCK

SERVES 6

Pressed duck is popular in Europe, and perhaps the most famous version is found at La Tour d'Argent in Paris, where *canard à la presse* (or, by historical claim, *caneton Rouennais à la presse*) is a daily house specialty. Few restaurants on this side of the Atlantic are prepared to press a duck, and even those still familiar with the voluptuary ritual, such as the 21 Club in New York, require advance notice. After roasting the birds, the dish is executed in view on a *table volante* or "flying table," where the breast meat is skinned and sliced, then set aside. The carcasses are then cut into pieces and squeezed in a press, later to work their fluid magic in a chafing dish. Obviously, this can be a spectacular ceremony at home, a luscious creation that is the pure essence of waterfowl—and really easy to do. A second recipe for the dish follows this one. Although duck presses are expensive and not widely available except from a specialty supplier such as the Orvis Company (Manchester, Vermont 05254), no serious game kitchen is complete without one.

The very best duck to press is a semidomesticated mallard, the kind you decoy by phone from Balducci or Lobel & Sons, or one such as a redhead from Core Sound, North Carolina, whose wild credentials exclude a fish diet.

Traditionally, the old shooting clubs served creamed pearl onions as a side dish, and, according to Romi Perkins, who is as skilled in the field as she is in the kitchen, the Cedar Point Club on Lake Erie was famous for its "apple" sauce accompaniment that consisted of 2 Comice pears to every 6 Granny Smith apples, adding sugar, cinnamon, freshly grated nutmeg, and grated lemon zest to taste. Romi also notes that Cedar Point regulars eschewed the traditional wild rice in favor of thinly sliced halves of whole wheat bread turned butter side down, then sauced, with the duck slices placed on top.

For a wine I'd suggest a California cabernet sauvignon by Stag's Leap, Cakebread Cellars, Robert Mondavi (Insignia), Château Montelena, Joseph Phelps, or Spring Mountain.

**3   mallard ducks *or* 6 teal
       or ringbill ducks**

**1   cup dry red wine,
       preferably cabernet
       sauvignon**
¼   cup cognac
½   cup (¼ pound) butter
**6   tablespoons red or black
       currant jelly**
4   shallots, minced
juice of ½ lemon
**salt and freshly ground
       black pepper to taste**

Preheat the oven to 475°F.

Remove and reserve the duck livers and roast the birds for 15 to 20 minutes, depending on the size of the ducks, but "done" is at an instant-read-out temperature in the breast of 130 to 140°F. The leg meat will not be cooked. On any wild duck it offers little to eat in any case and is better utilized in the press. (Restaurants such as La Tour send their plumper domestic legs back to the kitchen for finishing and serve them as a dividend course.) Skin, then carve the breasts into thin slices and transfer to a warm platter.

At table, pour ½ cup of the red wine and the cognac into a chafing dish. Add any juices collected from the carving, the butter, currant jelly, minced shallots, lemon juice, and duck livers, finely minced. Cover the dish and let simmer. With kitchen shears, cut up the carcasses and put these in the press with the remaining ½ cup of wine. Press the duck, extracting all blood and juices into a pan or sauceboat, and add to the chafing dish. Season with salt and freshly ground pepper. Reheat the duck in the sauce, then arrange on serving plates over beds of wild rice. Spoon the remaining sauce over each portion.

PRESSED DUCK

SERVES 4

2   large mallard ducks,
        including livers
3   tablespoons unsalted
        butter
½   cup prepared Dijon-style
        mustard
2   cups dry bread crumbs
1½   cups good-quality dry
        red wine
2   tablespoons cognac
1   tablespoon chopped
        shallots
salt and freshly ground
        pepper to taste

Preheat the oven to 350°F.

Trim off wing tips and any extra fat from the ducks. Roast for 20 minutes. While the ducks are roasting, puree the duck livers with the butter in a food processor fitted with the steel blade and set this mixture aside at room temperature.

Reset the oven to 375°F.

When the ducks have cooled slightly, remove the legs. Remove any extra fat from the legs and coat them with mustard and bread crumbs. Return the legs to the oven to finish cooking for 25 to 30 minutes.

Remove duck fat from the breast portions and remove the wishbones. Cut long oval-shaped pieces from each breast, holding the knife parallel to the cutting board. You should get 4 slices from each breast.

Chop the duck carcass into 1-inch pieces and place them in the duck press. Add a few ounces of wine and lower the press. Squeeze the juice into a container with the pureed liver and butter. Release the press, add more wine, and press again until all the juices and blood are extracted.

Use a sauté pan large enough to hold the breast meat in a single layer. Pour in the cognac and ignite it. Sprinkle the pan with the shallots and add the mixture of duck juices and pureed liver. Warm lightly, stirring constantly, until the sauce is slightly thickened. Do not let the mixture boil. Add duck breast slices and season with salt and freshly ground pepper. Warm the slices, but do not cook them; the breast meat should still be pink. Never boil this sauce, or it will separate.

Serve the duck and sauce on warm plates, with 3 soufflé potatoes per person. When the plates are cleared, serve the duck legs with a small salad of Boston lettuce and julienne mushrooms in a light vinaigrette.

WILD DUCK THE EASY WAY

In my opinion, one of the best of all wild duck preparations is not only simple but guaranteed to be delicious. A wild duck is virtually all breast; the diminutive legs and wings provide more sinew than meat, and there is hardly any sizable part elsewhere on these fowl. I don't even pluck the birds but simply skin the breasts out (at the midline from the apex of the breastbone with the point of a knife) and excise the meat, which can then be cut lengthwise into 2 fillets. Allowing a pair of fillets for each of 4 people, I marinate the duck for about 30 minutes in 1 cup of olive oil, the juice of 1 lemon or lime, and 2 tablespoons of soy sauce and cook over a hot charcoal fire—about 4 to 5 minutes on each side or to an internal temperature of 120°F for very rare or 140°F for medium-rare. Optionally, the breast meat can be sautéed either in fillet form or as a scaloppine, by gently pounding with the flat side of a chef's knife. For the sauté pan the duck can be marinated in vermouth or white wine, then dusted with seasoned flour and cooked in clarified butter over medium heat. Deglaze the pan with vermouth or wine and spoon over the fillets. Either way the result is comparable to prime filet mignon in texture and, if anything, more flavorsome. Accompanied by wild rice, watercress salad, and a currant or gooseberry preserve, it makes a superlative meal. The remaining carcasses, incidentally, need not be wasted as these can be simmered and added to your game stock inventory in the freezer—or made into a soup.

Pressed Duck.

DUCK AND RICE CASSEROLE

SERVES 4

2　large wild ducks *or* 4 small ducks (such as teal), dressed
3　celery ribs, cut into 2-inch pieces
1　onion, halved
1¼　teaspoons salt
¼　teaspoon pepper
3　ounces (about ½ cup) wild rice
3　ounces (about ½ cup) white rice
1　cup sliced mushrooms
½　cup chopped onion
½　cup (¼ pound) butter or margarine
¼　cup all-purpose flour
1½　cups half-and-half
1　tablespoon chopped fresh parsley
½　cup slivered almonds

Place the ducks in a large pot with the celery, halved onion, salt, and pepper. Cover with water and simmer for 1 hour, until the birds are tender. Remove the duck from the broth, cool, and cut meat into bite-size pieces. Strain and reserve the broth.

Cook the rice. In a skillet, sauté the mushrooms and chopped onion in the butter until the onion is soft. Add 2 cups of the reserved duck broth and then the flour; stir until smooth. Cook over medium heat until bubbly. Add the duck pieces, half-and-half, and parsley.

Preheat the oven to 350°F.

Spread the rice in a buttered casserole dish, pour in the duck mixture, and sprinkle with the almonds. Cover and bake for 15 to 20 minutes. Uncover and cook for an additional 10 minutes.

Wild Duck the Easy Way.

WILD DUCK BREASTS WITH CILANTRO BUTTER

SERVES 4

¼   cup fresh lime juice
¼   cup canola oil
3   tablespoons cilantro leaves
8   duck breasts
½   teaspoon salt
½   teaspoon freshly ground pepper

Cilantro Butter (recipe follows)

Mix together the lime juice, canola oil, and cilantro and place in a glass baking dish. Sprinkle the duck with the salt and pepper. Coat with marinade and refrigerate overnight.

Grill the duck breasts for 3 minutes per side, then transfer to a warm platter and top each with a slice of the Cilantro Butter.

CILANTRO BUTTER

½   cup (¼ pound) butter or margarine, softened
juice of 1 medium lime
3   shallots, minced
¼   cup minced cilantro

¼   teaspoon salt
½   teaspoon pepper
¼   teaspoon cayenne pepper

Mix the softened butter with the lime juice. Stir in the shallots, cilantro, salt, pepper, and cayenne. Transfer to plastic wrap and roll into a log. Refrigerate overnight.

DUCK SOUTH BAY STYLE

SERVES 4

2   large ducks (mallard,
       black, canvasback,
       pintail, or redhead) *or*
       4 smaller ducks (teal,
       wood duck, ringbill),
       dressed
salt and pepper to taste
3   tablespoons butter
4   shallots, chopped
½   cup cognac
½   cup dry red wine
1   quart Sauce Demi-Glace
       (see Index)
½   pound mushrooms
4   slices bacon

Preheat the oven to 450°F.

Season the ducks with salt and pepper. Roast them for about 30 minutes for the large ducks, 20 minutes for the smaller ducks, or until they reach an internal temperature of 140°F. Debone the ducks and reserve the meat. Chop the bones.

Melt 2 tablespoons of the butter in a heavy saucepan and sauté the shallots and duck bones together until the shallots are brown. Pour the cognac and red wine into the saucepan of bones, heat the mixture, and ignite it. When the flames die out, reduce the liquid by half. Add the Sauce Demi-Glace and again reduce by half. Strain the sauce and season to taste. Stir in the remaining tablespoon of butter.

Wipe the mushrooms with a damp cloth and trim base of stems. Cut large mushrooms into quarters or slices; leave small button mushrooms whole. In a heavy skillet, sauté the bacon until crisp; in a bowl crumble it into pieces. Sauté the mushrooms in the fat remaining in the skillet and add them to the bacon. Reheat the duck meat in a small amount of the sauce and arrange on a warm platter. Pour the balance of the sauce over the duck. Garnish the platter with the mushrooms and bacon.

MALLARD DUCK WITH PRESERVED FIGS

SERVES 4

1   mallard duck, about 5
    pounds
¼   cup clarified butter
½   cup dry white wine
1¼ cups duck stock
2   large sugar cubes
3   tablespoons white
    vinegar
3½ ounces (1½ tablespoons)
    preserved figs
juice of ½ lemon

Dress and truss the duck and place in a braising pot with 2 tablespoons of the clarified butter. Braise until the bird is medium-rare (internal temperature 140°F). Remove the duck and deglaze the pot with the white wine. Reduce this deglazing by a quarter and mix in the duck stock. Remove the trussing strings from the duck.

Meanwhile, prepare a caramel with the sugar cubes. Crush them and melt with 1 teaspoon of water in a heavy pot. Stop the cooking of the caramel by pouring in the vinegar and then the stock mixture. Reduce the mixture if needed to adjust the consistency; it should be thick but still runny. Pass the sauce through a fine sieve. Drain the figs well and add the fig juice and the lemon juice to the sauce. In a small saucepan, heat the figs in the remaining butter. Adjust the seasoning of the sauce. Arrange the duck on a platter with the sauce and the figs around it. Serve with dauphine potatoes and asparagus tips.

Terrine de Canard

Serves 12 or More

1 large duck (mallard, redhead, or canvasback) *or* 2 small ducks (teal, ringbill, or wood duck)
1 pound boneless pork, cut into large chunks
1 pound boneless veal, cut into large chunks
¼ cup chopped shallots
1 teaspoon dried thyme *or* 1 tablespoon fresh leaves
½ bunch fresh parsley, stems removed, chopped fine
½ cup cognac
½ cup chopped shelled pistachios
salt and pepper to taste
12 to 14 thin slices *lard gras* (fatback)
1 bay leaf

Debone the ducks and chop the meat, reserving the livers. Put the duck livers, pork, and veal through a food grinder. Transfer to a bowl and mix in the shallots, thyme, and parsley. Add the cognac and stir lightly. Mix with the chopped duck and pistachios. Add salt and pepper. Make a small patty of the mixture, cook it, and taste for seasoning. Re-season if necessary.

Line a terrine or loaf pan with fatback, letting the ends dangle over the ends of the pan. Fill with the pâté mixture and top with the bay leaf. Cover with a sheet of fatback and fold the ends over the top.

Preheat the oven to 375°F.

Place a large shallow baking pan or bain-marie in the oven. Place the terrine in the baking pan, then fill the baking pan with enough hot water to come halfway up the sides of the loaf pan. Bake for 2 hours.

Remove the terrine from the oven, cover with foil, and place a weight on top. Allow to cool. Refrigerate overnight. Serve with *cornichons* or Cumberland Sauce (see Index).

Grilled Duck Breasts with Fried Plantains.

GRILLED DUCK BREASTS
WITH FRIED PLANTAINS

SERVES 4

2   mallard duck breasts
6   garlic cloves
1   poblano chili
1   ancho chili
2   tablespoons olive oil
3   tablespoons sherry
      vinegar
½   cup honey
salt and freshly ground
      pepper to taste
freshly ground cumin
1   very ripe plantain
½   cup all-purpose flour
¼   teaspoon salt
¼   teaspoon pepper
¼   teaspoon ground
      cinnamon
1   tablespoon butter
2   tablespoons peanut oil
Honey and Chilies Sauce
      (recipe follows)
fresh cilantro sprigs

Separate each duck breast into 2 pieces. Cross-score the breasts with 3 or 4 incisions. Refrigerate. Peel the garlic cloves and cut into slivers. Using rubber or plastic gloves, cut open the chili peppers and remove the stems and seeds. Cut the poblano chili into julienne strips and chop the ancho chili. Pour the olive oil into a small saucepan and set over moderate heat. Add the garlic slivers and strips of poblano; stir for 1 minute. Add the ancho chili and stir often for 15 seconds. Pour in the vinegar and let the mixture reduce by half. Add the honey. Remove this glaze from the heat and let it steep for 20 minutes. Strain. If the glaze becomes too cool, it may be necessary to reheat it to strain out the garlic and chilies. Reserve the glaze and discard the solids.

Prepare a hot grill or preheat the broiler.

Season the duck pieces with a pinch each of salt, black pepper, and cumin. Oil the grill with a cloth dipped in peanut oil. Lay the duck breasts, skin side down, on the grill. You will need to move them around and turn them over occasionally to prevent flare-ups. When the duck is half-cooked, brush the glaze on the pieces.

Peel the plantain and, with a sharp knife, cut into slices on the bias. Mix the flour with ¼ teaspoon salt, ¼ teaspoon pepper, and the cinnamon. Coat the plantain slices with the mixture; shake off excess flour. Heat the butter and peanut oil in a skillet and fry the slices for 1 to 2 minutes, turning them only once.

Slice the cooked duck breast pieces into 4 or 5 thin slices. Spoon some of the prepared sauce onto 4 warm plates and arrange the slices of duck on the sauce. Arrange the plantain slices opposite the duck slices and garnish each serving with cilantro sprigs.

HONEY AND CHILIES SAUCE

6	ounces slab bacon
12	black peppercorns, bruised
¼	cup cumin seeds
2	ancho chilies
2	chipotle chilies
1	head of garlic
2	bay leaves
5	tablespoons butter
2	tablespoons olive oil
1½	cups diced carrots
1½	cups diced onions
1	cup diced leeks, white part only
½	cup diced celery
1	cup sherry vinegar
1	cup dry sherry
2	quarts degreased duck or chicken stock

Remove any rind from the bacon and cut the bacon into small dice. Toast the pepper-corns and cumin seeds in a dry skillet. Using rubber or plastic gloves, split the chilies and re-move the stems and seeds. Toast the chilies in a dry skillet until the skins are blackened. Cut the head of garlic horizon-tally into halves. Crumble the bay leaves.

In a large but fairly shal-low saucepan over high heat, cook the bacon until half-cooked. Add ¼ cup of the but-ter and the olive oil. Add the vegetables and stir thoroughly to coat them with the fats. Continue cooking, stirring only occasionally to allow some caramelization. When the vegetables are browned on the edges, use paper towels to blot excess fat. Pour in the vin-egar and, after about 30 sec-onds, pour in the wine.

Reduce the mixture to about ½ cup. Add the stock, pepper-corns, cumin seeds, garlic, bay leaves, and chilies. Reduce by half or slightly more; this will take about 45 minutes. Re-move the sauce from the heat and pour through a strainer into a clean glass or stainless-steel container. Push down hard on the vegetables to get all the flavor possible in the sauce. Chill the container, first by setting in a container of icy water, then by leaving in the refrigerator overnight.

When ready to serve, re-move the congealed fat from the top of the cold sauce. Heat the sauce in a shallow sauce-pan. When just thickened, swirl in the remaining table-spoon of butter with a whisk.

DUCK SALAD "21"

SERVES 6

4 duck breasts	2 tablespoons cooking oil	

MARINADE

½ cup red wine vinegar 1 cup dry red wine 3 tablespoons soy sauce	2 tablespoons chopped unpeeled fresh gingerroot	¼ cup olive oil ¼ cup chopped shallots 1 juice orange

SALAD

12 endive leaves, sliced lengthwise	4 bunches of mâche or Boston lettuce	16 arugula leaves 2 inner romaine lettuce leaves, cut on the bias

DRESSING

⅔ cup olive oil ¾ cup red wine vinegar 2 tablespoons prepared mustard 2 tablespoons soy sauce 1 tablespoon finely chopped shallots 2 teaspoons finely chopped fresh gingerroot 1 tablespoon chopped fresh parsley 2 tablespoons reserved marinade	

Remove the skin and bones from the duck breasts. Place all marinade ingredients except the orange in a stainless-steel or ceramic bowl. Cut and squeeze the orange, add the juice and orange pieces to the bowl, and marinate the duck in the mixture, refrigerated, for 12 hours.

Remove the duck from the marinade, reserving 2 tablespoons of the marinade. (The rest of the marinade can be frozen for reuse—it is excellent for pheasant. Boil and cool completely before reusing.) Place the greens in a chilled salad bowl and set aside. Mix all the ingredients for the dressing.

Heat a sauté pan until very hot. Add the cooking oil and sauté the duck breasts until brown but still rare (130 to 140°F internal temperature). Remove the breasts from the pan and cut into thin slices as for a London Broil. (The recipe can be prepared in advance to this point.) Return the slices to the sauté pan and toss for several seconds. Add the dressing to the pan and mix. Pour the duck and dressing into the salad bowl, toss, and serve.

DUCK WITH CHOKECHERRY SAUCE

SERVES 8

4   mallard ducks, each 4 to
        5 pounds
1   tablespoon salt
1   tablespoon sugar
1   teaspoon ground
        cinnamon
½   teaspoon ground cloves
½   teaspoon crushed dried
        rosemary
2   large oranges
¼   cup pine nuts or shelled
        pistachios
½   cup cherry brandy
Chokecherry Sauce (recipe
        follows)

Preheat the oven to 300°F.

Remove the giblets and necks from the ducks. Discard or save for another use. Combine the salt, sugar, cinnamon, cloves, and rosemary and sprinkle the mixture inside and outside of the ducks. Cut the oranges into quarters and squeeze the juice of 2 quarters into each duck cavity. Place the squeezed quarters in the cavities as well. Place the ducks on a rack in a roasting pan and roast for 3 to 3½ hours, depending on the weight of the ducks. Baste the birds with their own fat and juices every hour. Roast until they are golden brown. When the ducks are cooked, allow them to cool for about an hour.

Split the ducks into halves, remove the back-bones, and pull out the inside breast and thigh bones. You may also want to pull out the leg bones after you take out the inside thigh bones. Cut a circle around the upper leg bones, where there is meat. Hold the lower part of the leg meat with one hand and pull out the leg bone with the other hand. Discard the bones. (The ducks may be cooked several days ahead and refrigerated.)

Preheat the oven to 350°F.

Spread the nuts on an un-greased pie pan and toast for about 10 minutes, stirring occasionally, until the nuts are golden brown. (Pine nuts will toast in a little less time than pistachios.) Watch so they do not burn. Warm the cherry brandy.

When ready to serve, place the duck pieces on a baking sheet and reheat in the oven until they are hot all the way through and as crisp as desired, usually 10 to 15 minutes. Remove from the oven, at once pour the cherry brandy over them, and ignite it. When the flames die out, top each piece with 3 to 4 tablespoons of sauce and sprinkle them with the toasted nuts. Serve with wild rice.

CHOKECHERRY SAUCE

MAKES ABOUT 2 CUPS

1 cup chokecherry or other tart jelly or jellied cranberries 1 cup port	½ cup Mango Chutney (see Index) ½ cup fresh orange juice	In a saucepan set over moderate heat, combine all the ingredients and mix well. Reduce the heat and simmer for about 15 minutes. Use for game birds or domestic birds.

Overleaf: A flock of brant in flight.

Barbara Reiger's
Chesapeake Gander

Serves 6

3   medium onions,
        chopped
3   tablespoons butter
8   apples, peeled, cored,
        and cubed
4   cups stale bread cubes
salt and pepper to taste
2   fresh thyme sprigs *or* 1
        tablespoon dried
2   eggs, beaten
½   cup gin
1   young Canada goose, 6
        to 8 pounds, dressed

Preheat the broiler.

Sauté the onions in the butter until golden. In a bowl, mix the onions, apples, and bread cubes. Add the salt, pepper, thyme, beaten eggs, and ¼ cup of the gin. With your hands, work this mixture into a moist stuffing, fill the goose cavity, and tie off with string. Place the bird in a roasting pan breast side up and pour the re-

maining ¼ cup of gin over the breast. Broil for 15 minutes, until the breast is browned.

Reset the oven temperature to 350°F.

Cook for no more than 1 hour for superb rare meat. The internal temperature of the breast should not exceed 130°F.

GOOSE LIVER PÂTÉ

SERVES 6 TO 10

The livers of wild geese, although smaller than those factory-farmed for the foie gras trade, make a wonderful pâté. This delicacy was introduced by the ancient Egyptians, who let their penned geese gorge on figs to increase the size of that organ. By the Middle Ages the French, not content with cages, began nailing the birds' feet to the barn floor and force-feeding them, a process known as *gavage* or "cramming." Nuts, fruits, and grain were literally forced down the birds' throats through a funnel. Although the methods used today are more humane, I still prefer a foie gras made from wild birds to the often tasteless, tinned import versions with chemical additives. This recipe can be used for duck livers also.

½   cup (¼ pound) butter
1   medium onion, chopped
     fine
1   garlic clove, chopped
     fine
½   pound goose or duck
     livers
½   teaspoon dried thyme *or*
     1 teaspoon fresh
     leaves
1   tablespoon finely
     chopped fresh parsley
½   bay leaf
salt and pepper to taste
2   tablespoons cognac
clarified butter

In a sauté pan, melt 2 tablespoons of the butter over low heat. Add the onion and garlic and let them "sweat"; do not brown. When the onion is soft, add the livers and herbs, then season with salt and pepper. Cook the livers for about 3 minutes, remove the pan from the heat, and let cool. Mince the goose livers and pass through a sieve into a bowl. Add the herbed onion. Soften the remaining 6 tablespoons of butter and, with your hands, blend the mixture with the cognac until it is a smooth paste. Spoon the pâté into a ceramic pot and cover with clarified butter. The pâté will keep for several days in the refrigerator, or it can be frozen. Serve with hot toast.

Hunting railbirds in the marshes of Virgin

12. SNIPE AND
RAILBIRDS

In nineteenth-century America game birds of all kinds were plentiful, but there were no parameters for defining any fowl as "game," and there was no concept of management, least of all a sporting ethic. Even that great naturalist John James Audubon, a name now revered among conservationists, had not only an insatiable passion for hunting but a remarkable appetite for his quarry—even sampling fish-eating pelicans, which he found, not surprisingly, "unsavory." But in Audubon's day, birds simply represented food for the taking, and the marshes, hills, beaches, prairies, and obviously the sky seemed never-ending sources of supply. In what has been called the Golden Age of the American hunting scene, from the post–Civil War years to the beginning of the twentieth century, shore and marsh bird shooting for market and sport (more so for the market), fulfilled a shopping list for executive chefs in New York, Philadelphia, Baltimore, and Chicago restaurants that would be totally unfamiliar to the modern epicure: the dowitcher, red knot, godwit, golden and black-bellied plover, willet, long-billed and Eskimo curlew, clapper, king, Virginia and sora rails, and Wilson's snipe. Bringing from fifty cents to two dollars a dozen in the 1880s, virtually every species delivered by the hundred-pound barrel seemed doomed to extinction. Fortunately, the "utilitarian" concept of the meat hunter was gradually outlawed through the efforts of conservationists such as George

Bird Grinnell, Theodore Roosevelt, and Ira Gabrielson—men who were *both* naturalists and hunters, a prerequisite to the sporting ethic. Today only the rails and snipe remain as viably managed populations for harvesting by the gun, but despite their excellence at table they require more than average physical labor to collect, and comparatively few fortunate souls are ever invited to a railbird or snipe dinner.

Historically, railbirds[1] have been hunted in the company of a "pusher," a muscular guide familiar with the local tides and marshes who could skillfully and swiftly pole a flat-bottomed skiff through emergent vegetation such as wild rice, cordgrass, and dense bulrushes, where the rail feed—while the shooter stands comfortably balanced in the bow. A century ago this was a profitable occupation when birds were being delivered to market, but since pushing is hard work, and commercial harvesting is a thing of the past, it is no longer a popular exercise and the number of guides extant is not great. The only option is to hunt on foot, which often means mucking about in an aquatic nightmare for miles and muddy miles, sometimes in water belly deep—or deeper. The last and only time I hunted on foot was in the marshes around Barnegat Bay with the late Nelson Benedict, then outdoors editor of the *Newark Star Ledger*. Nelson brought along his faithful springer spaniel, who promptly became lost in a series of interlocking ditches when the tide went out. We spent the entire day in clouds of mosquitoes hunting for his dog.

By comparison, snipe territory is just wet landscape, but there are still boggy miles to negotiate and no guarantee of seeing birds, as snipe are migratory—abundant today and scarce or totally absent tomorrow. And unlike slow-flying railbirds, when flushed, snipe are swift, acrobatic fliers; the hunter who bags a half dozen is doing a very credible job. I have been told on great authority that snipe zig and zag only for the first ten yards; then it's an easy going-away shot. Unfortunately, after squishing a mile or two across a Florida hammock, I am either ten yards too early or, more probably, twenty years too late. Nevertheless, there is a faithful coterie of railbird and snipe enthusiasts along the Atlantic seaboard, myself included, as these most delicious birds provide glorious dining.

A member of the sandpiper family, our common or Wilson's snipe, *Capella gallinago*, also known as jacksnipe, is similar to the closely related woodcock in its rich flavor but is smaller in size, weighing about four ounces. The breast meat in peak season shows white spots or minuscule streaks of fat, which add greatly to the taste. The classic method of cooking the snipe, known as *bécassine* in France, is to dry-pluck the bird, leaving it undrawn, then roast it over charcoal; when the bird is finished, the trail is quickly removed and mixed with an equal amount of *pâté de foie gras*; this mixture is then spread on toast slices and the bird mounted on top. Properly trussed, neither the head nor the feet are

---

[1]The expression "thin as a rail" doesn't refer to a fence but rather the shape of these birds when viewed from the front or rear. Seen in profile, they are deep-bodied but are very thin laterally, which expedites their walking through dense reeds.

removed; the legs are pressed close to the body, crossed at the knee joints, and the head is turned under the left wing, the long bill passed between the thighs, then tied off with butcher's string. Nobody has ever explained why the bill must be tucked *à la gauche*; for that matter, Swedish epicures completely cut the bills off both snipe and woodcock before cooking, and the only reason given by my gourmet friend Lennart Borgstrom is that long noses on birds are considered unsightly. So much for tradition.

The most underutilized game bird in North America is also a member of the Rallidae, the American coot (*Fulica americana*) or "mudhen," which ranges in abundance across the continental United States and from Alaska to Ecuador. There are several reasons why comparatively few hunters ever enjoy a sautéed breast of coot. Although it looks like a duck, the coot doesn't fly into decoys; it also prefers to swim away rather than flush when disturbed, and when the bird does take off, it skitters for a long distance over the surface (the coot has lobed rather than webbed feet) to gather flying speed. In brief, it is an easy target until it becomes fully airborne, and few shooters have the patience to walk muddy banks or scull a skiff to get a sporting shot. Ironically, when a coot does get airborne, it is usually thirty or more yards out and winging swiftly, now making it a difficult quarry. As a result the coot is not much hunted, and generous bag limits of fifteen to twenty-five birds in different flyways reflect their underutilization. Despite an old reputation of being inedible, coot is both tender and delicious. The bird has a plump breast and legs, more chickenlike anatomically than a duck, but it *must* be skinned and all traces of fat removed. The meat is very dark and somewhat bloodier than that of a duck, but on a strict diet of aquatic plants—especially wild rice, sweet flag, marsh smartweed, and wild celery—the coot is delicately flavored. The French name for the related European coot, *poule d'eau*, or water chicken, reflects its appreciation at table. As a dividend, the coot is equipped with an oversize liver, which makes wonderful pâté (see recipe, page 151). Any reference to a "fishy"-tasting coot is due to the fact that several diving sea ducks, specifically the scoters and eiders, are regionally known as "coot," and these species do feed mainly on bivalves and fish. However, even these sea ducks' breasts can be improved by breasting the birds out immediately after killing and removing all skin and fat globules and cutting the meat into thin slices before sautéing in butter and wine to a medium-rare.

The sora rail is our smallest North American game bird, weighing in feather about four to five ounces (king rail and clapper rail weigh from ten to fourteen ounces). When dressed, a sora can be fitted inside of a hollowed baking potato with some butter and herbs, then wrapped in foil and cooked *ensemble*. Which reminds me of Soyer and the ortolan. Personally, I can't think of a moral reason for eating this songbird, actually a bunting (*Emberiza hortulana*), but it does appear at table, particularly in Italy and France. When that famed chef Alexis Soyer of the London Reform Club was asked to prepare an ortolan stuffed with truffles, he observed, "An ortolan cannot be stuffed with truffles, but I will gladly stuff you a truffle with ortolan." One of the most famous dishes is *Ortolan à la Périgourdine*. A large truffle is scooped out to create a case in which the tiny undrawn bird is enclosed, then mounted on a circle of bread. The scooped-out portion of the truffle is finely shredded to form a well around the case, then covered with a pat of butter before roasting. The birds are served with a rich demi-glace flavored with the juice of an orange. My only taste of ortolan occurred some thirty years ago, at Le Chapon Fin in Bordeaux, before I knew anything about the bird's origins; undeniably a most savory morsel, but alas, it later gave me a guilt complex.

ROASTED SNIPE

SERVES 4

4   snipe
salt and white pepper to
    taste
4   thin slices unsalted
    fatback
2   teaspoons butter or
    margarine
1   cup Game Stock (see
    Index) or chicken
    stock, or more as
    needed
1   tablespoon cognac
4   large croûtes, toasted
    fresh

Cut each bird at the neck and pull out the gizzard. Cut a small opening near the thigh and remove the stomach and intestines. The rest of the innards should remain in the bird. Cut off the claws. Scald the feet and pull off the outer skin. Flay the head and remove the eyes. Dry the birds well.

Preheat the oven to 400°F.

Rub the birds with salt and white pepper. Put the beak of the bird into the thigh. Cover each bird with a sheet of fatback and tie it in place with white string.

On top of the stove, melt the butter in a heavy ovenproof pan large enough to hold all the birds. When the butter starts to brown, place the birds, breast side down, in the pan. Brown them on all sides. Add the stock and roast the birds, uncovered, for 10 to 15 minutes. Baste them now and then with stock from the pan or add more stock if needed. Check the birds often; test for doneness with a wooden toothpick or a thin metal skewer.

When the birds are done, remove them from the oven and from the pan. Remove the innards and chop them fine. Skim and strain the pan juices. Add more stock if needed; there should be about ¾ cup altogether. Add the chopped innards and the cognac to the juices. Remove the fatback from the birds. Loosen the beak from the thigh of each one and split the birds. Arrange the birds on the toasted croûtes and spoon the pan sauce over them. Serve with French fried potatoes and a green salad.

13. VENISON,
THE ANTLERED GAME

With the widespread availability of game in the winter season, it somehow seems uninspired to serve that ubiquitous baked ham sugarly studded with pineapple at Christmas, no less a redundant turkey considering its recent appearance at Thanksgiving. We long ago settled on a saddle of venison with a sauce Grand Veneur as our festive family dinner, which I feel is more in the early American spirit of holiday dining. The venison is accompanied by pears poached in port, hearts of artichoke topped with chestnut puree, and straw potatoes. And Christmas being the very peak time for oysters, when the Malpeque, Belon, Cotuit, Wellfleet, Chincoteague, and Bristol are plump and sweet, a generous serving on the half-shell has become our traditional starter. New Zealand raspberries, to me the very best of that fruit, are also being delivered in December, and when marinated in aquavit, then topped with crème fraîche, they make a wonderful curtain call. Venison of some kind can be bagged with a telephone and a credit card, but qualitative differences exist not only in the experience of the purveyor and his source of supply but in the individual species comprising that generic term.

By definition, venison is any of the antlered game animals in the family Cervidae, which in North America includes our indigenous elk, moose, whitetail deer, blacktail deer, mule deer, and caribou. There are also exotic species on game preserves, notably the sika deer, axis deer, and fallow deer, which find their way to market in small quantities. With one exception only male deer are antlered; both sexes of caribou, a close relative of the semidomesticated reindeer, bear antlers. By loose kitchen definition the meat of our native pronghorn or "antelope" is also considered a venison, although it

Whitetail deer.

doesn't bear antlers and is in the family Bovidae—more closely related to a goat than a deer (the term *venison* comes from the Latin, *venatus*, which means "to hunt," so the definition was loose to begin with). The only true antelope on our continent are African exotics found on game preserves, and one species, the blackbuck, is marketed to a limited extent.

Exotic venisons are derived mainly from Texas. The propagation of African and Asian animals began on the fabled King Ranch back in 1929, originally for the sole purpose of hunting, but more recently on various private lands under the Species Survival Plan to maintain populations of endangered animals such as the black rhinoceros, Grevy's zebra, nilgai, addax, and scimitar oryx. Poaching and loss of habitat have taken a tremendous toll, particularly in modern-day Africa. It's estimated that about 100,000 exotics of various kinds are now established in Texas, with small numbers in Missouri and New Mexico. Some ranches offer trophy hunting for certain species, not only for the income but more importantly as a means of culling the herds. The sika and axis deer and the blackbuck antelope are well adapted to Texas rangeland, and their reproductive success requires careful management. The surplus animals are harvested, dressed under the supervision of a state meat inspector, and delivered to luxury restaurants all over the United States. However, our native animals, especially the elk, moose, and whitetail deer, provide the finest of venison, and to my taste it's a toss-up which of these is superior in texture and flavor.

Until 1973 the European red deer and the North American elk were considered separate species, but taxonomically they are now recognized as the same animal, *Cervus elaphus*. The name *elk* is a colloquialism derived from the German word *elch* (phonetically similar in Scandinavia, where it is *alg*, pronounced "aylg"), which in Europe refers to the moose—not the red deer. It has been suggested that the original Shawnee Indian name *wapiti* be used in this country, but elk is so long established that the change would only add to the confused terminology. The elk is the second-largest North American deer (to 1,100 pounds), surpassed in size only by the moose. Until the beginning of the nineteenth century, the elk was widely distributed in the United States, ranging from Maine to California, but it is now limited to the Rocky Mountains region, small areas of the Pacific Northwest, and portions of Manitoba, Saskatchewan, and Alberta. European red deer are most prolific in Scotland, Germany, Austria, Hungary, Romania, and Yugoslavia. Transplanted to Argentina and New Zealand, red deer thrived bountifully, to the point that venison has become a major export food in the latter country; in 1981 the value of its wild animal products amounted to $37,228,837. Today the red deer of New Zealand and, to a lesser extent Scotland, provide most of the venison delivered to the American marketplace. The world's largest importer is West Germany, where a roast saddle of *Hirsch* is the benchmark of culinary excellence at any game-oriented restaurant. From October to December, venison addicts flock to the Hotel Erbprinz (two kilometers off the Autobahn between Baden-Baden and Karlsruhe), the grill room in the Hotel Vier Jahreszeiten in Hamburg, or the Tantris Restaurant in Munich on Johann Fichte Strasse.

Germany's stag forests couldn't begin to supply the widespread demand.

New Zealand's ascendancy in the venison trade is a modern saga with peculiar ancient roots. In the year 1350, when the Maori people paddled in westerly currents and prevailing winds some 2,000 miles from Polynesia to New Zealand, they arrived in a biological vacuum, a land where no predatory animals or carnivorous fishes existed. However, the North and South Islands were one vast aviary, which included the now extinct moa bird, a flightless giant according to fossil records, often standing fourteen feet tall; in Maori legend it was extremely aggressive toward man. Most of the Maori's food hunting was for birds such as the shearwaters, silvereyes, and parrots, and this diet was supplemented by marine fishes, huge freshwater crayfish, and sweet potatoes—a South American tuber that these aquatic nomads had evidently collected and preserved for seeding on some earlier journey to the east. Uneventful centuries passed before the rabbit was introduced by European settlers in the 1840s, then the red deer in 1851. Subsequently into the vacuum were delivered chamois, sika deer, moose, thar, fallow deer, whitetail deer, rusa, and sambar deer. These exotics of singular appetite had no natural predators such as wolves or bears to keep their numbers in balance, and eventually in competition with domestic sheep, the overgrazed countryside eroded, causing alarming flood problems. By the early 1920s professional hunters or "cullers" were being paid bounties to kill off the herds. My old Kiwi companion of years past, Rex Forrester, presently hunting and fishing officer for the Tourist and Publicity Department of New Zealand, began work as a culler in 1947, and in his book *The Chopper Boys* he describes his early career:

I worked for several years in various districts. If we didn't shoot over 1000 deer in six months we were fired. Many got six-month tallies as high as 2500. Our flour was invariably weevily, the spuds were rotten, army biscuits by the ton. The latter would have been better directed to the post-war building boom, as they made admirable bricks.

We were sent into the mountains in November and ordered to stay there till May. It was a lonely, hard life, but it spawned a breed of Kiwi outdoorsmen envied both here and abroad. For where else but in New Zealand in this modern day and age could a man pit himself against nature and learn the arts of survival in the wilderness? Once he had learnt these things, hunting came easily, but he still lived a hermit's existence not much different from that of primitive man, with his only modern tool a battered ex army rifle.

Cullers explored and opened up the back country, pioneering tracks across alpine passes later to be followed by thousands of trampers, sports hunters, mountaineers and nature-lovers. They used to joke about maps which had the words "unexplored" stamped across them (some still do). There wouldn't be a mountain range or valley floor that hasn't been trodden by the boots of some lone culler.

By 1957, just one season of culling accounted for 63,583 deer, and with the advent of helicopter hunting in the 1960s, it was inevitable that New Zealand would find itself with a multimillion-dollar venison business and a product that was rapidly being exhausted. For that matter, according to Rex Forrester, the toll among the "chopper boys" was considerable; in a six-year period 208 helicopters crashed, many of them cartwheeling down mist-shrouded mountainsides in a ball of flame. Logically, the solution was to farm the deer, which could be managed in a controlled environment. The first auction of live animals took place in 1977, and today there are about 2,000 deer farms in New Zealand. Although a typical 500-pound red deer provides about 150 pounds of dressed-out and boned meat, commercially no part of the animal is wasted, not even the antlers.

The stag has long played a role in naturopathic medicine. During medieval times both the *pizzle* or penis and the testicles of red deer, called *daintees*, were considered delectable aphrodisiacs and, when cooked in a sweet and sour sauce, were ceremoniously served to privileged guests—those who sat above the salt at royal banquets. However, in the Chinese lexicon it's "the pearl of the brow of the deer" that lingers in modern-day pharmacopoeia. In Oriental markets (a trade dominated by Korean brokers) "elk horn in velvet" commands as much as $500 per pound, and considering the fact that the average stag wears about fifteen pounds of antler, this by-product of venison farming represents a lucrative industry. Stags shed their ossified or bone-hard antlers each year, and immediately a new growth starts. Antlers grow to an imposing size slowly, usually taking from five to six months, during which time they have a soft bloody core covered with a velvety skin and are spongy in texture. On New Zealand elk farms and those few ranches that exist in the United States, when the velvet is prime, the stag is tranquilized, the antlers are sawed off, and the stump is cauterized; a new set regenerates in the following year. At retail markets in Hong Kong and Singapore this horn appears in wafer-thin slices, like nearly transparent potato chips; these are steeped in water and herbs (ginseng is a popular additive) and served as a liquid extract or processed into pill, powder, and paste form. Even the inferior cast-off "hard horn" satisfies Oriental bargain hunters who want to treat various cardiovascular and genital ills, and while the pearl is yang rather than yin, there is no scientific evidence that it is efficacious—but the fact remains that the antler business amounts to thirty million dollars annually in the United States alone, based on the sale of export licenses (U.S. Fish and Wildlife Service).

The moose (*Alces alces*) is the largest member of the deer family, weighing up to 1,600 pounds. It is distributed in boreal forests from New Brunswick across Canada to Alaska and occurs in some northern states, notably Maine, Wyoming, and Montana. The name *moose* comes from the Ojibwa Indian language, a people who long ago learned to bring the animal within killing range with a birchbark horn; the moose horn can be used like a megaphone to imitate a lonesome cow or, when rattled against a tree, to create the sound of a bull raking his antlers. And when filled with water it can be poured artfully to imitate a urinating moose—for some reason a fatal attraction. The spread of antlers on a moose is awesome, and the fact that they will charge automobiles, even running head-on into railroad engines, makes the use of a birchbark horn a somewhat secular skill.

There is a great similarity between the venisons of elk and moose, and a roast of either one is as good as, in my opinion better than, the finest beef. Elk are by choice grazing animals, consuming tremendous quantities of grass from late spring into winter. Browse (the leaves, stems, and buds of woody plants), such as that utilized by other deer, is a minor food source in comparison. As a result, elk meat more nearly resembles beef in texture but without the fat marbling. Moose, on the other hand, although browsers, are adapted to a variety of forage—from ground vegetation such as the lowbush cranberry or blueberry to various aquatic plants. Moose meat, like that of elk, is of exceptionally delicate flavor. However, a number of variables can affect quality in all venisons, beginning with the time of harvest.

Among antlered game, the best venison will come from a mature buck deer, bull moose, or bull elk killed early in the season while still fat. When the males go into active rut, due to metabolic changes they cease eating and rapidly lose weight; they shouldn't be expected to provide gourmet fare during that period. Generally speaking, the rut lasts only three to four weeks, starting in late October, and is over by mid-November. If you are hunting in rutting season, only a young male of any kind or a doe (whose period of estrus lasts only about twenty-four hours) should be considered for table purposes. This may preclude collecting a trophy head, but the option can be measured in terms of prime meat. When the animal has been killed, the hunter's individual skill in field dressing, the ambient air temperature on location, and the speed of delivery to cold storage are critical factors. This can be something of a problem with a moose, for example, which will field dress at over 1,000 pounds and must be hauled over rough terrain a mile or more to the nearest tote road. By contrast, venison entering our commercial market is harvested under controlled conditions (vis à vis New Zealand game farms or estate shooting in Scotland).

For the North American hunter the major source of venison is our most popular big game animal, the whitetail deer (*Odocoileus virginianus*). Although figures on the annual venison harvest include the western blacktail and mule deers, the whitetail is dominant in a recent count of 2,269,848 deer taken by sportsmen in the United States—which represents over 61,000 tons of boneless meat. Whitetail deer have been recorded at weights exceeding 400 pounds, but mature northern bucks generally weigh 200 to 300 pounds with the largest occurring in northern states. Despite intense hunting pressure, the present whitetail population is estimated at twelve million, which exceeds any previous census. As with other deer, hunter harvest is an important tool in herd management, as the deer soon die from malnutrition on overbrowsed ranges. Browse is the staple in a deer's diet, but fruits and nuts, especially acorns, and agricultural crops are consumed whenever available. Thus, prime venison is associated with hardwood forests (oak, beech, wild cherry, dogwood, apple), which are common from Maine to Virginia and across the northern tier of states to Minnesota.

Among the exotic deer introduced to the United States, the fallow deer (*Dama dama*) has a very restricted range in the wild, providing little hunting, and this harvest is mainly on preserves. A native of western Asia, southern Europe, and North Africa, the fallow is a small deer with palmated antlers (similar to those of a moose). Nevertheless, quantities of fallow venison arrive at market by way of Texas ranches and also from one unique operation, Joseph von Kerckerink's 4,800-acre Lucky Star Ranch near Chaumont, New York. Von Kerckerink specializes in the fallow, and his annual October-to-December crop goes directly to such game-critical kitchens as La Caravelle, La Côte Basque, Le Veau d'Or and La Crémaillère. The Lucky Star product is in great demand for the very good reason that the animals are butchered as yearlings and delivered in fresh rather than frozen form. Personally, I find the fallow very similar in texture and flavor to that of the small European roe deer (*Capreolus caprea*), which is to say a very superior venison.

The eating of venison provided us with a common expression in the English language. At medieval banquets the lord of the manor, his family, and privileged guests sat at the high table, while those of lesser social rank sat at lower-level trestle tables (either permanent sideboards or boards laid across saw horses for the occasion). Venison meat was reserved for the high table, while the *umbles* or deer entrails such as the livers, kidneys and hearts were baked in an umble pie and served to the trestle tables. Thus evolved the expression "he eats humble pie," meaning that one lowers himself or is of a lower social station. Venison liver in particular is a great delicacy, and the umble pie was probably a tasty dish in its own right.

COOKING NOTES
SELECTION OF VENISON CUTS

Venison, whether butchered at home or by a professional at a locker plant or purchased at market, presents a variety of cuts that have specific uses in different recipes. The following is a general guide to what can be obtained from various parts of the animal.

Saddle

The most choice cut of venison, the saddle is cut from the lower back, separated from the pelvic or H-bone just above the hindquarters, extending to the rear of the shoulder (it will vary in weight according to the size of the animal, but at market saddles usually weigh from ten to thirteen pounds bone in). It contains two short loins or "backstraps" lying parallel to each side of the backbone. These can be cut free, the outer membrane removed, and cooked whole, or cut crosswise into boneless medallions, or sawed crosswise with bone in to produce T-bone steaks and loin chops. Generally speaking, a saddle of venison, as served in restaurants, is a boneless backstrap, but it is sometimes presented at large dinner parties in whole form bone in with the backstraps cut free for serving.

Tenderloin

Two long fillets (referred to as the filet mignon) are found directly *under* the saddle lying parallel to the backbone. These small tenderloins are usually cooked whole or sliced into medallions and are very choice cuts. This part of the deer never exercises and is as tender as Japan's pampered Kobe beef but with a delicate game flavor.

Shoulders and Neck

When deboned, the forelegs or shoulders provide excellent pot roasts when the meat is rolled and tied. However, the topmost portion along the back can be cut into rib-eye fillets or rib-eye chops. When one is butchering a deer, the carcass is usually divided in half, separated at the terminus of the rib cage, and two strips of meat can be excised from either side of the backbone in the same fashion as cutting out the backstraps. Continuing with the knife up the back, the neck also produces boneless strips that make excellent stew meat or can be rolled into a roast.

Haunches

When deboned, the hind legs (commercially, "hinds"), or more familiarly the haunches, provide the top round, outside round, rump, and sirloin tip (or knuckle), all of which make excellent roasts. They can also be sliced across the grain and made into steaks or medallions. The haunches are a more valuable cut than the shoulders.

Ground Venison

Venison burger meat is usually made from trimmings of the lower neck, shanks, rib meat, breast, and flank. However, because all venison is lean, either beef suet or unsalted pork fat must be added at a ratio of one pound of ground suet to five pounds of ground venison. Although pork fat is preferred, it reduces the frozen shelf life to about two months as it acquires a rancid flavor if kept longer. To be realistic, all burger meat should be used shortly after grinding as even beef suet adds little more to storage time, which is about six months. Trimmings can also be used in making sausage, pâté, soups, and stocks.

LARDING AND BARDING

Venison fat is a tallowlike substance with a disagreeable taste. It is the source of what innocent chefs refer to as a "gamy" flavor, which is not the true flavor of the meat. All fat should always be carefully removed from any cut of venison. Usually beef fat or salt pork is substituted on cuts such as roasts that require long cooking periods, and this is accomplished by larding or inserting ¼-inch strips of fat into the meat with a larding needle or by barding, which is simply wrapping thin sheets of fat around the meat and tying it in place with butcher's string. Either method prevents the venison from drying out; larding also improves its appearance. For larding you need a long-handled grooved needle designed to insert the strips of lardoons. To "pique" the venison, pierce the meat with the point of a knife at equidistant places on the roast and with the split end of the needle insert the lardoons in each opening, running them through and bringing them out about half an inch from the insertion. This leaves tails of fat covering the surface of the meat, which will be lubricated and nicely browned.

VENISON RAGOUT

SERVES 6

4   pounds venison
     shoulder, cut into 1½-
     to 2-inch cubes
3   cups dry red wine
1   cup cider vinegar
4   medium onions,
     quartered
4   medium carrots, peeled
     and cut into chunks
7   peppercorns
4   cloves
1   large bay leaf
2   teaspoons salt
½   teaspoon crushed dried
     rosemary
¼   teaspoon dried thyme
½   cup vegetable oil
4   beef bouillon cubes and
     1 quart hot water *or* 1
     quart venison broth
additional hot water if
     needed

2 to 3 tablespoons all-
     purpose flour

Place the venison in a large nonmetallic bowl or crock and add 2 cups of the wine, vinegar, onions, carrots, and all spices and herbs. Cover and let stand in a cool place or the refrigerator for at least 24 hours, turning the meat occasionally so that all pieces are exposed to the marinade. Venison may marinate for up to 5 days.

When you're ready to prepare the ragout, remove the meat and pat the cubes dry. Strain the marinade, reserving the vegetables and seasonings and discarding the liquid. In a stew pot, heat the vegetable oil and quickly brown the venison over high heat. When richly browned on all surfaces, add the remaining cup of red wine, the bouillon cubes dissolved in the hot water, and the vegetables and seasonings reserved from the marinade. Add additional hot water to cover, if necessary. Bring just to a boil but do not boil. Lower the heat at once, cover, and simmer for about 1½ hours or until the meat is tender. Transfer the meat to a heated serving dish. Skim the fat from the pot liquids and stir in the flour to thicken the gravy if desired. Pour the gravy over the meat and serve with parsley potato dumplings or potato pancakes and applesauce.

Overleaf: A venison stew.

VENISON STEW

1   bottle good-quality dry
     red wine
1   carrot, sliced thin
2   shallots, sliced thin
2   bay leaves
1   fresh thyme sprig
6   peppercorns
salt to taste
1   cup vegetable oil
3   pounds boneless venison
     leg or shoulder, cut
     into 1- to 2-inch cubes
1   cup (½ pound) clarified
     butter
3   tablespoons all-purpose
     flour
1   medium onion, sliced
½   pound blanched pork
     belly, diced
½   cup crème fraîche or
     heavy cream
1   tablespoon chopped
     fresh parsley

Combine the wine, carrot, shallots, bay leaves, thyme, peppercorns, salt, and vegetable oil in a ceramic bowl. Place the meat in the marinade, making sure all pieces are covered. Let stand for at least 8 hours or overnight.

Remove the meat from the marinade and dry each piece thoroughly. Strain the marinade and discard the vegetables.

Heat some of the butter in a Dutch oven over very high heat. Brown the pieces of meat quickly. Remove the pot from the heat and sprinkle the meat with the flour. Stir for a few minutes and return the pot to the stove over medium heat. Add the strained marinade, stirring with a wooden spoon. Put the lid on the Dutch oven and let the stew simmer over low heat for about 1 hour, checking and stirring occasionally.

While the meat is cooking, cook the sliced onion in butter over medium heat until browned. Remove from the heat and keep warm. Fry the pork belly in a sauté pan until crisp. Dry between 2 paper towels and reserve.

When the meat is cooked, transfer it to an earthenware casserole. Add the reserved onion and pork belly. Strain the sauce and pour it over the meat. Reheat without boiling. Add the crème fraîche and sprinkle with chopped parsley. Serve with cooked wide egg noodles or spaetzle (see Index).

OLD LUCHOW'S VENISON RAGOUT

SERVES 6

2	cups dry red wine
1	cup red wine vinegar
8	peppercorns
2	bay leaves
3	juniper berries, crushed
4	carrots, sliced
2	onions, sliced
3	large garlic cloves, peeled and crushed

a small handful of chopped fresh parsley

4	celery ribs, chopped
2	fresh thyme sprigs *or* 1 teaspoon dried
3	pounds boneless venison leg or shoulder, cut into 1½- to 2-inch cubes

all-purpose flour
salt and pepper to taste

5	tablespoons butter
5	tablespoons vegetable oil
½ to 1 cup beef stock, as needed
1	cup sour cream

Red Cabbage (recipe follows)

Mix 1 cup of the wine, the vinegar, peppercorns, bay leaves, juniper berries, carrots, onions, garlic, parsley, celery, and thyme in a large glass or ceramic bowl. Add the venison and marinate for 3 to 5 days in the refrigerator.

Preheat the oven to 350°F.

Remove the meat from the marinade and pat dry. Pour the marinade through a strainer; discard the liquid and reserve the vegetables. Coat the meat with flour seasoned with salt and pepper. Brown quickly in butter and oil in a heavy casserole. Add the vegetables reserved from the marinade, the remaining cup of wine, and enough beef stock to nearly cover the meat. Bake, covered, for 2½ to 3 hours, adding beef stock if necessary. At the end, stir in the sour cream. Serve with red cabbage and noodles.

RED CABBAGE

1	cup (½ pound) butter
1	head of red cabbage, sliced thin
2	apples, cored and sliced
2	onions, sliced
1	large bay leaf

½	cup red currant jelly
salt and pepper to taste
2	smoked ham hocks
¼	cup water
6	tablespoons white vinegar

In a heavy casserole with a tight-fitting lid, melt the butter. Add the remaining ingredients except vinegar, bring to a boil, and cook, covered, over low heat for 2½ hours. At the last minute, add the vinegar.

VENISON GOULASH

SERVES 4 TO 6

1 teaspoon salt
½ teaspoon pepper
1 tablespoon sweet
   Hungarian paprika
1 fresh thyme sprig *or* ½
   teaspoon dried
½ cup all-purpose flour
2 pounds boneless venison
   from hindquarters or
   foreleg, cubed
5 tablespoons butter
2 medium onions,
   chopped

1½ cups Game Stock (see
   Index) or beef stock
2 large garlic cloves,
   peeled and put
   through a press
10 large mushrooms, sliced
1½ cups sour cream

Mix the salt, pepper, paprika, and thyme into the flour. Dredge the venison cubes in the seasoned flour. In a large skillet, preferably cast iron, sauté the venison in 3 tablespoons of the butter until brown. Remove from the pan. Sauté the onions in the remaining butter until browned. Add the stock and garlic and stir. Return the venison to the pan, cover, and cook for 30 minutes. Add the mushrooms and stir in the sour cream. Cook for 7 to 10 minutes, until tender and juicy, stirring often. Serve over rice or noodles.

SADDLE OF VENISON BADEN-BADEN

SERVES 8 TO 10

1   saddle of venison, including bones trimmed from both sides
1   cup red wine, preferably from the region of Baden
1   onion, chopped coarse
13 juniper berries
10 black peppercorns
½   cup (¼ pound) plus 1 tablespoon unsalted butter
1   tablespoon oil
1   onion, sliced
1   carrot, sliced
1   teaspoon all-purpose flour
1   cup warm water
salt and pepper to taste
4   strips cut from sliced bacon, fat part only
freshly ground white pepper
4   large pears, peeled, halved, and cored
½   cinnamon stick
juice of 1 lemon
red currant jelly, preferably with whole berries, or gooseberries
½   cup sour cream

Cut away all of the very thin membrane that covers the meat or trim the tenderloin. Reserve the bones and marinate the meat, refrigerated, in the red wine with the onion, 8 of the juniper berries, and the peppercorns for 1 or 2 days.

Remove the meat from the marinade, strain the marinade through a fine-mesh sieve, and reserve the marinade. Make incisions on both sides of the spine bones along the saddle, about ½ inch deep. Pat the meat dry with paper towels.

In a saucepan over very high heat, roast the bones, cut into pieces, in 1 tablespoon of the butter and the oil. Add the sliced onion and carrot. Continue cooking until the mixture is browned, stirring frequently. Dust with flour and cook for another 1 or 2 minutes.

Pour in the warm water and scrape up all dark bits from the bottom and sides of the saucepan. Add the reserved marinade and reduce to ½ cup. Season with salt and pepper and keep warm.

Preheat the oven to 450°F.

Prepare the saddle of venison for oven roasting: Put the fat bacon strips into the incisions along the bone. Mix the white pepper with the remaining juniper berries, sprinkle this seasoning over the meat, and pat it in to make it stick.

Melt the remaining ½ cup butter, pour a third of it over the meat in a roasting pan, and put it in the preheated oven.

Immediately reset the oven to 400°F.

Roast for 35 to 40 minutes, depending on thickness. Baste it twice with the remaining butter and salt it after about 20 minutes of roasting time.

Meanwhile, poach the pears gently with the cinnamon stick in water acidulated with the lemon juice, until tender but not soft. When cool, fill with currant jelly.

To serve, cut the meat away from the bones. Carve the 2 longish pieces (the backstraps) diagonally in not-too-thin slices. Then reassemble these on the bones to achieve the original look of the saddle of venison. Arrange on an oblong platter, garnished with the pears. Further accompaniments should be chanterelle mushrooms, sautéed in butter, and spaetzle (see Index). Just before serving, stir the sour cream into the game broth and pass the sauce at table.

VENISON
KOCHMEISTER STYLE

SERVES 10 TO 12

5 to 6 pounds venison
     backstrap
2½ cups dry red wine
juice of 1 lemon
2   cups water
3   tablespoons red wine
     vinegar
3   onions, diced
6   peppercorns
2   bay leaves
2   cloves
¼   teaspoon dried thyme
¼   teaspoon dried tarragon
½   cup all-purpose flour
¼   teaspoon coarsely
     ground pepper
3 to 4 tablespoons butter or
     margarine
¼   teaspoon salt
3   carrots, sliced
3   tablespoons tomato paste
4   gingersnaps, grated
3   tablespoons dark brown
     sugar

2   tablespoons lemon juice
1   cup dried red currants
salt to taste

Place the venison fillet in a bowl. Pour 2 cups red wine, juice of 1 lemon, 1 cup of the water, vinegar, 1 diced onion, peppercorns, bay leaves, cloves, thyme, and tarragon over the meat and marinate, refrigerated, for 24 to 30 hours. Remove the meat from the marinade and pat dry. Strain the marinade and reserve the liquid.

Mix the flour and ground pepper together. Coat the venison with flour. Heat the butter in a Dutch oven or a large pot and brown the meat on both sides. Add the salt, carrots, remaining 2 diced onions, tomato paste, 1 cup of the strained marinade, and 1 cup water. Cook, covered, over low heat for 2½ to 3 hours, turning the meat occasionally. Place the meat on a heated platter.

Strain the sauce through a sieve and press the vegetables through the sieve. There should be about 2½ cups of sauce; if less, add a little more of the reserved marinade. Pour the sauce into a saucepan and add the gingersnaps, sugar, remaining ½ cup wine, lemon juice, currants, and salt if necessary. Bring to a boil and simmer until thickened. Pour the sauce over the meat and serve with spaetzle (see Index).

VENISON RAGOUT
BELGIAN STYLE

SERVES 6

¾   cup all-purpose flour
2   teaspoons salt
¼   teaspoon black pepper
3   pounds boneless venison
        (top round, outside
        round, rump,
        shoulder, or sirloin
        tip), cut into 2-inch
        cubes
½   cup peanut oil
½   pound white onions,
        sliced
4   garlic cloves, peeled and
        chopped
¼   cup cognac
1   bay leaf
1   teaspoon dried thyme
2   cups beer
12   large white mushrooms,
        sliced

Mix half of the flour with the salt and pepper and sprinkle it on a work surface. Dredge the cubed venison in the flour, coating each chunk thoroughly. Pour half of the peanut oil into a large skillet and brown the meat evenly over moderate heat. When the venison is crusty, transfer the meat to a Dutch oven or large casserole with a slotted spoon.

Preheat the oven to 350°F.

Pour the remaining oil into the skillet and cook the onions and garlic until softened and faintly browned. Transfer to the casserole. Pour the cognac into the skillet to simmer and deglaze the pan with a wooden spoon. Add the bay leaf, thyme, beer, mushrooms, and remaining flour and continue simmering and stirring until the mushrooms are limp. Pour this mixture into the casserole dish.

Bake the ragout, tightly covered, for 2 hours or until the venison is tender. Remove the casserole dish and let cool, then place in the refrigerator to stand for 24 to 36 hours. When ready to serve, reheat the covered casserole at the same temperature for 1 hour or until it is heated through. Like all game stews, this one is improved by ''resting'' and reheating.

ANTELOPE IN THE
STYLE OF BENTLEY'S

SERVES 4

This dish can be either grilled or sautéed.

1½ pounds antelope
        backstrap or boneless
        leg slices

MARINADE

½ cup olive oil
1 teaspoon dried thyme
    leaves

1 tablespoon dried
    rosemary leaves

1 tablespoon cracked black
    pepper
2 garlic cloves, peeled and
    chopped

SAUCE

2 tablespoons drained capers

1 tablespoon anchovy paste *or* 3 anchovy fillets

⅓ cup tomato puree *or* ¼ cup pureed sun-dried tomatoes

¼ cup Sauce Demi-Glace (see Index) *or* 2 beef boullion cubes dissolved in ¼ cup water

¾ cup Marsala (the low-cost California variety works well)

freshly ground pepper to taste

Allow a 6- to 7-ounce serving per person. This would normally be 3 medallions 1 inch thick from the backstrap or 2 1-inch-thick slices from the boned leg. Mix all marinade ingredients and marinate the meat at room temperature for 2 to 3 hours. Drain the meat, reserving the oil from the marinade.

To sauté, put the oil from the marinade in a sauté pan and heat almost to the smoking point. Without overcrowding, add the drained meat, leaving on the bits and pieces of garlic and herbs from the marinade that have adhered to the meat, and sear to rare or medium-rare. Do not burn the oil as it will impart a bitter flavor to the sauce.

To grill, cook over a hot fire to the same degree of doneness, allowing the flames to envelop and seal the meat. This will occur when the marinade drips into the fire.

In either case, remove the meat when done and place on a warm platter or in a low oven.

To the hot sauté pan, add 2 tablespoons of the reserved olive oil, the capers, and the anchovy paste. Sauté briefly and add the tomato. Reduce slightly and add the beef demi-glace and Marsala. Reduce the whole mixture until thickened. Place the meat on plates and place the sauce on top or place the sauce on the plates and arrange the medallions on top. Add freshly ground pepper to taste.

MEDALLIONS OF CARIBOU WITH CREAM AND GREEN PEPPERCORN SAUCE

SERVES 2

2 ¾-inch-thick medallions from loin of caribou
salt to taste
¼ cup clarified butter
3 tablespoons Calvados or applejack
1 large shallot
½ teaspoon drained water-packed green peppercorns
1 cup lightly thickened Game Stock (see Index)
½ cup heavy cream

Season the medallions with salt. In a sauté pan, sauté them in 3 tablespoons of the clarified butter until golden on both sides. Pour off the fat, then pour in the Calvados, heat it, and ignite it. When the flames die out, remove the medallions from the pan and keep them warm.

Peel and mince the shallot. Put the remaining tablespoon of butter into the sauté pan and add the shallot and the green peppercorns. Sauté until the shallot pieces are translucent, then add the stock. Stir to deglaze the pan and reduce the mixture by half. Pour in the cream and let the sauce simmer (do not let it boil) until reduced to the desired consistency.

Return the medallions and any juices to the sauce and heat to serving temperature. Or serve the caribou with a spoonful or ribbon of the cream sauce and serve the rest of the sauce separately.

Noisettes of venison and pears with sauvignon sauce.

Overleaf: Roast of Venison Black Forest.

ROAST OF VENISON BLACK FOREST
(ROTI DU CHEVREUIL "FORÊT NOIRE")

SERVES 6

1   saddle of venison, deboned, including bones trimmed from both sides
1   bottle cabernet sauvignon
3   carrots, chopped
2   onions, chopped
1   fresh thyme sprig *or* 1 teaspoon dried
1   fresh rosemary sprig *or* 1 teaspoon dried
3   bay leaves
½   cup vegetable oil
3   Granny Smith apples
½   cup sugar
1   lemon, cut in half
½   cup (¼ pound) plus 7 tablespoons unsalted butter
1   pint blueberries
½   cup red wine vinegar
salt to taste
Spaetzle (recipe follows)

Marinate the venison, refrigerated, for 2 nights in the red wine with the carrots, onions, and herbs. Drain the meat, reserving the marinade liquid and vegetables separately. In a big pot, sauté the bones until browned in 3 tablespoons of the oil, add the vegetables from the marinade, cover with water, and cook for 6 to 8 hours over low heat. Strain the stock and set aside.

Slice the ends of the apples, peel, and cut in half. Scoop out the core and a little more with a melon baller. Poach the rounds in a saucepan with water to cover, 1 teaspoon of the sugar, the lemon, and 2 tablespoons of the butter; do not overcook. Set the apples aside. In a small pan, simmer the blueberries, remaining sugar, and vinegar for 5 minutes. Set aside.

Preheat the oven to 400°F.

Sauté the venison in 5 tablespoons oil and 5 tablespoons butter to seal in the juices and put immediately into the oven for 15 to 20 minutes, depending on the size of the fillets and the degree of doneness desired. It is best kept medium-rare.

Remove the venison from the oven and keep warm. Degrease and then deglaze the pan with all the red wine reserved from the marinade. Reduce by two-thirds and add the strained stock. Reduce to the thickness desired, by about half. Finish the sauce by melting in the remaining ½ cup butter. Add salt to taste. Slice the venison and reheat in the oven for 1 or 2 minutes. Fill the apple rounds with the blueberries. Arrange the venison and filled apples on 6 hot dinner plates and spoon sauce over the venison. Serve with spaetzle.

SPAETZLE

4   eggs
salt to taste
pinch of ground nutmeg
1   cup all-purpose flour
1   tablespoon semolina
     flour
5   quarts water for boiling
     spaetzle
1   tablespoon vegetable oil
butter to taste

Break the eggs into a large bowl. Beat lightly with a fork, then add the salt and nutmeg. Gradually add the flour and semolina. Work well to form a smooth dough. Let this dough rest for at least 1 hour.

In a large pot, bring 5 quarts water to a rapid boil. Add some salt and the oil.

Have ready on the side a bowl of cold water. Then press the dough through a large-holed strainer (or a special spaetzle strainer) into the boiling water. Boil until it is cooked. Transfer to the bowl of cold water, drain, and toss with butter to serve.

VENISON STEAKS
WITH WILD MUSHROOMS

SERVES 4

4   **venison steaks cut from the loin, 7 to 8 ounces each**
7   **tablespoons olive oil**
½   **teaspoon salt**
1   **teaspoon freshly cracked black peppercorns**
1   **quart port**
36   **black Tellicherry peppercorns**
¼   **pound slab bacon**
5   **tablespoons butter**
1   **head of garlic**
1½   **cups diced carrots**
1½   **cups diced onions**
1   **cup diced leeks, white part only**
1   **cup diced celery**
2   **quarts degreased Game Stock (see Index) or veal stock**
2   **bay leaves, crumbled**
2   **cups fresh wild mushrooms (chanterelle, oyster, or shiitake)**
salt and pepper to taste

Rub the venison steaks lightly with 3 tablespoons of the olive oil and season with ½ teaspoon salt and the cracked black peppercorns. Refrigerate. Pour the port into a saucepan and add the whole peppercorns. Cook over mod-erate heat for about 20 min-utes. You will need 2 cups of the wine for the sauce. Re-serve peppercorns and port separately.

Cut any rind from the bacon and cut bacon into small rectangular pieces (lardoons). In a heavy skillet, sauté the lit-tle lardoons until done to your taste. With a skimmer, trans-fer them to a plate covered with paper toweling. Leave the bacon fat in the skillet and add 2 tablespoons of the re-maining olive oil and 1 table-spoon of the butter. Cut the head of garlic crosswise into halves and add to the skillet along with the carrots, onions, leeks, and celery. Continue to cook, stirring only occasion-ally. Allow the vegetables to brown on the edges. Pour in the reserved 2 cups port and continue to cook until only a very small amount of liquid re-mains. Pour in the stock and add the bay leaves. Reduce the sauce by half and strain it; there should be about 2 cups strained sauce when finished. Discard the vegetables and other solids and chill the sauce. (This sauce can be made 1 or 2 days in advance.)

Trim and clean the mush-rooms, slice them, and roll into moist absorbent toweling; keep them cool. Heat a very large heavy skillet and coat with 1 tablespoon of the re-maining olive oil and add 3 ta-blespoons of the remaining butter. Sauté the mushrooms until just cooked. Season with salt and pepper and transfer to a bowl; keep them warm.

Wipe out the skillet and coat it again with the remaining ta-blespoon of olive oil. Turn heat to high and put the steaks in the pan; if the pan is not large enough to hold them all, cook them in batches. Sear steaks on both sides to the de-sired doneness. However, keep in mind that venison is very lean; if steaks are cooked past rare, they will be very dry-tasting.

Transfer the steaks to a platter and pour any liquid re-leased by the mushrooms into the skillet. Use this liquid to deglaze the pan and carefully scrape up any collected bits of meat with a flat-bottomed wooden spatula. Remove the sauce from the refrigerator and discard the fat congealed on top. Heat the sauce in a saucepan and set it in a warm place. Add the cooked lardoons and 2 cups prepared sauce to the skillet and let the mixture reduce over moderate heat. Whisk in the remaining tablespoon of butter and the reserved peppercorns. Spoon some of the sauce onto warm plates and arrange the steaks on top. Arrange the mushrooms over the steaks. There may be sauce left over; refrigerate to store it.

Note:

After straining sauces one afternoon, I popped a black peppercorn into my mouth to investigate its flavor and texture after the time it had spent simmering in the sauce base. To my surprise it was soft, almost like a green peppercorn, and still interestingly spicy. You may choose to omit them from the dish, except for their flavor, but unless they were overly dried out to begin with, you will find them soft enough to chew.

Overleaf: The Explorers, Florida.

EXPLORER'S PREMIERE

SERVES 6

6 2-ounce pieces boneless blackbuck antelope
salt and pepper to taste
¼ cup butter *or* 3 tablespoons olive oil
2 cups Red Currant Sauce (recipe follows)
3 ounces foie gras
3 ounces boneless top round veal
3 ounces chicken leg meat
leaves from 2 fresh thyme sprigs
¾ cup heavy cream
1 teaspoon salt
¼ teaspoon pepper

2 tablespoons pine nuts
3 quail, deboned
¼ cup packed light brown sugar
1 tablespoon dark sesame oil
2 cups Green Peppercorn Sauce (recipe follows)

Season the antelope with salt and pepper. Sauté the pieces in the butter or olive oil in a skillet for 2 minutes on each side, until medium-rare. Place the antelope pieces in the Red Currant Sauce.

Grind the foie gras, veal, and chicken together twice. Mix with the thyme, heavy cream, 1 teaspoon salt, ¼ teaspoon pepper, and the pine nuts. Stuff the quails with the ground mixture, then coat the birds with a mixture of brown sugar and sesame oil. Steam them for 5 minutes, then smoke them for 7 to 10 minutes. Slice the birds and fan out the slices on a base of Green Peppercorn Sauce.

RED CURRANT SAUCE

MAKES ABOUT 2 CUPS

½   tablespoon chopped
    shallots
1½ teaspoons chopped garlic
¼   cup butter
¼   cup fresh red currants
½   cup port
1   cup veal stock

1   cup Sauce Demi-Glace
    (see Index)

Sauté the shallots and garlic in 1 tablespoon of the butter in a saucepan. Add the currants and wine. Reduce the mixture to ¼ cup over moderate heat. Add the veal stock and Sauce Demi-Glace and bring to a boil. Whisk in the remaining butter, a small piece at a time, and serve as soon as the sauce is ready.

GREEN PEPPERCORN SAUCE

MAKES ABOUT 2 CUPS

1 tablespoon chopped shallots
1½ teaspoons chopped garlic
¼ cup butter
1 fresh thyme sprig *or* ½ teaspoon dried
½ cup Pinot Noir
1 cup Sauce Demi-Glace (see Index)

1 tablespoon drained water-packed green peppercorns

Sauté the shallots and garlic in 1 tablespoon of the butter in a saucepan. Add the thyme and wine and reduce to ¼ cup over moderate heat. Add the Sauce Demi-Glace. Bring to a boil, then strain into a clean saucepan. Add the peppercorns. Whisk in the remaining butter, a small piece at a time, and serve the sauce as soon as it is ready.

ROAST LOIN OF AXIS DEER WITH CORN CAKES

SERVES 4

When boning the deer, be sure to save all bones and trimmings to use for the sauce.

¼ cup vegetable oil
1 teaspoon minced fresh rosemary *or* ½ teaspoon dried
1 teaspoon minced fresh thyme *or* ½ teaspoon dried
1½ teaspoons minced garlic
salt to taste
black pepper and white pepper to taste
1½ pounds boneless axis deer loin
bones and trimmings from the deer
1 cup Sauce Demi-Glace (see Index) or Sauce Espagnole (see Index)
1 teaspoon minced shallots
3 tablespoons butter
3 fresh thyme sprigs
2 tablespoons fresh lingonberries
½ teaspoon drained water-packed green peppercorns

¼ cup raspberry vinegar
2 tablespoons lingonberry preserves
clarified butter
Corn Cakes (recipe follows)

Mix the vegetable oil, minced herbs, ½ teaspoon of the garlic, and salt and pepper to taste to make a marinade. Place the deer loin in a glass or enameled container and pour the marinade over it. Turn to coat all sides of the meat. Marinate in a cool place for 3 hours.

Preheat the oven to 350°F.

Place the bones and trimmings from the meat in a heavy saucepan and brown in the oven for about 10 minutes. Remove the bones. Add the sauce, bring to a boil on top of the stove, and simmer. In a small saucepan, sauté the

shallots and remaining teaspoon of garlic in 1 tablespoon of the butter. Add the thyme sprigs, lingonberries, green peppercorns, and raspberry vinegar. Reduce this mixture slowly until it is almost dry. Scrape what remains into the brown sauce and simmer for 10 minutes. Bring the lingonberry preserves to a boil and add to the brown sauce. Bring the sauce to a boil, then strain it into a clean pan. Set aside.

Remove the deer loin from the marinade and pat it dry. In an ovenproof pan, melt enough clarified butter to cover the bottom of the pan and in it sear the deer meat until golden on all sides. Then put the pan in the oven and roast for about 7 minutes for medium-rare.

Reheat the sauce if it is cold and whip in the remaining 2 tablespoons of butter, a small piece at a time. Do not let the sauce boil again. Slice the loin and serve with the sauce and Corn Cakes.

Roast Loin of Axis Deer with Corn Cakes.

CORN CAKES

¾   cup all-purpose flour
½   cup cornmeal
½   teaspoon baking powder
salt and pepper to taste
1   egg
¾   cup half-and-half
¼   cup chopped onion
½   cup corn kernels
2   tablespoons sugar

½   cup julienned potato
vegetable oil

In a bowl, mix the flour, cornmeal, and baking powder with a little salt and pepper. Mix in the egg and half-and-half and whip the mixture until smooth. Add the onion, corn kernels, sugar, and potato. Drop the batter by large spoonfuls onto a heavy griddle brushed with vegetable oil and cook over medium-high heat until bubbles appear on the top. Use a broad spatula or pancake turner to flip the cakes over and cook on the other side. The cakes should be golden brown on both sides.

VENISON HUNTER STYLE

6   pounds saddle of
         venison or elk on the
         bone
½   pound carrots
½   pound celery
½   pound onions
1   small bunch fresh
         parsley
½   cup vegetable oil
1   cup tomato paste
6   quarts water
1   bay leaf
1   teaspoon dried thyme *or*
         1 tablespoon fresh
1   teaspoon crushed black
         peppercorns
1   teaspoon salt, or more to
         taste

5   tablespoons chopped
         sun-dried tomatoes
1   cup water
1¼ cups brandy
¼   pound fresh wild
         mushrooms (oyster
         mushrooms,
         chanterelles, or
         morels)
¼   pound (4 to 6 large)
         shallots
1   cup (½ pound) clarified
         butter
½   cup all-purpose flour
1   cup heavy cream
large pinch of white pepper

Preheat the oven to 375°F.

Cut the venison meat from the bones and trim off all silverskin and fat from the meat. Discard fat. Place the bones in a roasting pan along with the silverskin. Brown bones evenly, turning them occasionally, for about 30 minutes. Do not let them burn. While bones are roasting, wash carrots and celery, but do not peel them. Chop them and the unpeeled onions into coarse pieces. Wash, dry, and chop the parsley.

Remove the roasting pan from the oven and set over moderate heat on top of the stove. Add the oil, chopped vegetables, and tomato paste. Mix all ingredients well. Stir the mixture frequently so it does not burn. When vegetables are browned, deglaze the pan with 3 quarts of the water. Scrape the bottom of the pan to release all meat juices stuck to the bottom. Stir everything well and bring to a boil, then pour the whole mixture into a 3-gallon stockpot. Add the bay leaf, thyme, peppercorns, parsley, and 1 teaspoon salt. Pour in another 3 quarts water; mix well. Bring the stock to a simmer and cover. Simmer for 3 hours, checking the water level every hour. The stock should reduce but not dry out.

Pour the finished stock through a strainer into a clean pot. Discard the vegetables and bones. Return the stock to the heat and bring to a simmer. Taste it and adjust seasoning if needed. Reduce the strained stock to about 2 cups. During this final reduction, skim off and discard oils and foam that rise to the surface. (The stock may be prepared several days ahead. Refrigerate it until it is needed.)

There should be at least 3 pounds of venison fillet remaining after deboning. Cut it into 16 portions, each weighing 3 ounces. Lightly pound each portion on the cut side. Put the sun-dried tomatoes into a bowl and cover with 1 cup water and 1 cup of the brandy. Let them reconstitute for about 1 hour. Wash and trim the mushrooms and cut into strips. Peel and chop the shallots.

Heat about half of the clarified butter in a large sauté pan. Dust the venison slices with flour and shake off the excess; they should be lightly coated. Sautéing the slices in batches so as not to crowd them, and adding more of the clarified butter as needed, sauté the venison until done to your taste. Transfer to a plate and keep warm. In the same pan, sauté all the wild mushrooms along with the chopped shallots for about 1 minute.

Heat the remaining ¼ cup brandy in a small pan, then pour it over the mushrooms and ignite it. When the flames die out, deglaze the pan with the 2 cups strained stock and the cream. Scrape the bottom of the pan to release all flavors of venison and mushrooms. Mix the sauce well and bring to a simmer. Drain the tomatoes and add them to the sauce. Mix. Taste and add salt and white pepper if needed. Return the venison steaks to the sauce and heat to serving temperature. Serve with rice.

MEDALLIONS OF VENISON
WITH GORGONZOLA BUTTER SAUCE

SERVES 4

1   whole small whitetail backstrap *or* ¾ mule deer backstrap, about 2 pounds
1   cup olive oil
1   tablespoon cracked black peppercorns
1   tablespoon chopped garlic
3   tablespoons lemon juice
1   teaspoon minced shallots or scallions
¼   cup dry white wine
¼   cup heavy cream
2   tablespoons crumbled Gorgonzola cheese
½   cup (¼ pound) cold butter
½   teaspoon white pepper

Place the game in a glass or enameled container. Make a marinade from the oil, cracked peppercorns, garlic, and lemon juice and pour it over the meat. Let it marinate for at least 1 hour. Turn the meat occasionally to allow the marinade to flavor all sides. Meanwhile, prepare a charcoal fire or preheat a gas grill or broiler.

To make the sauce, combine the shallots, wine, and cream in a saucepan over moderate heat and reduce to half of the original volume. Lower the heat and add the crumbled cheese; stir until melted. Cut the cold butter into 4 pieces and add to the sauce, a piece at a time, stirring all the while. Season with white pepper. Set the sauce aside in a warm place but not over direct heat as it could cause the sauce to separate.

Put the meat close to the heat source to allow the olive oil coating to flare up and create a hot fire. Keep turning the meat to allow the outside to char without overcooking the middle. Remove the venison from the heat when it is rare (130°F) or at least no more than medium-rare (140°F). Slice, arrange on individual plates, top with the sauce, and serve.

ELK TENDERLOIN
WITH CARAMELIZED ONIONS

SERVES 8 TO 10

1   elk tenderloin
½   cup vegetable oil
4   teaspoons cracked black
     peppercorns
1   teaspoon salt, plus
     additional to taste
1   teaspoon plus a pinch of
     crumbled dried thyme
2   large yellow onions
½   cup (¼ pound) clarified
     butter
½   teaspoon sugar
⅔   cup sour mash bourbon

Cut the tenderloin into 1½-inch slices, preparing 1 or 2 slices per person. Make a marinade with the oil, 3 teaspoons of the cracked peppercorns, 1 teaspoon salt, and 1 teaspoon thyme. In a glass or enameled pan, marinate the elk steaks for about 30 minutes, turning occasionally.

Peel and slice the onions. In a sauté pan, use part of the clarified butter to cook the onions over moderate heat until they begin to turn dark brown at the edges. Remove onions from the pan. Increase heat to high and add enough butter to coat the bottom of the pan. Just before the butter smokes, add some of the elk steaks, being careful not to crowd them. The object is to get a good crust on the outside of the meat without overcooking the middle. When the steaks are rare to medium-rare, place on a warm plate and set aside.

Add the pinch of thyme, the sugar, remaining 1 teaspoon peppercorns, and salt to taste to the pan and continue to cook, adding enough butter to keep the bottom of the pan moist. When the pan is hot but not burning, deglaze it with the bourbon and quickly return the cooked onions. Stir them around the pan so that they become coated with pan juices. Spoon onions over the steaks and serve immediately.

Remember, texture is important. The contrast of the crusty, almost charred steaks with the soft caramelized onions is the secret of this dish. Serve with crispy hash brown potatoes on the side and pour a good zinfandel.

TERRINE OF VENISON

SERVES 4 TO 6

6   ounces boneless venison
    meat
2   ounces venison liver
4   shallots
1   fresh parsley sprig
2   pinches of dried thyme
1   pinch of ground allspice
¾   tablespoon salt
3 to 4 tablespoons applejack
    or Calvados
a few turns of the
    peppermill
1   egg
2½ ounces fresh (unsalted)
    pork fatback, chopped
½   pound fresh (unsalted)
    pork fatback, cut into
    thin sheets
1   carrot, cooked
1   apple
1   bay leaf
½   cup all-purpose flour
¼   cup water
Les Légumes du Chevreuil
    (recipe follows)

Cut the meat and liver into
small pieces, peel and mince
the shallots, and mince the
parsley. Mix these ingredients
with the thyme, allspice, salt,
applejack, and freshly ground
pepper in a glass or ceramic
bowl. Allow the mixture to
marinate for a few hours.

Add the egg and chopped
fatback to the mixture in the
bowl, then run the whole mixture through a meat grinder
fitted with a fine die or mince
in a food processor, but do not
puree the mixture. Line a 3-
cup terrine with the thin
sheets of fatback, reserving
enough for the top. Push the
carrot through an apple corer
to get a long cylinder. Pierce
the apple around its core with
the corer to get 5 or 6 cylindrical pieces of apple.

Preheat the oven to 400°F.

Pack a third of the mixture
into the terrine. Lay half of the
carrot and 2 or 3 lengths of
apple on it. Cover with another third of the mixture and
the remaining carrot and apple

pieces; finally, pack in the last
of the ground mixture. Cover
with the remaining sheet of
fatback. Place the bay leaf on
top. Place the cover on the terrine and seal it with a paste
made of the flour mixed with
the water.

Set the terrine in a bain-
marie and bake for 1 hour and
15 minutes. When done, remove the lid. Cover the top of
the pâté with a sheet of aluminum foil and place a ½-
pound weight on top. Let the
terrine cool under refrigeration for several hours or overnight.

When you are ready to
serve the terrine, loosen the
mixture from the sides of the
mold with a thin-bladed knife
and turn it out on a cutting
board. The fat can be scraped
off if you wish or can remain
as a border all around. Use a
sharp knife to cut the pâté into
thin slices. Arrange on plates
and garnish with olives or
cornichons or a spoonful of
lingonberries (no lettuce,
please). Or serve with vegetable puree as follows.

Les Légumes du Chevreuil
(Vegetables for Venison)

In olive oil, briefly cook some green leaves of leek, turnip greens, spinach, or any seasonal greens with some garlic and seasoning and a few tablespoons of white wine. When tender, puree the vegetables and let them cool.

With some chopped bacon, cook some red vegetables—carrots, red cabbage, shallots—with seasonings and a few tablespoons of red wine. When the vegetables are tender, puree them and let them cool.

To serve, spread the green puree on one side of the plate, the red puree on the other side. Carefully arrange a slice of pâté on the purees.

Roasting a whole hog on the barbecue.

14. WILD BOAR
AND JAVELINA

The wild boar (*Sus scrofa*) is the genotype of our modern swine, which, according to Chinese manuscripts, was first domesticated some 3,000 years ago during the Shang dynasty. A diabolical spirit in mythology, at medieval banquets the boar's head displayed on a separate platter represented the triumph of Christ over evil. The Boar's Head Festival that began during the reign of King Wenceslas in twelfth-century England is one of the oldest traditions of the Christian church, known as the Feast of Epiphany (marking the end of the Christmas season on January 6th). This tradition continued in the great manor houses of the American colonial period and is still celebrated in many churches today.

The ferocity of a cornered boar with its paired self-sharpening tusks is not only legendary but very real. The ancient art of hunting the boar with dogs and spear was considered an ultimate test of man's courage. Xenophon, in his hunting treatise *Cynegeticus* (c. 400 B.C.), cautioned that a barbed spear must be used to prevent the boar from running up the shaft and disemboweling the hunter. In Greek mythology, Adonis was killed by a boar and in his resurrection became the god of swine. A boar can upend and fatally gore a horse, as British troops learned when "pig-sticking" was a macho sport in India during the eighteenth century. Although I have hunted boar in Germany, Austria, and Argentina, my only painful swine confrontation occurred while trout fishing on the Little Deschutes River in Oregon. Some farmer's stray Poland China sow, of a portly 200 pounds, came ambling along the bank, and, after a few kind words, I turned my back and was violently butted—actually propelled ass over teakettle into the stream. But domestic pigs have a long history of reverting to type—which confuses some kitchens.

In our culinary view, there are three kinds of pigs: the domestic breeds (such as the familiar Hampshire, Yorkshire, Poland China, and Chester White), the feral hog, and the European wild boar. The feral hog, which is the second most hunted animal in my home state of Florida, was originally from domestic stock and arrived near Boca Grande on the voyage of Hernando de Soto in 1539. On subsequent Spanish visits, more and more swine were landed, and early settlers raised them under semiwild conditions. Many hogs escaped and were left to roam the woods, where they were hunted by white men and Indians alike. After generations of living in the wild, the razor-sharp tusks and the hair became longer; some animals developed a ridge of hair on the back, thus prompting the name "razorback," which is a colloquialism and does not indicate a different breed. Today the annual harvest in Florida is usually given at 36,000 hogs, but it fluctuates considerably. In one season (1973–74), the kill reached 84,128, far exceeding the deer harvest of 57,122 in the same period. Feral hogs occur in smaller numbers in the southern United States from Kentucky to Texas, but the only other significant population is in the coastal mountains of California, which provide hunters with about 16,000 wild swine per year, mainly in that area from Mendocino to Santa Barbara counties. The California feral stock originated from domestic hogs liberated by Spanish Jesuit missionaries beginning in 1769. Hawaii also has a substantial population of wild hogs, which predates mainland introductions as they apparently originated with the early Polynesians. It is likely that these swine are descendants of the domestic South Sea pig of Asiatic origin. A comparatively small number are harvested each year in various public hunting areas, particularly on the big island of Hawaii.

The European wild boar can be a very large animal, up to 500 pounds or more. This swine was delivered to North Carolina in 1912 by one George Moore to stock a small preserve near Hoopers Bald. It has been recorded that these pigs originated in Russia and were transshipped from Germany; however, the logic of this escapes me, as wild boar were abundantly present in the latter country and more likely came live-trapped from the Black Forest. In any case, hogs retaining true European wild boar characteristics, as well as feral hybrids, occur in western North Carolina and eastern Tennessee. These are hunted in the wildlife management areas of Cherokee National Forest and Great Smoky Mountains National Park, as well as on private preserves open to paid shooting, of which there are a number in Tennessee and also Pennsylvania.

Although a large boar makes a fine trophy for the hunter, it is the shoat that is famed for its delicate pork flavor. This preference is not mine alone, as a distinction is made between adult animals and the young in all classic European restaurants: the wild boar in Italy is called a *cinghiale*, but it is the *cinghialetto* of less than forty pounds that is preferred at table, while in France the *sanglier* is prime as a young *marcassin*. The same thing is true of our feral hog in Florida and California; however, any animal up to eighty pounds in dressed weight, which is purely subjective on my part, will provide quality pork, assuming that it has been feeding on a forest diet of mast, typically acorns and beechnuts, as well as on wild grapes, palmetto berries, and roots of various kinds.

What produces praiseworthy pork is a geographic differential. The very best European wild boar I recall eating was at a restaurant in Belgium in the forest at Lorce, called La Vallée. It is famous for both its mousse of woodcock and *marcassin* in green pepper sauce. The chef claimed that after summering on whortleberries his porkers "finish" themselves off with a pristine diet of chestnuts and truffles (hogs are professionals at gathering these subterranean fungi) in the fall season. My old friend Jake Boyd, who live-traps feral hogs on his Florida ranch, puts the pigs on a six-week diet of mangoes, which produces the most exotic fresh ham to grace any game table. The leanest pork in my experience is found on Florida's ferals, and this is especially true of young animals. It is compensatory with the species; there is more subdermal fat on hogs found at higher or cooler elevations, as swine lack thermoregulatory sweat glands. A wild shoat from the Everglades region has sweet, succulent white meat and a very minimum of fat, so one must be especially careful not to overcook or dry it out—which is a common state of the art at country barbecues, where invariably the hog has been skinned rather than wire-brushed to remove the bristles, a painstaking process in the field. Without larding, barding, or oil basting, it can be a total loss.

Roasting a Whole Hog

Most chefs are in harmonious accord with that ancient Roman satirist, Decimus Juvenalis, who perfectly described a wild boar as "the animal appointed by nature to appear at banquets." A whole roast pig deserves to be served to the sound of trumpets. The mechanics of cooking a whole game or domestic animal, whether wild boar, domestic pig, mountain sheep, domestic lamb, mountain goat, or domestic kid, are essentially the same, with perhaps a few exceptions depending on size. In Spain, for example, it's the toothsome suckling pig that is relished by connoisseurs; three-week-old animals weighing seven to eight pounds are the hallmark of those restaurants specializing in *cochinillo asado*, which is roasted in clay pans in woodburning stoves. At Botins in Madrid, where they've been in business since 1725, the pans are sloshed with white wine and rosemary, then the butterflied pigs are basted with lard (suckling pigs are not fat) until the skin is crisped.

The *kalua* pig of Hawaii is cooked in an *imu* or underground oven, really a hole in the ground, not unlike some Maine clambakes. The pit is lined with heated lava stones, and some of these are packed in the body cavity before the animal is lowered into the hole. The pig is then buried in ti and banana leaves, which are covered by wet burlap sacks. A large piece of canvas is placed over the sacks to prevent heat and steam from escaping. Some Honolulu beach hotels make a tourist spellbinder out of it, with muscular beachboys blowing soulful notes on their conch shells as the trussed hog is paraded to the pit. The *imu* method can be duplicated by mainlanders, but digging the pit, heating the rocks, and finding enough corn husks to substitute for the foliage would render me hors de combat.

Few private homes are equipped with an oven large enough to cook the average feral hog or wild boar. Roasting over an open fire outdoors with the hog turning on a spit is the ideal alternative. I have no formal recipe, because to some extent we are talking in abstracts. Chiefly, it's a matter of maintaining a hot charcoal or wood fire where the boar will turn. The fire should be placed in such a fashion that the heat will be directed at the animal from an angle—you'll need a drip pan below the hog anyhow. If you are cooking it with skin on (my preference, but it requires hard work with scalding water and a wire brush to remove the hair), the hide should be punctured in various places from time to time to allow the fat to drip away until the skin becomes crisp. If you are cooking with skin off, it will require frequent basting once the fat has been rendered. If the hog is very fat, which is generally true of the domestic kind, I would suggest slicing some of it away before you begin roasting.

The important thing is to avoid undercooking (the normal pork safeguard against trichinosis) and to arrive at the correct internal temperature of 155°F. This should be taken in the hams and through the shoulders as deep as possible but without touching bone. Accurate reading requires a meat thermometer with a long probe. If you're using a Meat Thermicator, bear in mind, when cooking the hog with skin on, the needle won't make a dent in its hide; puncture the surface with a sharp knife so you can insert the probe without damaging it. The actual cooking time is highly variable. It depends on the heat of your fire, its distance from the hog, the ambient outdoor temperature, and, of course, the size of the boar. In theory you should be cooking at about 280°F. An eighty-pounder (dressed weight) might take four hours under windless conditions to as long as seven hours in a wind and cold weather—with the hog no more than eighteen inches from the coals. Bill Bonnette, who runs a celebrated game kitchen at Bonnette's Hunting Preserve in Lake Park, Florida, cooks his wild pigs for ten hours, but with the skinned pork thirty-two inches from the fire. So the only viable guideline is internal meat temperature, no matter how small or large the animal.

Many chefs routinely marinate their hogs before cooking. I do not, unless it's an old feral pig; it isn't a question of game flavor, a meat quality that I am otherwise devoted to, but wild swine become unduly porcine with age. A good citrus marinade that dates all the way back to the conquistadores is plain sour orange juice; sour oranges are a variety native to Florida (popular in making pies) and not spoiled fruit. Their acidity can be duplicated by diluting any available orange juice with an equal volume of grapefruit juice. To marinate a whole pig, slide it into one of those supersize heavy-duty plastic garbage bags, pour in the juice and rinds, tie the end closed, and let sit for from four to six hours, turning it occasionally. For basting, which is essential, if you cook a skinned pig, you can stay with a citrus base such as one part Italian garlic dressing to two parts sour orange juice, or you can use one of those commercial country barbecue sauces similarly diluted.

To roast an eighty-pound boar, you will need at least eight bags (twenty-pound size) of charcoal to maintain a hot fire for a prolonged period; 200 pounds of charcoal is probably a safer minimum in cold autumn climates. The barbecue pit has to be big. At home I use my smokehouse, which I designed to serve both purposes. It has a cement floor, rear and sides, with a redwood roof and doors. The roof and doors can be folded back, and the horizontal steel rods (in lateral series), which normally hold the wire mesh panels for smoking, will support an animal up to eighty pounds. I don't need a motor-driven spit to rotate the pig, because the meat gets a good circulation of heat and smoke with the roof and baffle doors closed. Too, I rarely cook a hog of over forty pounds, which is plenty big for family entertaining. To expedite the cooking, I butterfly the animal by splitting it down the middle and laying it flat on the belly side. I toss big handfuls of wet hickory and oak chips on the fire, giving the pork a rich, smoky flavor. This is probably the simplest method, and if you don't have a smokehouse, or a covered grill big enough to hold a pig, a firebox can be jury-rigged with cement blocks and steel rods.

I don't know of any commercially made spits suitable for roasting whole hogs or other game of substantial size. Those few practical ones that I have seen were designed and built by their owners, and the best of these was constructed by Stanley Leen of Leen's Lodge at Grand Lake Stream, Maine. Stanley is a master of hog cookery and for many years has featured a pig cookout for his guests at camp. His festive *pièce montée* usually scales at eighty pounds, a considerable weight to rotate with rhythmic precision. Stanley's unit consists of a $\frac{1}{10}$-horsepower shadded pole electric motor that operates at 1,500 rpm, with a reduction gear box that brings it down to twelve rpm. By means of a ten-to-54 tooth chain sprocket, it's reduced to 2.2 rpm. This turns a whole animal over twice a minute on a one-inch-diameter stainless-steel shaft seven feet in length. To get any whole animal rotating in a regular rhythm so it sputters to a golden crust on all sides, it must also be correctly balanced and trussed on the spit. This requires running the spit through the hog's anus, parallel to and below the backbone, then out the mouth. Unless it's balanced, the hog will flip and flop, scorching in some areas and not cooking in others. The legs must be tucked in and trussed with steel wrapping wire and the snout secured to the spit with pointed steel prongs.

JAVELINA

Javelina is the common name for the collared peccary or "musk pig" (*Dicotyles tajacu*) in Texas, Arizona, and New Mexico, which is the extent of its range in the United States. However, it is also found throughout Mexico to Central America. The javelina superficially resembles a pig but is not related to the swine, belonging to the family Tayassuidae. Unlike pigs, which have gallbladders and simple stomachs, the javelina lacks a gallbladder and has a complex stomach. Javelina feed principally on mast and berries and a wide variety of plant species, including spiny cacti in desert regions. The javelina has thick bristly hair that grows especially long around the head and neck; thus the name collared peccary. There is a second species, the white-lipped peccary, which ranges from southern Mexico into the rain forests of South America. Although the whitetail deer provided the bulk of animal protein to the ancient Maya in Mexico, the peccaries, less susceptible to those pitfalls and snares portrayed in the codices, were also an important food and offered live for ceremonial sacrifice.

Smaller than wild boar, adult javelina weigh from thirty to sixty pounds and are delicious eating. There are three musk glands (thus the euphemism "musk hog") along the midline of the back that emit a powerful odor, but these do not affect the meat and can be removed with the skin. A young sow javelina is excellent, but I would not cook or eat an old boar. There is that much difference between the two. The meat is not as light in color as that of pork but is of similar texture and has virtually no "wild" or musky taste. It is delicious when barbecued over mesquite coals. Wear rubber or plastic gloves while you're doing the skinning; otherwise the musk smell gets on your hands and doesn't readily disappear.

COOKING WILD BOAR IN FOIL

Ever since that pioneer Dutch O'Leary invented his oven, which went through a slow process of evolution (pivotal characters with the unlikely names Beaver Charlie, who redesigned the original Dutch oven, making it twice as deep, and Steeljaws Newhouse, who had it made with an upturned lid so the camp fire coals could be placed on its top), not many revolutionary tools have been designed for the outdoor chef beyond the barbecue grill and aluminum foil. Foil is a versatile utensil and plays an important role in cooking game meats that tend to toughen and dry. When properly wrapped or sealed so the steam doesn't escape, foil works as a pressure cooker. A wild pig with skin on doesn't present any real problem as the skin and underlying fat help keep the meat moist, but the vast majority of hunters skin the animal out. When exposed to direct heat, a skinned pig will become tough and chewy no matter how carefully it is cooked.

Few outdoor chefs have roasted as much native pork as wildlife biologist Lou Gainey, who was Everglades regional director of the Florida Game and Freshwater Fish Commission for twenty-four years. The Gainey method, which is the best I know of, is to brown and sear, bringing the internal temperature to about 80°F, then place it on a large sheet of foil before heavily coating it with chopped onion and a suitable barbecue sauce. Securely wrapped and left on the fire for two to three hours, depending on the size of the cut, it becomes tender and juicy. It can be tested for doneness (150°F) with the Meat Thermicator needle through the foil. To prevent tearing the wrap, thus causing steam to escape and scorching the meat, I use heavy-duty foil in the eighteen-inch width or a double wrap of the lighter weight. Any homemade or commercial brand barbecue sauce is suitable as long as it and the chopped onion are applied generously to steam and create a liquid bath. This method works equally well with venison hams and even game birds such as pheasant and wild turkey.

COOKING WILD BOAR

Expert Lou Gainey builds a fire of charcoal and wood for barbecuing wild boar. The large grill allows him to vary the intensity of the cooking heat from one area to another.

  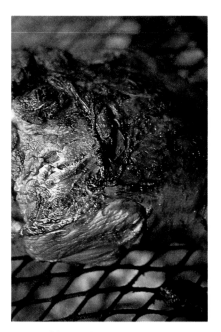

When the coals are glowing and covered with a fine ash, he places the boar on the grill to sear and brown it.

When the boar is well browned, and the internal temperature has reached about 80°F, Gainey transfers the boar to foil covered with chopped onions and barbecue sauce.

Then he slathers the boar with more sauce and onions, coating the meat thoroughly with the mixture to keep it moist and flavorful.

Gainey wraps his hand in a heavy towel to turn the browning boar on the grill. He uses a long branch to stoke the fire under th
pieces that are being seared.

Flaming logs sear the meat while ashen coals finish cooking the foil-wrapped pieces.

Succulent wild boar barbecued by the Gainey metho

SMOTHERED WILD BOAR
A LA FRANÇAISE

SERVES 6

4   pounds boneless wild
     boar, cut from hams of
     a young animal
     (*marcassin*)
2   cups Uncooked
     Marinade (recipe
     follows)
¼   cup vegetable oil
1   cup clear Game Stock
     (see Index)
1   bouquet garni made of
     parsley, thyme,
     rosemary, and bay leaf
salt
½   cup fresh blood
garnishes such as bacon,
     mushrooms, onions as
     desired

Cut the boar into 1-inch cubes. Put the meat in a glass or ceramic container just large enough to hold it all. Pour the Uncooked Marinade over the meat and let it marinate in a cool place for 24 hours.

Lift the pieces of meat from the marinade and pat them dry. Reserve the marinade. In a large pan, brown the meat in the oil, turning the pieces to color them on all sides. Transfer the meat to a platter and pour off the fat from the pan.

Deglaze the pan with some of the red wine from the marinade. Reduce the deglazing by half, then pour in the rest of the marinade and the stock. Add the bouquet garni and season lightly with salt. Return the meat to the pan, cover, and cook for 1 to 1½ hours. (If the meat was taken from an older boar, cook for at least 2 hours.)

Lift out the meat, being careful not to include any of the vegetables or spices. Reduce the cooking liquid by a third, then pour the mixture through a very fine sieve into a clean saucepan. Add the browned meat and any juices that have accumulated. Just before serving, thicken the sauce with blood.

Add to the stew blanched cubes of bacon, mushroom caps sautéed in oil, little onions browned with meat glaze, as desired. Serve the stew with buttered noodles and heart-shaped croutons sautéed in clarified butter.

UNCOOKED MARINADE

2   onions
2   carrots
2   celery ribs
3   fresh parsley sprigs,
     including the stems
2   cups dry red wine
1   bouquet garni made of
     parsley, thyme,
     rosemary, and bay leaf
3   juniper berries
3   cloves
12 white peppercorns

Peel the onions, scrub and scrape the carrots, and wash the celery ribs and parsley. Cut the vegetables into thin slices and chop the parsley, including the stems. Combine with the wine and the bouquet garni and whole spices.

Smothered Wild Boar à la Française.

Wild Boar Chops "Tavern"

SERVES 4

1	medium onion
1	carrot
8	peppercorns
1	teaspoon dried thyme
1	teaspoon dried rosemary
½	bay leaf
2	cups dry red wine
2	teaspoons red wine vinegar
2	tablespoons vegetable oil, or more if needed
8	wild boar rib chops, each 7 to 8 ounces

salt and pepper to taste

2	tablespoons butter
1	cup Game Stock (see Index)

Apples Stuffed with Cranberries (recipe follows)

Chop the onion and carrot, crush the peppercorns lightly, and combine with the herbs, red wine, vinegar, and 2 teaspoons of the oil. Arrange the chops in a glass or enameled container and pour the mixture over them. Marinate in a cool place for 12 to 14 hours.

Remove the chops from the marinade; set liquids and solids aside. Trim the chops and season lightly with salt and pepper. In a large skillet, sauté the chops in the remaining 4 teaspoons oil and 4 teaspoons of the butter over high heat until pink or medium-rare. If the pan does not hold all the chops in a single layer, sauté them in batches. If the pan becomes too dry, add more oil, 2 teaspoons at a time.

Transfer the chops to a baking dish and keep warm. Pour the oil from the pan and add the reserved marinade and all the solids. Simmer until reduced by half. Add the stock and reduce by a third. Adjust the seasonings and strain the sauce through a fine sieve into a clean saucepan. Add the remaining 2 teaspoons of butter to the sauce and keep it warm.

Arrange the chops on a large platter and garnish with the stuffed apples. Serve the sauce separately.

Apples Stuffed with Cranberries

SERVES 4

¾ to 1 cup sugar

2	cups water

lemon juice

small piece of cinnamon stick

4	apples
½	cup cranberries

Make a light sugar syrup with ⅔ cup of the sugar and 2 cups water. Add a few drops of lemon juice and the piece of cinnamon stick. Wash and core the apples and with a vegetable peeler remove a thin strip of peel around the middle of each apple. When the sugar is completely dissolved in the water and the syrup is transparent, gently place the apples in the syrup and poach them over moderate heat for 10 to 12 minutes or until tender but not mushy; they should hold their shape. Set them in a glass baking dish, reserving the syrup.

Meanwhile, wash the cranberries and remove any stems.

Put the cranberries in a small saucepan and pour in ½ cup of the syrup used to poach the apples. Bring to a boil and simmer for about 10 minutes, stirring occasionally. Most of the berries will pop, and the mixture will thicken. Taste a berry; you will need to add more sugar; over low heat, add the sugar, 1 tablespoon at a time, until the fruit is sweet enough for your taste. Let the cranberries cool, then spoon them into the poached apples. (These apples may be served cold, but if you prefer to have them hot, they may be reheated in the baking dish while the sauce is being prepared.)

TIMBALE OF WILD BOAR AND PHEASANT

SERVES 4

¾   pound boneless lean
       wild boar
salt and white pepper to
       taste
¼   pound skinless, boneless
       pheasant breast
2   egg whites, beaten
       lightly
5   tablespoons Flour
       Panade (recipe
       follows)
¼   pound shelled pistachios
6   tablespoons milk
⅞   cup heavy cream,
       whipped
⅔   cup heavy cream
⅓   cup pheasant demi-glace
1   tablespoon vegetable oil
1   tablespoon butter

Cut the boar meat into strips and season lightly with salt and white pepper. Cut the pheasant meat into strips and season lightly with salt and white pepper. Set the pheasant aside in a cool place. Grind the boar meat twice through the finest blade of a meat grinder. Add the lightly beaten egg whites. Slowly mix the Flour Panade into the meat mixture to make a forcemeat. In a food processor fitted with the steel blade, puree the pistachios with the milk and fold the puree gently into the meat mixture. Push the forcemeat through a fine-mesh sieve into a clean bowl. Slowly fold in the whipped cream, 1 tablespoon at a time. Chill the mixture.

Simmer the unwhipped heavy cream until reduced by half. Add the pheasant demi-glace and simmer. Mix the reserved pheasant strips with the oil and sauté quickly in a preheated pan. Add the pheasant to the cream sauce and simmer for 1 minute. Chill this mixture also.

Preheat the oven to 275 to 300°F.

Butter 4 6-ounce soup cups and line the inside with the forcemeat, filling the cups about three-quarters full. Fill the inside with the chilled pheasant mixture and cover evenly with the rest of the forcemeat. Place the cups in a bain-marie and bake for 20 to 25 minutes.

FLOUR PANADE

1 cup water
5 tablespoons butter
pinch of salt
¼ pound (about 1 cup) flour

Bring the water, butter, and salt to a boil in a small saucepan. Reduce the heat to moderate and slowly add the flour, stirring constantly. The mixture will thicken to dough consistency and should pull away from the sides of the pan. Push the mixture through a fine-mesh sieve and wrap it in buttered waxed paper until needed; it will keep in the refrigerator for 24 hours.

Herd on the Move, *by William Hanes. The Thomas Gilcrease Institute of American History and Art, Tulsa, Oklahoma*

15.

BUFFALO, THE HORNED GAME

Upon seeing the American bison in 1539, Hernando de Soto identified it by the Spanish name *búfalo*, a name in fact belonging to various species of Asian oxen. In de Soto's day the bison roamed not only the plains of the Far West but by the uncounted millions all the way from Illinois south to Georgia and north to Pennsylvania and western New York. By the 1770s these herds had been exterminated in the central plains, and by the 1880s they were virtually extinct everywhere. The bison has a bizarre history to say the least.

During the European invasion of the "Wild West," the slaughter of buffalo by sporting royalty was prophetic. The nobility of Victorian England, Scotland, Ireland, and, as an added starter, the Grand Duke Alexis of Russia (who hunted with George Custer) galloped into the country while buffalo were still a thundering herd of mindless millions. The original tourist in these sagebrush safaris was a titled Englishman, and even Jim Bridger, who honchoed many bloody expeditions, never encountered the likes of Sir St. George Gore. Wealthy beyond imagination, Gore arrived at St. Louis in 1853 for the sole purpose of shooting every feathered biped and wild beast in sight. That it would cost $500,000, a staggering sum over a century ago, didn't discourage Sir Gore in the least. Outfitted with 112 horses, twenty Red River wagons, a train of six mule rigs, and forty-eight hounds, and tended by fifty bewildered buckskinned guides and gunsmiths, he journeyed for two years through Colorado, Utah, Wyoming, and Montana with his brass bedstead, marble-topped commode, and an arsenal suitable for the First Marine Division in a major firefight. Gore was particularly keen on buffalo and kept a squad of loaders

in a sweat at his double-barrel .56-caliber Hawkens guns, which blew away bison at a range that would match the best of the contract hunters to come. Only the finest wines in crystal goblets graced Sir Gore's camp table, and his game arrived in a veritable bath of red currant sauce instead of Bridger's frontier favorite—vinegar and chopped onions. Currant sauce, which Charles Francatelli, Queen Victoria's venison-mad chef, had recently put in a recipe (*The Modern Cook*, published in 1845), was not merely melted jelly, but an amalgam of three-quarters of a cup of red wine, the pared rind of one lemon, twelve cloves, and one cinnamon stick to each cup of simmering jelly. While few historians may remember why Gore Canyon, Gore Pass, and the Gore Mountains entered Colorado geography, fewer still know his fate. When Jim Bridger went off to the Utah war, Gore burned all his equipment at Fort Union. Only the obdurate parts of the bedstead and commode survived. Sir Gore threw these in the river and went home to England and was never heard from again.

In the 1870s, woodburning engines of the Kansas Pacific Railroad and the Atchison Topeka and Santa Fe roared and belched across the land like alien monsters whose only mission was to obliterate the past and future of the Plains Indian. For a brief period buffalo hides brought fabulous prices on the world market. In a week a professional hunter could kill and skin a hundred or more animals, earning more than $500 for his labor; one tanned pelt commanded over $1,500 in the London and Paris fur trade. But with the flood of amateur fortune seekers, many the dregs of eastern society, the slaughter soon outran Dodge City's capacity to cope with it. Herds were often broadsided by passengers shooting from trains and the meat left to rot. The air vibrated with the sound of bluebottle flies. There was simply too much meat to salt and ship. Thousands of acres of hides were stacked on the prairie, and often these hid the railroad stations from view. That delicacy, buffalo tongue, was easy to excise and deliver to market, so the surviving animals were pursued in a charnel house atmosphere until the shaggy beasts were virtually extinct. Only the starving Comanches fought back, and the ultimate obscenity was pronounced by General Philip Sheridan on the cultural impact of that holocaust: "The only good Indians I ever saw were dead." Nobody described the carnage more succinctly than Chief Black Elk in 1883, on the Madison River in Montana:

It was the summer of my twentieth year that I performed the ceremony of the elk. That fall, they say, the last of the bison herds were slaughtered by the Wasichus [white men]. I can remember when the bison were so many that they could not be counted, but more and more came to kill them until there was only a heap of bones scattered where they used to be. The Wasichus did not kill them to eat; they killed for the metal [gold] that makes them crazy, and they took only the hides to sell. Sometimes, they did not even take the hides, only the tongues; and I have heard that fire boats came down the Missouri River loaded with dried bison tongues; they just killed and killed because they liked to do that. When we hunted bison, we killed only what was needed.

Buffalo hunter's headdress and drum.

But these were the golden years of the American cowboy, and if the buffalo was missed, few voices were raised at its passing. Game of some kind seemed to exist in endless supply.

Perhaps the greatest culinary tribute paid to the buffalo in print was a bestselling recipe book called *50 Bison Dishes* by a Mrs. Vernon Palme, but when Harper & Brothers published it in 1886, the herds were on the verge of extinction. Ironically, the author choked to death on a fish bone before publication, and the art of bison cookery was without champion or subject.

I had my first taste of buffalo more than twenty years ago in the form of a burger. I was fishing for trout in Wyoming's Grand Canyon of the Snake River with Ted Hale, whose profitable hobby was raising bison on his ranch near Afton. One noon Ted grilled some patties over a wood fire. I expected something dry and gamy; instead, those buffalo burgers were not only juicy but tasted like prime fresh-ground sirloin with a somewhat denser texture.

Buffalo has 25 to 30 percent more protein than beef, so it is a richer, "meatier" meat. What I didn't know at the time was that it has less than half the cholesterol of beef, less than a third the fat, and many fewer calories. And these hardy animals thrive without being dosed with antibiotics or hormones. Ted's succulent burgers inspired many wonderful meals of steaks and roasts in subsequent years, culminating in my frequently adding buffalo to our semiannual Chevaliers de Tastevin dinners in Palm Beach, where it always draws rave notices.

The American bison (*Bison bison*) is a member of the family Bovidae. There are two subspecies, the plains bison (*B. bison bison*) and the wood bison (*B. bison athabascae*), with natural free-ranging herds restricted to Yellowstone National Park, Wyoming, and Wood Buffalo National Park, Northwest Territories. There are state and federal herds elsewhere managed for scientific purposes, as well as fenced-in private herds managed and sold as livestock. Today the buffalo meat on our market comes from semidomesticated animals on about 700 commercial ranches. I am not sure that *domesticated* is the right term for bison. One evening Ted Hale asked me to grab a pitchfork and help him feed his herd. We went out in the meadow with a tractor-driven hay wagon, and before long we were surrounded by hungry buffalo. They weren't about to wait for service; half-ton animals rammed the wagon from all sides and chugalugged flying grass while I did acrobatics on top of the load, as though exercising on a trampoline. Ted stayed on the tractor seat, shouting words of encouragement. In one minute I came to appreciate the tenacity of a Sioux hunter on his pony, charging into the uproar and dust clouds with his bow and arrow. Charles Russell, Frederic Remington, George Catlin, and many other artists immortalized the chase, but the sheer power of the bison cannot be translated into paint.

COOKING NOTES

Buffalo meat is purveyed by specialty butchers, and it's available directly from USDA–inspected producers, who express every cut from shrink-wrapped frozen patties to steaks and roasts and even quarters and halves. Due to the lack of fat marbling, buffalo should not be cooked as long or at as high a temperature as beef. I rely on my Meat Thermicator to get the proper internal temperature, with rare at 120°F, medium-rare at 130°F, and medium at 140°F. In practice everything that can be accomplished with beef is suitable for buffalo.

BUFFALO JERKY

Jerky is air-dried, kiln-dried, or oven-dried strips of meat from big game animals, notably the buffalo in commercial production and the antelope and various deer as a home product. Salt and other condiments may or may not be added, and the meat may or may not be smoked. In appearance and texture, jerky resembles dark strips of leather; it has a long shelf life and will keep indefinitely when frozen. The name *jerky* evolved from the process of "strapping out" the meat when nailed to a tree or barn, by manually jerking the muscle sheaths loose (with the grain), reducing it with a knife into jerks of about a foot in length, three-quarters of an inch thick, and two to three inches wide. All membrane and fat is removed, and the condiments are pounded into the meat fiber with a mallet. When completely dehydrated, the meat shrivels to 20 percent of its original weight.

Some form of jerky probably dates back to troglodyte man, as salting and air-drying both fish and game is a very ancient process. As a subsistence food for the plainsmen and early American explorers, jerky was welcome fare on the trail, as we see in an entry of Captain Meriwether Lewis's journals dated September 17, 1804: "We rested ourselves for about half an hour and regaled ourselves on half a biscuit each and some jerks of Elk which we had the precaution to put in our pouches in the morning before we set out, and drank of the water of a small pool which had collected from the rain."

Although jerky is not a widely popular food item today, it is still utilized by backpackers, hunters, and fishermen in the Rocky Mountains region. It is easy to make at home, and buffalo jerky is marketed particularly in Wyoming and Montana. Personally, I've used jerky as a trail supplement for many years—like potato chips, it's habit-forming. However, it is not a food that one instantly chomps on; its leathery texture requires initial mouth softening, much as you would enjoy a lollipop.

An allied but dissimilar air-dried meat product was pemmican. The Cree Indian word is *pimikân*, which means "journey meat." In this case it was pounded fine and mixed in equal parts with fat or marrow, often augmented by nuts and berries and compressed into sheets or cakes. Pemmican, like jerky, was a food for Indian travel, especially among the Cree, Assiniboin, and Chippewa. It was also a popular food among the French-Canadian *voyageurs*. The "Pemmican War" between the fur traders of the Hudson Bay Company and the Northwest Fur Company (1812–21) was aptly named for the combat ration that supported its participants.

BARBECUED BUFFALO STRIP STEAKS WITH DEEP-FRIED ONION RINGS

SERVES 4

1   ancho chili
2   tablespoons bourbon
4½   cups olive oil
2   garlic cloves, peeled and
        cut into slivers
2   tablespoons roughly
        chopped fresh oregano
1   bay leaf
4   10- to 12-ounce fresh
        buffalo strip steaks
salt and pepper to taste
½   cup hot red pepper
        flakes, or less to taste
2   to 3 red onions
1   quart buttermilk
2   cups all-purpose flour
1   teaspoon salt
4   teaspoons cracked black
        peppercorns
2   teaspoons cayenne pepper
4   teaspoons hot red
        pepper flakes
vegetable oil for deep frying
Barbecue Sauce (recipe follows)

Wearing plastic or rubber gloves, split the ancho chili, remove and discard the stem and seeds, and cut the pepper into 3 pieces; toast the pieces in a dry skillet over high heat until the skin is blackened. Prepare a marinade by combining the bourbon, ½ cup of the olive oil, the garlic, oregano, bay leaf, and chili pieces in a glass or enameled container. Mix all the ingredients together. Season the steaks with salt and pepper, put them in the marinade, and cover the container with plastic wrap. Marinate in a cool place for 1 hour, then turn the steaks over and marinate for another hour. Or, if you prefer, the steaks can be marinated overnight in the refrigerator.

To prepare the onion rings, heat the remaining 4 cups oil in a large heavy pan. When the oil is fairly hot, add the ½ cup hot red pepper flakes. Reduce the heat to warm and let the oil heat for 5 minutes. Turn off the heat and allow the oil to steep for 30 minutes, or longer for spicier results. Strain the oil and discard the pepper flakes. Cut the onions into medium-thin rings. When the oil has cooled, put the onions in enough of the oil barely to cover them and let them marinate for 1 hour. Lift the onions out of the oil and put them in a clean bowl. (The marinating oil can be saved to be used one or more times, if refrigerated.) Add the buttermilk to the bowl of onions and set aside. Season the flour with 1 teaspoon salt, the peppercorns, cayenne, and 4 teaspoons hot red pepper flakes. Set aside until ready to cook the onions.

Prepare a hot grill.

In a deep-fryer, heat the vegetable oil to 360°F. Lift the onions from the buttermilk, drain, and coat them with the seasoned flour. Lift steaks from the marinade; it is not necessary to dry them. (The marinade can be saved for other uses.) Put the steaks on the grill and grill to desired doneness. Turn steaks over and brush or spoon on some of the barbecue sauce. Grill for a minute, then repeat with the other side. Shake excess flour from the onions and fry them, in batches if necessary, in the hot oil. When brown and crisp, lift the onions to a bowl lined with paper toweling.

Serve the steaks with the onions, with bowls of warm barbecue sauce for dipping. Another way to serve them is to slice the steak, arrange the slices in a fan shape on a plate, and spoon a little of the bourbon marinade over the slices.

BARBECUE SAUCE

MAKES ABOUT 6 CUPS

2   poblano chilies
2   jalapeño chilies
2   chipotle chilies
2   red bell peppers
1   red onion
2   celery ribs
3   garlic cloves
¼   pound smoked bacon
9   tomatoes
¼   cup olive oil
¼   cup butter
1   bay leaf, crumbled
½   cup maple syrup
½   cup sherry vinegar
1   teaspoon cumin seeds, toasted and ground
1   teaspoon hot red pepper flakes
2   teaspoons cracked black peppercorns
1   tablespoon minced fresh tarragon *or* 1 teaspoon dried
1   tablespoon minced fresh oregano *or* 1 teaspoon dried
½   teaspoon salt (optional)

Using rubber or plastic gloves, cut open all the hot chili peppers, discard stems and seeds, and cut the peppers into small dice. Soak the pieces of chipotle pepper in cold water while preparing the rest of the ingredients (these chilies are very hot). Prepare the bell pepper in the same way. Dice the red onion. Scrape and trim the celery and dice it. Peel and mince the garlic. Remove any rind from the bacon and cut the bacon into small dice. Peel and seed the tomatoes and cut into medium dice.

Put the olive oil and bacon dice in a heavy saucepan and cook over moderate heat until bacon is half cooked. Add the butter and cook until it foams. Add all the hot peppers and cook and stir for 15 minutes. Add the garlic, onion, bell pepper, celery, and bay leaf. Cook the mixture slowly and steadily for 10 minutes or so, until the vegetables begin to brown at the edges. Add the maple syrup and stir, then add the vinegar and stir again. Add the tomatoes, cumin seeds, and red and black pepper. Continue to simmer, stirring constantly until the sauce is thick and well flavored. Stir in the fresh herbs and finally adjust seasoning. You may wish to add ½ teaspoon of salt.

BUFFALO IN THE STYLE OF TUSCANY

1½ pounds buffalo
      tenderloin (fillet)
½ cup olive oil
1 teaspoon dried thyme
      leaves
1 teaspoon dried rosemary
      leaves
1 tablespoon cracked black
      peppercorns
2 garlic cloves, peeled and
      minced
1 tablespoon anchovy
      paste *or* 3 anchovy
      fillets
2 tablespoons drained
      capers
¼ cup pureed sun-dried
      tomatoes *or* ⅓ cup
      tomato puree
½ cup Sauce Demi-Glace
      (see Index) or beef
      stock
6 ounces Marsala
freshly ground pepper to
      taste

Allow 6 ounces buffalo for a serving; this should be 2 medallions cut about 1 inch thick. Place the meat in a glass or enameled container. Combine the oil, herbs, peppercorns, and garlic and pour over the meat. Marinate it at room temperature for 2 to 3 hours, turning the slices occasionally to be sure they are coated all over.

If you plan to sauté the meat, pour enough of the oil marinade into a skillet to coat the bottom and heat it almost to smoking. Add the meat, leaving on the bits of garlic and herbs that adhere to the slices. Sear the slices on both sides until rare or medium-rare. Do not burn the oil; that would impart a bitter flavor to the sauce.

If you plan to grill the meat, cook over hot charcoal to the same doneness, allowing the flames to envelop and sear the meat, which occurs when the marinade drips into the fire. When the buffalo is cooked, place the medallions on a warm platter and keep warm in a low oven.

Spoon 2 tablespoons of the remaining marinade into the skillet used to sauté the meat or use a clean skillet if you have grilled the meat. Add the anchovy paste and capers. Stir, cook briefly, then add the tomato puree. Reduce the mixture slightly, then add the Sauce Demi-Glace and wine. Continue to reduce until the sauce is thickened to your taste.

Arrange the medallions on warm serving plates and spoon the sauce on top or spoon the sauce onto the plates and place the medallions on the sauce. Sprinkle lightly with freshly ground pepper. Serve with sautéed porcini or chanterelle mushrooms and fresh snow peas and accompany with a cabernet sauvignon.

BUFFALO STEAKS WITH CHARDONNAY AND WILD MUSHROOMS

SERVES 6

5 pounds strip-eye buffalo
1 bottle Chardonnay
1 large onion, chopped
4 medium carrots, chopped
1 bouquet garni made of 1 sprig fresh thyme, 2 bay leaves, fresh parsley stems, tied together
6 beef bones for marrow (see Notes)
1 pound fresh chanterelles (see Notes)
1 pound fresh oyster mushrooms (see Notes)
1 pound fresh porcini (cèpes; see Notes)
1 pound snow peas
2 bunches fresh parsley
11 tablespoons unsalted butter
2 tablespoons corn oil, or more if needed
¼ cup minced shallots
salt and pepper to taste
2 cups beef bouillon

Put the buffalo in a glass or enameled container. Make a marinade from the wine, onion, carrots, and bouquet garni. Pour the marinade over the meat and let it marinate overnight. Soak the beef bones in cold water overnight.

The next morning, lift out the buffalo and cut it into 3 double steaks. Strain the marinade; discard the solids and reserve the liquid. Clean the mushrooms and trim as needed. Slice the mushrooms, but chop the stems of the porcini. Rinse and drain the snow peas; remove the stems and any strings. Wash and dry the parsley and chop fine. Set a large sauté pan over moderate heat and put in 2 tablespoons of the butter and the corn oil. Sauté the steaks to desired doneness, allowing about 15 minutes for medium-rare.

While the steaks are cooking, prepare the vegetables. Melt 5 tablespoons of the butter in a large pan and sauté the mushrooms until browned. Add 2 tablespoons of the minced shallots and half of the chopped parsley. Season with salt and pepper. Set aside.

_____

Preheat the oven to 400°F.
_____

Remove the sautéed steaks to a baking sheet. Tip extra fat out of the skillet, then melt 1 tablespoon of the butter in the pan. Add the remaining 2 ta-

blespoons of shallots and cook gently just to soften; do not let shallots brown. Add the strained marinating liquid to the pan and reduce by half. Add the bouillon and again reduce by half. While the sauce is reducing, scrape the marrow from the beef bones and cut it into ¼-inch slices. Bring a small saucepan of salted water to a rapid boil, add the marrow to the water, and at once remove the pan from the heat. Let the marrow poach for 2 minutes, then add the slices to the sauce. Finish the sauce by stirring in the remaining 3 tablespoons of butter and add the remaining chopped parsley. Adjust the seasonings. Keep the sauce hot.

Place the steaks in the preheated oven to warm them before serving. Bring the pan of mushrooms again to sautéing temperature and add the snow peas to cook quickly for 5 minutes. Remove the steaks and slice into 6 pieces. Arrange them on plates with the vegetables and a spoonful of the sauce. Serve the rest of the sauce separately.

Notes:

Ask your butcher for 2-inch pieces of beef shin bones and have him split the bones. After soaking the bones in cold water, scrape out the marrow cold. If you prefer, the bones can be wrapped in foil and heated in a 350°F oven for about 30 minutes. Let the bones cook, then scoop out the marrow. If you heat the bones, the marrow will not need to be poached and will be too soft to be sliced.

In some parts of the country all of the mushrooms called for can be found fresh in the fall. If they are not available, substitute other cultivated or wild mushrooms or dried mushrooms. Dried porcini are generally available year-round. Purchase 6 to 8 ounces dried to replace the pound of fresh mushrooms and let them soak in water or a mixture of water and wine for at least 30 minutes before preparing to sauté them. Rinse them to remove any sand and discard any stems. The soaking liquid may be filtered to use as part of the liquid in a recipe.

The Colorado Rockies

16. THE OTHER HORNED GAME ANIMALS

Next to the bison, among the other horned animals of the family Bovidae found in North America, the wild sheep is the most choice meat at table. The related mountain goat, musk-ox, true antelope, and unrelated western pronghorn suffer by comparison. It is not known when sheep were first domesticated. They were animals of sacrifice in many ancient religious ceremonies, and it is believed that domestication (more than 200 breeds) started in Asia during the Neolithic period. The true wild sheep, however, is among the finest of all game, for unlike in other wild ungulates the fat is marbled in the muscle tissue, which keeps the meat moist during cooking.

The first description of the wild sheep's excellence was recorded by Franciscan missionaries on the California peninsula in 1702. Their flavor and texture is totally different from that of domestic breeds, and the ribs of a bighorn cooked slowly over an open campfire are a delicacy without peer—as distinctive as the lamb of the *près salé*, that salt marsh product of Brittany's Gironde River estuary. But the ultimate in sheep dining would be those Skyline Medallions (see recipe in this chapter) as done by my old friend Russ Thornberry of Bow River valley days in Alberta. Mr. Thornberry is not only a chef of great talent but a big game guide who climbs enormously rugged peaks with disheartening ease, one of the prerequisites to a proper sheep dinner.

The wild sheep of western North America include the Rocky Mountain and desert bighorn sheep (*Ovis canadensis*) and the Dall's and Stone's sheep (*Ovis dalli*). The rams of either species have massive curled horns and are highly prized big game species both as trophies and at table. Wild sheep are difficult to come by. They are wary animals with keen eyesight and are easily alarmed, requiring arduous stalks in mountain habitats where the hunter must be sound of wind and limb—which brings to mind an incident that occurred some years ago near the summit of Mauna Kea on the island of Hawaii. We were hunting merino sheep at an altitude above 10,000 feet. The merino is a feral variety brought to the islands by Captain George Vancouver in 1793 that thrives on lava slopes in an ethereal world of mist. Although the air temperature was eighty-five at sea level in Kailua Kona, when Ernie Alberecht and I began stalking rams the following morning, watching them appear and then evaporate in dense white blankets below and above us, the thermometer probably registered thirty degrees. It was like hunting ghosts: first spotting the animals, then, after several hundred yards of scrambling over a cindery *aa* field, visibility dropped to zero and the herd vanished. During one of these frustrating stalks a shroud of mist lifted, and there stood a muscular barechested Japanese, bow in hand and a quiver of arrows slung on his back, wearing a tucked crotch cloth with heavy canvas wrapped around his feet and legs tied in rawhide thongs. I have met primitive hunters in Africa and the jungles of South America, but this reincarnation of a samurai in the frigid reaches of Mauna Kea was a tableau so ancient that I felt captured in a time warp.

The merino and other kinds of feral sheep, while certainly tasty, are not in the same culinary class with true wild sheep (unlike a comparison of the wild boar and the feral pig, as the latter is superior in my opinion), but the opportunity to hunt the genotypical bighorn or Stone's is a rare event. For reasons of herd management, a special permit is necessary in the better public hunting areas, which is issued by means of an annual drawing. The odds against a successful application are formidable (well over one hundred to one), so a wild sheep dinner is a rare event. In Canada the prime range is found in the Yukon, Northwest Territories, Alberta, and British Columbia, while in the United States it is in the high country of Alaska, Montana, Wyoming, Idaho, and, to a lesser extent, California, Utah, and Arizona.

Wild sheep are most abundant and reach their greatest size in central Asia. The ultimate trophy is the Marco Polo sheep (*Ovis poli*) found on the Pamir Plateau of Turkistan at elevations above 15,000 feet. However, the largest are the argali sheep (*Ovis ammon*) of Tibet and Mongolia, which may weigh more than 300 pounds. The only wild species in the Old World is the delicious mouflon sheep (*Ovis musimon*), originally found in the mountains of Sardinia and Corsica, which has been introduced with some success in

Hawaii and on the game ranches of Texas; the latter state also holds a large population of the North African Barbary sheep (*Ammotragus lervia*).

The king of the horned game animals, purely on the basis of its lordly perch at the very top of our continent, is the mountain goat. Billies are more skilled climbers than sheep and thrive in aeries that would give an old ram acrophobia. Actually, the mountain goat (*Oreamnos americanus*) is not a true goat but is best described as a goat-antelope, with its closest relative being the chamois of Europe. The meat of our mountain goat can be rated only as edible; unlike the domestic goat that provides delicately flavored and tender meat in the form of a milk-fed kid, the ubiquitous *cabrito* of Hispanic cuisines, the mountain goat is both tough and strongly flavored. It can be heavily marinated and pot-roasted, but to my taste it is not worth the effort. The Hawaiian method used in cooking feral goats (marinating slices of meat in teriyaki sauce, vinegar, ginger, and garlic, then barbecuing on charcoal) may improve the flavor, but I have never tried this and am now too old to climb where eagles fear to nest. The related chamois (*Rupicapra rupicapra*) inhabits the Alpine regions of Switzerland, Austria, France, Germany, and Yugoslavia. An extremely agile and wary animal found in rugged terrain of rocky ledges and scree slopes, it is considered a great trophy and prized at table. The chamois feeds on plants, including wild herbs and flowers, and the meat, similar to kid in texture, is very delicate in flavor. Chamois, or *gams* in German (*gamsgeiss* for the female and *gamsbock* for the male) are small animals, weighing from forty to sixty pounds. Their appearance at table in Europe is primarily at private dinner parties as the result of a hunt. Transplanted to New Zealand, they have thrived in the Mount Cook area.

The North American pronghorn, commonly called "antelope," is not a true antelope, nor is it a goat-antelope despite its generic scientific name (*Antilocapra*); it is the sole surviving member of a unique family that evolved on our continent millions of years ago. It is not related to the African antelopes such as the blackbuck that has been introduced to American preserves. The pronghorn occurs in seventeen states, mainly from Oregon eastward into the Dakotas and in parts of south central Canada and southward to northern Mexico. It is most abundant in the sagebrush regions of Wyoming and Montana. It has been estimated that our pronghorn population represented forty million animals in the early 1800s, equaling the historical bison herds in density. This pristine abundance has declined due to the inevitable loss of habitat but stabilized at about 700,000 today. While our wild sheep and mountain goat elude the hunter through their dexterity at high altitudes, the pronghorn on the buttes and plains has both incredibly keen eyesight and speed of foot; when running, it has been clocked in sprints up to sixty miles per hour—which suggests a culinary problem.

From a kitchen standpoint the pronghorn gets mixed reviews. In my opinion, at its best, it is not on a par with a bighorn sheep or an elk, animals that are found in the same geographical distribution. One of the peculiarities of the pronghorn is that its hollow hair, so effective an insulator for its thin skin in extremely hot and cold weather, causes the meat to sour unless the animal is skinned immediately after killing; the hunting season for pronghorn begins in September in Wyoming and Montana, when I've experienced midday air temperatures in the high eighties. The fact that it will usually snow in the same month is of little consequence as the great majority of pronghorns are harvested in the first legal week of shooting. Often a hunter will leave the animal unskinned for hours, and this makes a critical difference between a very palatable meat and one that requires a gustatory enthusiasm that I lack.

Skyline Medallions of Wild Sheep

SERVES 4

½   cup chopped onion
1   cup sliced fresh
        mushrooms
¼   cup butter
1   cup all-purpose flour
½   teaspoon salt
½   teaspoon black pepper
1   pound sheep backstrap
        or round steak, cut
        into ½-inch medallions
1   beef bouillon cube
1   cup hot water
1   cup whipping cream
1   tablespoon prepared
        mustard

Sauté the onion and mush-rooms in the butter. When the onion turns golden and starts to brown, remove the onion and mushroom mixture from the skillet and set aside.

Mix the flour with the salt and pepper and dredge the meat medallions in the seasoned flour. Sauté them slowly in the remaining butter from the onion and mushroom mixture. Add more butter if necessary and cook until the meat is done medium. Remove the meat from the skillet and set aside.

Dissolve the bouillon cube in the hot water and then pour into the skillet with the remains from cooking the meat. Stir and simmer until the liquid begins to thicken slightly.

Now add the whipping cream to the bouillon mixture and stir and simmer again until the mixture thickens to a medium gravy consistency. Turn off the heat and add the onions and mushrooms. Mix together well, add the mustard, and stir it gently into the mixture. Place the medallions on a bed of steamed brown rice and pour the sauce over them.

Black Bear. © Stock Imagery/1991

17. BEAR

The number of people who hunt bear or eat bear meat is infinitesimal compared to other game consumers. But the fact remains that an estimated 30,000 black bears are harvested in North America each year,[1] and bear meat of various origins does appear in specialty restaurants. The meat of a young bear that has dieted on plant food is rich and tender. But one must know a bear's credentials, as quality is strictly dependent on the source of supply. The meat of an *old* bear is dark, coarse, and tough; the fat is rank, and every speck must be completely removed even before freezing. Compounding the problem, it must always be cooked well-done, as bears, like hogs, can be carriers of trichinosis (never utilize bear liver as it has a high concentration of vitamin A, which can be toxic to man). Bear meat reaches its nadir when the animal has been nocturnally foraging in the village garbage dump, which is all too common in rural areas of the eastern United States and Canada. In a wild habitat the omnivorous black bear normally feeds on grasses, bulbs, tubers, berries, and nuts of all kinds, especially pine nuts. Both the black and the more carnivorous grizzly can absorb almost as much protein from plant material as do herbivores.

I recall with sympathy a dinner party given many years ago by social matriarch Margaret Hudson Marks, in honor of actor Basil Rathbone. Margaret divided her time

---

[1]An uncounted number are killed illegally, especially in southern Appalachia, to supply bear gallbladders and paws to Oriental black markets. The gallbladder, supposedly medicinal and an aphrodisiac, brings four-figure prices; bear paws are edible, and the claws are turned into decorative jewelry.

among Baden-Baden, her home at Florida's posh Seminole Club, and her forested estate at Turnwood, New York, but the origin of the bear's haunch escapes me. It was a formal buffet occasion, with an ice *pièce montée* nearly the size of a national monument of *Ursus americanus* standing on its hind legs at the table's center. I suspect the cooked bear had dallied too frequently in some domestic wasteland, as its texture and aroma reminded me of a leaky rubber boot left in the hot sun to dry. Even that swashbuckler Rathbone stabbed his portion again and again, then studied it, as though Errol Flynn were irretrievably stuck on his épée. Fortunately, the groaning board was well stocked with less exotic dishes, and the dinner memorably climaxed with individual Grand Marnier soufflés the diameter of a chef's hat.

The black bear is the only edible bear from a gourmand's standpoint, although I would limit the choice of cuts to the saddle, haunch, or rib sections of a young bruin. Since this book makes an effort to be comprehensive, the best I can say for really prime bear meat is that it's comparable to a good grade of beef. It is considered a great delicacy among the people of Lapland and the Indians of northeastern Canada. However, as with the pioneer Americans, protein availability undoubtedly plays an important role in its reputation.

When the first settlers came to southeast Florida, game was plentiful, especially deer, wild turkey, and bear. Black bear not only were abundant in the piney woods but, in the summer months, became beachcombers in their search for turtle eggs. Young bear, easily ambushed on the sand, were considered the best of all foods, but because of the hot weather, after one or two meals of fresh bear steaks the balance was salted down in the manner of corned beef. However, Florida's beaches yielded more than turtle eggs and bear meat. According to Charles W. Pierce, in *Pioneer Life in Southeast Florida* (edited by Donald Walter Curl, University of Miami Press, Coral Gables), those palm-studded strands now in the bikini littoral were a valuable junkyard:

> Up to 1882 the manner of living, with few exceptions was most primitive. The gun, fishline, net and the ocean beach were the sources from which we obtained our food and whatever else we needed. The ocean beach was our treasure chest that supplied us with articles of trade at the store in Sand Point. When supplies were running short, a settler would spend a week or so on the beach collecting old metal. It was not hard to gather four or five hundred pounds in a week of beachcombing.

The metal, copper, iron, and brass fittings were salvaged from shipwrecks, then so common to the hurricane coast of Florida. Their cargoes often provided welcome dividends and joyous celebrations in the form of wine and rum; the most mysterious of the wine wrecks occurred in 1886, when the entire beach from Miami to Indian River was littered with oak barrels. According to Pierce, an otherwise accurate recorder, "One hundred gallon casks of Spanish claret lay strewn along the coast, so close together that one could have walked for a mile without having to step off a cask." Yet no recently fated ship was found, and seemingly it was the cargo of an entire fleet. The most enduring wreck, however, had occurred in 1878, when the 175-ton Spanish bark *Providentia* went aground with 20,000 coconuts aboard; planted by the homesteaders, they put the "Palm" in Palm Beach. It seems ironic now that the strand on which the elegant Breakers Hotel, home to Wall Street's magnificoes, now stands was once a bear run.

Bears are of the family Ursidae, which in North America includes the black bear (*Ursus americanus*), the grizzly or brown bear (*U. arctos*), and the polar bear (*U. maritimus*). The largest land carnivore of the grizzly group is the giant "brownie" of Kodiak Island, Alaska. It may weigh more than 1,500 pounds and attain a length of more than nine feet. The grizzlies, wherever they occur, are not timid, and unprovoked attacks on man are well documented. Black bears generally avoid humans in wilderness areas; however, they lose their timidity in national parks, often appearing "tame" at roadsides, seeking tourist handouts. But a sow with cubs, whether black or grizzly, is potentially dangerous in any habitat. Despite some fancy shooting by James Butler "Wild Bill" Hickok, that legendary gunslinger was badly mauled by a sow grizzly while he was working as a wagon master in New Mexico.

Although I have never hunted bears, nor do I have any desire to, over the years I've had some uncomfortable moments while being eyeballed by vagrant grizzlies in Alaska, and one nocturnal marauder almost turned our cabin into splinters at God's Lake in Manitoba. My closest encounter occurred while exploring the fishing in a remote area of western Hudson Bay by helicopter—courtesy of a Canadian survey crew. Dropped on a tiny island, really a large gravel bar, I caught sea-run brook trout, which I piled on the bank to supply the camp, for about an hour while the pilot went off on some mission. At that point I spotted a huge, dirty white beast coming my way in a rolling gait over the barrens, nose to the wind. The pack ice had melted, and a polar bear was foraging inland. With nothing but a fly rod in hand, I watched the hairy monster closing fast, licking his chops, smelling either fish or, more likely, the acrid odor of fear. At the very last moment we were eyeball to eyeball across a narrow neck of water when the helicopter returned and, recognizing my plight, the pilot hovered over the old bruin's rear end and chased him across the tundra. However, this retreat was conciliatory, as the bear, standing on its hind legs, first tried to down the Bell Ranger. Nevertheless, I find bears fascinating and have never found a good reason to seek an ursine entrée when a hamburger will do.

BLACK BEAR LAPP STYLE

SERVES 4

This is an authentic peasant dish of Norway and Finland.

1½ pounds defatted bear meat, cut into 1-inch cubes
1   large onion
6   tablespoons butter
2   bay leaves

1   teaspoon ground allspice
salt to taste
1   cup fresh lingonberries or cranberries

Preheat the oven to 275°F.

Brown the meat and onion in butter in a cast-iron Dutch oven. Add the bay leaves, allspice, and salt. Add the berries and cover with water. Bake, covered, in the oven for approximately 3 hours. Serve with white rice or noodles.

Caution

Trichinella, the parasite known as muscleworm, which causes the illness trichinosis in humans, was found to be one hundred times more common in Montana bear meat, for example, than it is in pork. Montana researchers who screened bear meat during the 1986 season found *Trichinella* in about 10 percent of the animals tested. Freezing the meat does not kill the parasite, which can survive for at least two years in the frozen state. Only thorough cooking, which requires a minimal internal temperature of 140°F, will prevent trichinosis. Eating a rare bear steak is no different from playing Russian roulette.

18. Rabbit and Hare

The rabbit is the most widely hunted small game animal in the New and Old World. About thirty million rabbits are harvested by sportsmen each year in the United States alone, while another thirty-one million pounds of meat are produced on commercial farms. Every ethnic cuisine has its classic, and the popularity of rabbit as a restaurant item has grown significantly in the last decade. Whether *hasenpfeffer, ragoût de lapin, coniglio in umido*, or simply jugged hare, this low-cholesterol food is incomparable for sheer kitchen versatility; it can be cooked by just about any method, and the chickenlike texture of wild or domestic rabbit has universal appeal. The nondomesticated hares, somewhat stronger in taste, are preferred by gourmets for that very reason. It may be an anodyne to prejudiced palates that many game birds and animals, and seafoods for that matter, must bear a foreign label before they find public acceptance. An American tourist will often return home raving about a *leveret à la moutarde* he enjoyed in Alsace or a *gâteau de lapin aux herbes* as done in Provence, but let it be called young hare in mustard sauce or a jellied rabbit in fresh herbs, and the Peter Rabbit syndrome sets in. The European doesn't suffer from anthropomorphism, and indeed rabbit and hare cookery is regionally dictated by ancient tradition.

One of the more memorable meals that I enjoyed in recent times was a melt-in-the-mouth *râble de lièvre*, a saddle of hare as prepared by the Haeberlin brothers at the Auberge de l'Il at Illhausen, which in my opinion is one of the best restaurants in France. Another was John Baptiste Reynaud's Juniper Hare at Leith's restaurant in London, which consists of a rich stew made from the legs and neck, topped with slices from the succulent roast

Alain Jorand of St. Honoré with his Baron of Rabbit with Tarragon Cream.

saddle (see Index for recipe)—clearly worth a long detour. I don't know anybody who makes Ali-Bab's version of *lièvre à la royale* anymore, a popular dish in the early 1900s that encompassed ten pages in his book *Gastronomie Pratique.* Ali-Bab (non de plume of food critic Henri Babinsky) devised a sauce containing so many ingredients that I assume he just didn't like the taste of hare. I was weaned on Catskill rabbits, pan-fried like chicken, and a more toothsome delicacy than those fat cottontails we used to hunt in October weather, after a series of frosts, when the forest floor was painted crimson and gold with oak and maple leaves, I have rarely tasted. Later in the winter, in the mountains around the West Branch of the Delaware, we would seek the white snowshoe hare for a more robust flavor, like comparing a young Beaujolais to a mature Bordeaux.

Rabbits occur abundantly on all principal land masses. Members of the family Leporidae, which includes both hares and rabbits, have short gestation periods (from thirty to thirty-two days) and will, shortly after, reproduce again, a fecundity that was cursed by ancient cultures. During the reign of Antigonus of Macedonia "their [the rabbits'] posterity became so numerous that the people were obliged to implore the gods to preserve the harvest, and to annihilate their formidable enemies." The Greek geographer Strabo, seeing the Balearic Islands being rendered nearly uninhabitable by rabbits, sent ambassadors to Rome to ask Augustus for troops, "and Roman arms were once again victorious." Doe rabbits have been known to produce as many as twenty-three in a litter (although six to nine is average), which along with numerous black bear created a formidable problem for pioneer American farmers, the rabbit rapidly consuming herbaceous crops and the bear domestic livestock. Nevertheless, the European hare (*Lepus europaeus*) was introduced to Australia in 1870 for meat production, and most of these escaped from captivity with disastrous consequences to that continent's crops and grazing lands, reaching its nadir in the 1950s. I have seen vast "rabbit control" areas in New Zealand that were as awesomely barren as moonscapes. But the culinary value of these rabbits fortunately prevails. After thousands of years of domestication many breeds and varieties have been selectively developed throughout the world (The American Rabbit Breeders Association recognizes thirty-eight breeds and eighty-seven varieties of domestic rabbits), and by far the two most common, the kinds packaged frozen for supermarkets or delivered fresh by specialty butchers, are the New Zealand and Californian. On balanced diets these farmed animals grow more rapidly and to a much larger size than the wild species, with a potential growth to sixteen pounds (the record is twenty-three pounds), but they are usually processed as fryers at three to five pounds or seven to ten weeks old. Mature roasters of eight to ten pounds are much less in demand in the United States than in Europe. The meat of all domestic rabbits is white and mild in flavor, whereas wild rabbit is darker in color but no less tasty, simply different.

COOKING NOTES

If your rabbit or hare is one that was harvested in the wild, three days of aging in the refrigerator will greatly enhance its flavor, preferably cut into serving pieces and held in a bath of wine and vinegar (one-half bottle of white wine to three ounces of wine vinegar) or the same amounts of red wine for dark-meated hare, to which you add a bouquet garni and a teaspoon of crushed black peppercorns. For one that was collected at market twelve hours of marination is sufficient. A young hare is much the best, which is an animal of about six pounds; if you're judging at market, young hare and rabbits have sharp claws and the ears are soft and thin, while old have blunt claws and the ears are very firm. An important menu distinction is made in France, the young hare being a *leveret* and the older a *lièvre*. The choice portions are the saddle, hind legs, and shoulders, in that order. Properly dressed, the average wild rabbit of 2½ to three pounds can be cut into eight pieces; however, you really need two of these for a dinner party for six (the yield is about three pounds of meat), because the rib cage section has little meat and is more like a dividend than a sustaining portion. A store-bought rabbit or hare of six pounds or more can be cut into sixteen pieces: two pieces from each of the hind legs, four crosscut pieces from the saddle, four pieces from the rib cage, and two pieces from each of the forelegs. Actually the forelegs and rib cage are best reserved for soups or stews. Frozen packaged rabbit comes already dressed, and if you are hunting in a specialty food shop, the butcher will tend to these details.

Caution

All *wild* rabbits and hares are subject to tularemia, an infection caused by a bacteria *Pasteurella tularensis*, which is transmitted by an insect vector, notably the deerfly. It is uncommon, but when dressing wild rabbits, I consider it essential to wear rubber gloves as the organism can pass through human skin. Freezing will not kill the bacteria, but thorough cooking will; never eat a rare wild rabbit or hare. Tularemia has *never* been recorded among domestic rabbits, and in many years of hunting I have never met anybody who has suffered the disease. Nevertheless, one must be aware of its existence and take precautions.

HARE IN THE STYLE OF THE TUSCAN HILLTOWNS

SERVES 6

There are countless recipes in Italian cuisine for the hare (*lepre*) and rabbit (*coniglio*), and these are regionally dictated by ancient tradition. I once queried Marge Galante about Italian methodology, and her comments are worth preserving. Mrs. Galante is that kitchen wizard who, with husband Renato, a former captain on the Italian Steamship Line, owns Balzarini (210 Hampton Road, Southhampton, New York), one of those rare restaurants where the three critical criteria—food, ambience, and peer status—rank in equal measure:

"The Maremma is an area in Tuscany where civilization presses only lightly on ancient marshes and swamps. Rabbit and hare are part of the local diet almost to the point of boredom. Americans may consider pizza the all-Italian takeout food, but Tuscan housewives regularly pick up spit-roasted pheasant, partridge, and quail. Venison may be rare, but there's enough wild boar or goat to warrant inclusion of recipes in regional cookbooks. Once the game is properly aged, the marinating process begins. Refrigeration is not a national fetish in Italy, and the highly spiced marinades of previous centuries are still part of the culinary vocabulary. Hare and rabbit thrive in a bath of red wine and vinegar, sometimes fortified with cognac or brandy, and usually flavored by judicious quantities of bay leaves, thyme, rosemary, sage, peppercorns, and garlic. Raisins, sugar, and pignoli are ingredients in one recipe for hare, bringing this version of the dish even closer to its medieval or Renaissance forebears. This recipe is popular throughout all the northern provinces."

1 **6-pound hare**
all-purpose flour for dredging
3 **garlic cloves**
¼ **cup olive oil**
1 **fresh rosemary sprig**
1 **medium onion, chopped fine**
1 **carrot, chopped fine**
2 **celery ribs, chopped fine**
4 **cilantro sprigs, chopped fine**
1 **bay leaf**
½ **cup dry red wine**
½ **pound tomatoes, peeled, seeded, and cut into large pieces**
salt and freshly ground pepper to taste
2 **tablespoons golden raisins**
1 **tablespoon candied citron**
1 **tablespoon candied orange peel**
¼ **cup pine nuts**
1 **ounce unsweetened chocolate, grated**
3 **tablespoons red wine vinegar**

Cut the hare into serving pieces and flour lightly. Crush the garlic cloves and heat in the olive oil in a large sauté pan with a generous sprig of rosemary. When the oil is very hot, add the hare and sauté until the pieces begin to brown. Remove from the pan.

Make a *soffritto* by sautéing the onion, carrot, celery, cilantro, and bay leaf in the oil remaining in the pan until golden brown. Add the red wine and raise the heat to evaporate it, then add the tomatoes. Return the hare to the pan and simmer, covered, for 1½ hours or until just tender.

Add the salt and pepper, raisins, citron, orange peel, pine nuts, and chocolate. Simmer over very low heat for 10 minutes and add the wine vinegar. Turn the heat to high for 1 minute. Adjust the seasonings and serve.

CAMP-STYLE RABBIT STEW

SERVES 6

Frozen options are included here because these ingredients are often hard to find in fall hunting country.

2 fat rabbits, each about 3 pounds, dressed and cut into serving pieces
1 quart chicken broth or stock
1 cup dry white wine
3 cups water
2 teaspoons salt
1 bay leaf
¼ teaspoon dried thyme
3 cloves
3 peppercorns

4 large fresh parsley sprigs, stems removed
2 cups fresh or frozen green peas
12 fresh or frozen baby carrots
3 celery ribs, sliced thick, tops removed
4 large scallions, cut into ½-inch pieces
12 fresh or frozen baby onions

Place the rabbit pieces in a stew pot and add the broth, wine, water, salt, herbs, and spices. Bring to a boil, then lower the heat. Skim the surface as needed and simmer, covered, for 1 hour and 15 minutes or until the meat is almost tender. Add the peas, carrots, celery, scallions, and onions if fresh, simmering until the vegetables are cooked. Frozen baby onions won't stand much heat, so if using these, add them during the last few minutes. Remove the bay leaf and correct the seasoning if needed. Serve in large soup bowls with vegetables and broth and crusty sourdough bread for dunking. Buttered noodles and a green salad may be served on the side.

Rabbit in Mustard-Cream Sauce

Serves 4

2   rabbits, each about 3 pounds, dressed and cut into serving pieces
¼   cup olive oil
¼   cup unsalted butter
1   large onion
½   cup Dijon-style mustard, or more to taste
1   cup dry white wine
2   cups Sauce Demi-Glace (see Index), or more as needed
¾   cup heavy cream
½   cup cognac
salt and white pepper to taste

Reserve the rabbit livers for another use. Heat 3 tablespoons of the oil and 3 tablespoons of the butter in a large heavy pan and sauté the rabbit pieces, in batches if necessary, turning them to color on all sides. When the pieces are golden brown, transfer them to a platter.

Peel and mince the onion. In another heavy pan, large enough to hold all the rabbit pieces, heat the remaining oil and butter. Cook the onion over very low heat until almost translucent, but do not let it brown. Add the browned rabbit and all the juices on the platter and cook the rabbit and onion together for a few minutes. Add the mustard, wine, and enough Sauce Demi-Glace to cover the rabbit pieces. Add the cream and cognac and mix gently. Cover the pan and simmer the mixture for about 1 hour and 20 minutes. Check for tenderness and for taste. Add seasoning as needed and more mustard if you like.

BARON OF RABBIT
WITH TARRAGON CREAM

SERVES 6

3   barons of rabbit, saddle
     and hindquarters
     attached
2   tablespoons vegetable
     oil
1   bottle Riesling or
     zinfandel
juice of ½ lemon
2   fresh thyme sprigs
1   bay leaf
3   fresh tarragon sprigs
salt and pepper to taste
⅔   cup heavy cream
1   tablespoon chopped
     fresh tarragon
1   tablespoon coarse-grain
     prepared mustard
½   cup (¼ pound) butter
lemon juice to taste for
     finishing the sauce

Ask your butcher to dress the rabbits. Prepare a marinade with 1 tablespoon of the oil, the wine, juice of ½ lemon, thyme sprigs, bay leaf, tarragon sprigs, and salt and pepper. Pour the mixture over the rabbit in a glass or enameled container and turn the rabbit in the mixture to be sure it is coated all over. Marinate it overnight in the refrigerator.

Preheat the oven to 400°F.

Remove the rabbit from the marinade and pat it dry. Reserve the marinade. Season the rabbit with salt and pepper and place in an ovenproof pan coated with the remaining oil. Roast for 25 minutes. Remove the meat from the pan and let it rest while you prepare the sauce.

Remove the excess fat from the roasting pan and deglaze it with the wine from the marinade. Over moderate heat, let the liquid reduce by half. Add the cream and reduce again to the desired thickness. Remove the pan from the heat and add the chopped tarragon and mustard. Whisk in the butter, bit by bit. Finish the sauce with lemon juice to taste. Serve with linguine and sautéed fresh mushrooms.

LOIN OF RABBIT
WITH STUFFED FRESH FIGS

SERVES 6

6   rabbits, each 2½ to 3
     pounds
2   medium onions, diced
1   medium carrot, diced
3   garlic cloves, peeled and
     crushed
1   bay leaf
1   tablespoon juniper
     berries
2¾ cups Gewürztraminer
½   cup cider vinegar
2   tablespoons vegetable
     oil
¼   cup tomato paste
2   cups chicken stock
1   fresh rosemary sprig *or* 1
     teaspoon dried
1   fresh thyme sprig *or* 1
     teaspoon dried
salt and pepper to taste
½   cup (¼ pound) butter
¼   cup diced dried apricots
arrowroot as needed
Stuffed Fresh Figs with
     Pecan and Apricot
     Chutney (recipe
     follows)

Remove forequarters and hindquarters from rabbits and save for another use. Remove the loins, debone them, and save the bones for the sauce. Combine half of the diced onions, the carrot, garlic, bay leaf, juniper berries, 2 cups of the wine, the vinegar, and the oil to make a marinade. Pour it over the rabbit loins in a glass or enameled container and marinate in a cool place overnight.

_____

Preheat the oven to 350°F.
_____

Put the bones and trimmings in a roasting pan and add the vegetables from the marinade. Brown in the oven. After the bones have browned and the vegetables have become almost caramelized, add the tomato paste to the pan. Deglaze the pan with ¾ cup of the remaining wine and add the chicken stock, the liquid from the marinade, and the herbs. Simmer the mixture for 1½ hours, then strain. Set aside.

Split 6 of the loins lengthwise into halves. Take 1 whole loin and 2 halves and braid (see photos). Repeat with the remaining pieces. Secure the meats with wooden skewers. Sprinkle the loins with salt and pepper and seat them in 6 tablespoons of the butter in a hot pan, browning the meat on both sides. Finish cooking in a 350°F oven until the meat is medium-rare, about 25 to 30 minutes.

To finish the sauce, sauté the remaining onion and the apricots in the remaining 2 tablespoons butter over moderate heat until the onions are translucent. Add the strained stock and reduce the mixture to 1½ cups. Strain once again, then thicken with arrowroot if needed.

Remove the skewers from the meat. Cut 3 slices from each loin and fan them on a plate with the unsliced portion at the back. Spoon some sauce onto each plate. Garnish with stuffed figs (recipe follows) and winter vegetables.

STUFFED FRESH FIGS WITH PECAN AND APRICOT CHUTNEY

SERVES 6

2 tablespoons pecan pieces
½ cup chopped dried
    apricots
1 teaspoon cider vinegar
3 tablespoons apple juice
1 teaspoon dry sherry
1 teaspoon grated orange
    zest
6 large fresh figs

Preheat the oven to 350°F.

Toast the pecans on an un-buttered pan in the preheated oven for 12 to 15 minutes. Let them cool. Soak the apricots in a mixture of the vinegar, apple juice, and sherry until soft-ened. Add the pecans and the grated orange zest and com-bine. Sauté the mixture in a small saucepan over moderate heat for about 10 minutes, stir-ring. Cut the figs open along one side and stuff them with the chutney. Serve as a gar-nish for game.

BRAIDING LOINS OF RABBIT

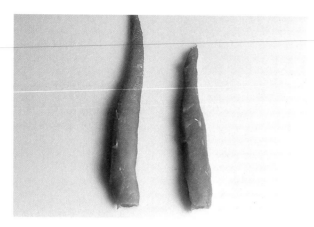

1. *Start by laying out 2 rabbit loins on a work surface.*

2. *With a thin-bladed sharp knife, carefully cut a shallow slit down the center of one of the loins.*

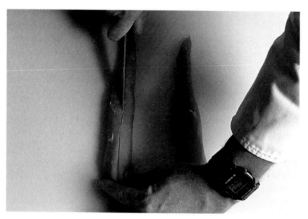

3. *Draw the knife down the length of the loin . . .*

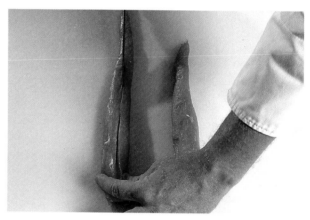

4. *. . . continuing the slit to the tip of the loin.*

5. *Now deepen the slit by cutting through again . . .*

6. *. . . all the way to the tip.*

7. *Carefully insert the knife into the slit at the top of the loin . . .*

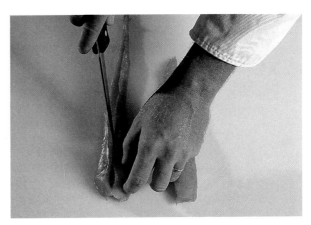

8. *. . . extending the cut as close to the top as possible to widen the opening without separating the 2 halves.*

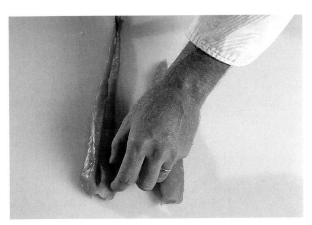

9. *Again run the knife down the slit to make sure you have cut all the way through.*

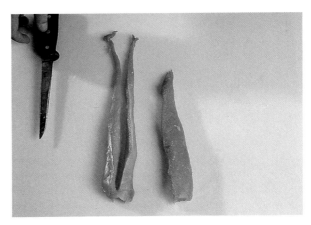

10. *You should now be able to open up the cut loin.*

11. *Pick up the cut loin and place the halves around the other loin as shown.*

12. *Carefully tuck the whole loin inside the other so it fits snugly into the cut loin at the top.*

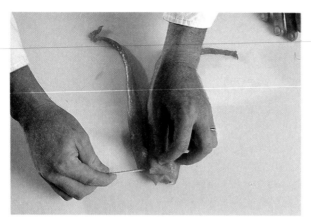

13. *Insert a sturdy toothpick (or a piece of a bamboo skewer) into one side.*

14. *Holding the middle loin in place . . .*

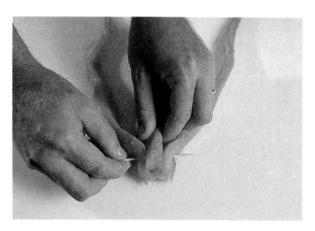

15. *. . . push the toothpick or skewer through all 3 pieces.*

16. *The pick should hold the strips of meat firmly in place.*

17. *Gently straighten the loin strips.*

18. *Spread them as shown to prepare for braiding.*

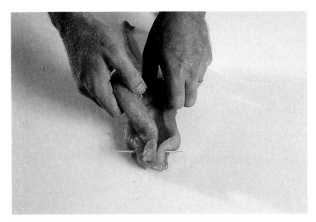

19. *Start the braid by picking up the middle (whole) loin with one hand.*

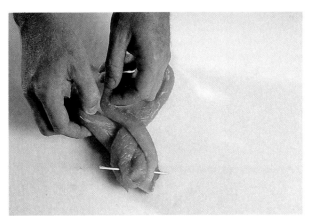

20. *With the other hand, cross the 2 loin halves underneath the whole loin (shown from the bottom).*

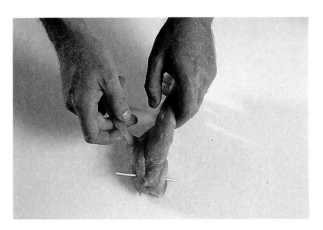

21. *Now begin weaving the strips . . .*

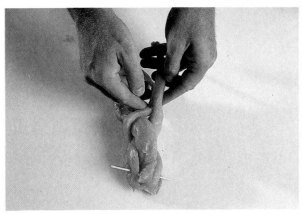

22. *. . . alternately moving the outer strips to the center as for a standard braid.*

23. *Continue braiding . . .*

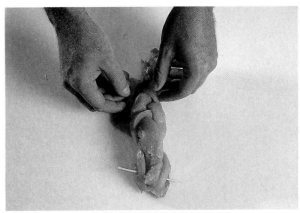

24. *. . . weaving the strands tightly but gently to avoid tearing the meat . . .*

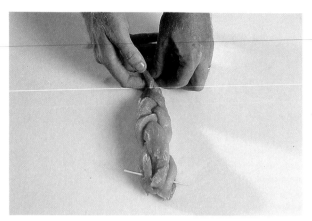

25. . . . *until you reach the tips of the loins and the braid is completed.*

26. Here are the same steps, showing the loins from a different angle:

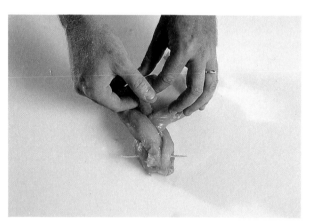

27. *Begin by crossing the outer strips under the center strip.*

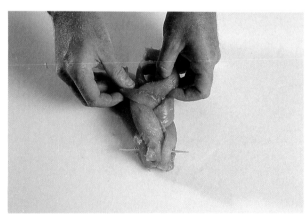

28. *Then continue braiding as shown . . .*

29. . . . *alternating strips . . .*

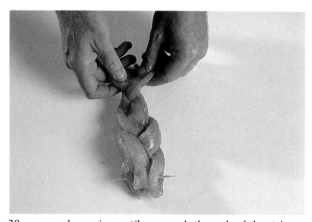

30. . . . *and weaving until you reach the ends of the strips.*

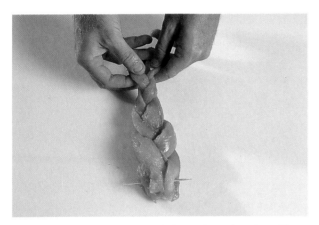

31. *Here is the completed braid shown from the other side.*

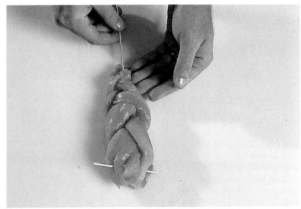

32. *To keep the braid intact, insert a bamboo skewer into the narrow end and push it toward the top.*

33. *Push the skewer through the braid until it emerges at the wide end.*

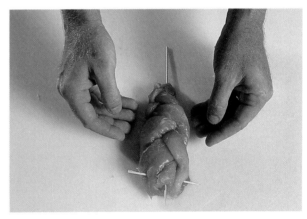

34. *Gently push the braided meat up the skewer from the narrow end to compact and round the braid.*

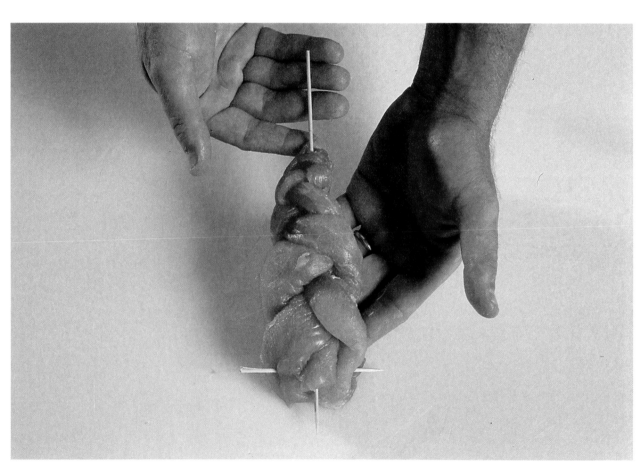

The finished rabbit loin braid, ready to be cooked.

MR. REYNAUD'S JUNIPER HARE

Jean Baptiste Reynaud is the managing director of Leith's restaurant in London, and his recipe consists of a rich stew made from the legs and neck of the hare, topped with slices from the succulent pink roast saddle. Ideally the pieces of hare should be marinated for 3 or 4 days in the wine. The stew part of the dish may be cooked the day before or even frozen well in advance and reheated when required.

1   hare, 4 to 5 pounds
½   pound carrots, peeled
       and sliced
¼   pound onions, peeled
       and sliced
1   celery rib, sliced
1   teaspoon salt
1   teaspoon crushed black
       peppercorns
1   bouquet garni made of
       bay leaf, 1 fresh
       thyme sprig, 1 bunch
       fresh parsley, tied
       together with string
½   bottle dry white wine
6   tablespoons red wine
       vinegar
all-purpose flour
vegetable oil for frying

½   cup chicken stock or
       water
1   garlic clove, crushed
¼   cup juniper berries
2   teaspoons tomato puree

Have the butcher cut the hare legs and the neck into pieces. Keep the back (saddle) whole but, using a small sharp knife, remove the outer layer of membrane and sinew. Place the pieces of hare, saddle included, in a glass or ceramic container and add all the vegetables, the salt, crushed peppercorns, and bouquet garni. Cover with the white wine and vinegar and leave in the refrigerator for 4 days. Move the pieces every 24 hours to ensure even marinating.

Remove all the pieces of hare and strain the vegetables, reserving the marinade. Pat the hare dry with a cloth. Set aside the saddle. Dust the rest of the pieces with flour. Heat a little oil in a frying pan and brown the floured joints well on all sides. Lift out and fry the vegetables.

Put all the vegetables and fried hare into a large sauce-pan and cover with the marinade. Add the stock or water, crushed garlic, juniper berries, and tomato puree. Bring to a boil, skim off any froth and fat, then simmer until really tender, 2½ to 3 hours. (A bit of overcooking will not hurt: on the contrary.) If the sauce is rather thin, lift out the solid ingredients and boil rapidly to reduce to a syrupy consistency, then pour back over the meat. Check the seasoning for salt and pepper.

Preheat the oven to 425°F.

Seal the saddle by sautéing briskly in hot oil in a shallow pan until brown all over. Then roast in the preheated oven for only 10 minutes. The flesh should still be pink near the bone. Carefully remove the 2 large fillets of roasted flesh from either side of the backbone and the 2 tiny fillets from underneath. Cut them into thin slices. Arrange these pink slices of saddle on top of the stewed hare and serve immediately.

CIVET DE LAPIN

SERVES 6

2   cottontail rabbits, cut
       into serving pieces
blood from the rabbit
2   quarts dry red wine
¼   cup cognac
1   fresh thyme sprig
3   garlic cloves, peeled and
       chopped
2   bay leaves
salt and pepper to taste
2   large onions
½   pound bacon
1   cup all-purpose flour
½   pound small white
       button mushrooms
juice of 2 lemons
2   pounds carrots
6   slices white bread
6   tablespoons clarified
       butter

Dress the rabbit, being sure to keep the blood; refrigerate the blood. Cut the rabbit into serving pieces and place in a glass or enameled container large enough to hold all the pieces. Make a marinade with the red wine, cognac, thyme, garlic, and bay leaves. Add a pinch of salt and a pinch of pepper. Pour the marinade over the rabbit and turn the pieces to be sure all are covered. Marinate the meat for 24 hours in the refrigerator.

The next day, peel and chop the onions. Cut the bacon into small cubes, put them in a pan of cold water, and bring to a boil. Pour off the water and sauté the bacon cubes until they are crispy. Lift the bacon cubes out of the pan and transfer to a plate but leave the fat in the pan. Remove the rabbit from the marinade, reserving the marinade, and pat the pieces dry. Put the chopped onion into the skillet with the bacon fat and set it over moderate heat. Add the rabbit pieces and let everything brown on all sides. Sprinkle with the flour and let

everything cook for 10 minutes longer, turning often. Add the marinade with all the flavoring ingredients, bring to a boil, and let the stew simmer, uncovered, for 1½ to 2 hours. While the rabbit is cooking, prepare the garnishes.

Wash and trim the mushrooms and put in a small saucepan. Add the lemon juice and a little salt and pepper. Bring to a boil and simmer for 2 to 3 minutes. Drain the mushrooms, transfer to a plate, and set aside. Scrub and scrape the carrots and cut them into olive shapes. Cook them in boiling salted water for about 5 minutes. Drain. With a heart-shaped cookie cutter, cut a large heart from each slice of bread. Brown the slices in clarified butter until golden brown on both sides.

When the rabbit is tender, turn off the heat, transfer the

Civet de Lapin.

pieces to a serving dish, and keep them warm. Reduce the sauce if necessary; it should have the consistency of a light syrup. Strain the sauce. Pour a ladle of the sauce into the reserved rabbit blood and pour the mixture back into the rest of the sauce. Do not let the sauce boil again after adding the blood. Season with salt and pepper to taste.

Garnish the rabbit with the bacon cubes, mushrooms, and carrots. Pour the sauce over it and arrange the heart-shaped croutons around the edge of the dish. Serve with spaetzle (see Index).

SAWMILL FARM RABBIT CHASSEUR

SERVES 6

2   rabbits, each 3½ pounds, dressed
1   large Spanish onion, diced
4   large carrots, diced
7   tablespoons vegetable oil
1   quart canned Italian-style peeled whole tomatoes
2   teaspoons salt
½   teaspoon ground black pepper
6   fresh tarragon sprigs *or* 1 tablespoon dried
½   teaspoon ground cloves
12   whole shallots, peeled
6   mushrooms, cut in half
6   bay leaves
⅓   cup all-purpose flour, approximately
3   tablespoons butter
6   garlic cloves, peeled
2   cups dry white wine
3   cups veal stock
1   tablespoon tomato puree

Cut each rabbit into 7 pieces—4 legs and 3 pieces of loin. Sauté the onion and carrots in 3 tablespoons of the oil until tender. Discard the oil and transfer the vegetables to a roasting pan large enough to hold all of the rabbit pieces. Pour off and reserve the liquid from the canned tomatoes. Puree the whole tomatoes in a food processor, then add the puree to the sautéed vegetables and spread the mixture evenly on the bottom of the roasting pan. Add half of the reserved tomato liquid. Add the salt, pepper, tarragon, cloves, whole shallots, mushrooms, and bay leaves.

Preheat the oven to 350°F.

Coat the pieces of rabbit lightly with flour and sauté them, in batches if necessary, in the butter and remaining oil for 8 minutes on each side. For the last 4 minutes, add the whole garlic cloves. Transfer the rabbit pieces and garlic to the roasting pan, placing them on top of the vegetables. Pour off the oil from the frying pan and deglaze the pan with the white wine. Bring it to a boil, then add veal stock and 1 tablespoon tomato puree. Let the mixture boil for 4 minutes. Pour it over the rabbit and vegetables. Cover the roasting pan with aluminum foil. Bake for 1 hour and 45 minutes.

A hearty game stew.

19. GAME STEW

Duringthe gastronomic debauchery that flourished in the fourteenth century, a medieval feast was triadic in form, with fish, game, and birds presented in sequence. There were often ten to sixteen different dishes in each course. Starting with a *musclade* of minnows followed by the *jollys* of salmon, one went through lamprey and various fish to porpoise and whale (both were considered fish). Then came roe deer and red deer, wild boar and hare before launching into the *grete byrdys rosted*, which encompassed plover, curlew, woodcock, heron, swan, stork, pheasant, ostrich, bustard, and lesser feathered bipeds such as the lark, figpecker, thrust, and ortolan. I don't know how good King Henry's lads were able to get back in their tin suits—but there was a fillip after each meal consisting of a *trappe* of *stuwe*, presumably for anybody who passed out between courses. In that bygone era of overkill, I wouldn't have made it much beyond the salmon's *jollys*, but I'd have done a lot of polite finger lickin' until the stew came along.

I can't think of any more satisfying meal than a robust game stew. There are those in the parish who would say the same thing about a ragout of beef or lamb, but that wild, unadulterated flavor elevates it from mere food to a transcendent ecstasy. A game stew doesn't cook; it catalyzes into a shower of rich juices and aroma. My fledgling experiments with game stew, however, were less than a joy to behold. These date back to schooldays, when a Stevens model 107 single shot in sixteen gauge cost $7. Boyhood enthusiasm was part of the problem. We were always in a hurry to get on with the hunting, so a midday squirrel, rabbit, or grouse hadn't even cooled before its brief tenure over the coals. To make matters worse, we used an aluminum pot because it was light and easy to carry. Our recipe was simple—cover the critter with "crick" water, then throw in an onion and carrot. The result was half-scorched, rubbery meat that we *had* to agree was the best we ever tasted. Teenage nimrod philosophy. It would have been more logical to bring along a peanut butter sandwich, but then an important element of hunting would have been lost. Every sportsman should learn how to cook a few basic dishes early on, especially if he travels off the beaten path. It can be a matter of comfortable survival in remote places; it is also an outdoor discipline with its own rewards. I've had meals in the woods that were as ambrosial as those in the hallowed precincts of La Tour d'Argent or La Couronne. Greater in some respects. But learning begins at home. You can't "practice" when you're a hundred miles from the nearest grocery store and every item in the grub box counts. One of the easiest meals to put together is a stew of any kind. It doesn't matter whether you use rabbit or an African sand grouse—meat simmered with vegetables equates to celestial dining.

Hearty game stews were the staple of many pioneer families in America and as disparate in content as their geography. Those settlers of the 1870s around Biscayne Bay in the vicinity of Miami, Florida, thrived on a stew called "soffgie," made from bear, opossum, racoon, or, more often, venison and thickened with the root of one of the cycads (*Zamia integrifolia*). Cycads are bushes closely related to the pines. After grinding, the root was used as a flour staple by the Big Cypress or Mikasuki Seminoles. The Indians called what is now the New River in Miami *Kuntihatchi* because of the great quantities of "coonties" root found in that region. Charles W. Pierce (*Pioneer Life in Southeast Florida*) observed:

> Farther on, on what was known as the "hunting grounds" lived John Addison, and beyond him a mile or so to the south at a place later known as Cutler, lived William Fuzzard. He was the last settler to the south on the west side of the bay. Fuzzard was manager of a Boston company that had built a steam starch factory for the making of starch from comtie, or coontie root, a sort of dwarf sago that grows all over the pine woods on the west side of the bay. This starch and the plant it is made from is called comtie by the Indians who taught the white man to use it as food. The Indians made a stew of all kinds of meat, but mostly venison, and when well cooked they thickened it with comtie and then called it "soffgie."

Among game stews, Brunswick stew is the most famous squirrel presentation, a papillary passion of Thomas Jefferson and John Adams, and while its origin is claimed by several geographic Brunswicks, its authorship was probably in Brunswick County, Virginia. It was a favorite dish in the colonial capital of Williamsburg. Rabbit was often substituted for squirrel, and indeed one is as good as the other, but modern restaurants usually build it around chicken, which is a non sequitur. Long absent from the American culinary scene is the cowboy's son-of-a-bitch stew, made from the heart, liver, kidneys, tongue, sweetbreads, and marrow gut of ruminant calves (beef or game). Hot chili peppers and onion provided the alembics for the distillation of these innards. It was said that a good SOB stew could burn the tailgate off a chuck wagon. This reminds me of the pre-Castro era, when Vic Barothy had his houseboat operation on the Rio Jucaro. We shot the migrating white-crested pigeons or *torcazas* at Cayo Matias between bouts on the bonefish flats. Chef Emanuel turned our squab into a noble stew, although it was a mite incendiary with the chilies. His personal pot, isolated on the back burner, would leave any Norte Americano breathing fire like a dragon. Personally, I want a game flavor to dominate and use condiments only sparingly. Colonel Ray Camp, one of the great outdoor writers of a generation past and ramrod of New York's Gourmet and Wine Club, immortalized Barnstable Coot Stew, although his "coot" was really a scoter. Scoter is luscious if you remove all the fatty tissue from the breast and souse the meat in your favorite marinade for about ten hours. Despite blandishments against marination, a little citric or acetic acid does wonders for game.

Venison stew is perhaps the most popular rendition, and for it to be really good you want a prime animal. Some methods of cooking will disguise imperfect flavors to a large extent. Frying is a good example. But stewing is opposite in effect; it gradually concentrates an essence—the ultimate flavor. Therefore, proper stew requires choice cuts of meat. Many people relegate the trimmings, or shanks, breast, flank, and neck to the pot after boning them out. Except for the neck (which can be made into a tasty stew by first simmering it for a couple of hours until the meat is easily forked from the bones), the other cuts are not going to make a classic ragout. I certainly wouldn't use the succulent tenderloin for anything but roasting or grilling, but the shoulder, rump, or round is ideal. You can turn the scraps into venisonburgers by adding ground pork or beef fat, but the cumulative effect is a McDonald's reject. Scraps can be utilized in making a clear soup with a couple of oven-browned bones, an onion, some celery, and seasoning. Slowly reduce the liquids by two-thirds. Strain it and you have a delectable broth, or it can be used as a stock instead of water when making a stew, which greatly enriches the flavor.

An important step in keeping venison tender is to take the time to excise as much of the sinew in the connective tissue as possible when you're cubing the meat. This can be done with a small sharp knife. Under heat the elastic sinew contracts, literally toughening the venison as it cooks. Sometimes pieces that went in the pot almost two inches square will bounce on your plate like miniature rubber balls. The sinew is not easy to cook, chew, or digest.

All stews are simple in construction. Even the old Chesapeake Bay fisherman's oyster stew is nothing more than a little country smoked ham or bacon cubed and crisped in the pan, a dollop of bay water added to simmer before slipping in the oysters with their inevitable soupçon of marsh mud. On a cold morning in a duck blind, it's pure nectar.

The great thing about a stew is that you can get a number of meals out of it. On my annual trek to Montana for the fall brown trout, which coincides with the big game and bird seasons, base camp is Tom McNally's home at Ennis. Although we do some innovative cooking (Tom has composed sonnets such as railbird breast steamed with butter and herbs enclosed inside a baking potato), having a stew on hand is insurance against those late-night returns, after a day of hunting or fishing, when poplars are shivering in the wind and a stick-to-the-ribs meal is for lords spiritual and temporal. Our favorite is elk, undeniably the classic red meat in wild or domestic kingdoms. NcNally has a cast-iron Dutch oven big enough to serve as a base plate for 120 mm mortar. Which is about the right size. Of course the longer a stew sits, the better the flavor and texture. It can be refrigerated and reheated, and it freezes perfectly.

The only hazard in making a stew is burning it, and that's not uncommon if you use a thin metal pot. You can't beat heavy cast iron with a tight-fitting lid, because it maintains a uniform heat. Cast iron may show a trace of rust at times, but it's harmless; in fact it's a kind of natural Geritol. For maintenance, after scalding the pot (no soap), take a paper towel and wipe the interior with a little vegetable oil. Stewing is done at a simmer, which by definition is cooking at 170 to 180°F. Eyeballed in camp without using a thermometer, the liquid "shakes," with tiny bubbles popping in the surface. Gradually the volume will reduce to a fragrant infusion. Depending on how long it cooks, or how often the stew is reheated, add just enough water to keep it from evaporating to an irreducible mush or becoming scorched. A bit of sherry or dry white wine helps.

There are two schools of thought on when to add the vegetables. In what is now euphemistically known as *nouvelle cuisine*, the carrots, onions, and celery look like they were faceted by a myopic lapidary and are tossed in at the last minute to retain their vitamin "integrity." Personally, if I want an honest vegetable, I'll munch on it before eating a stew. A stew is a marriage of flavors after a long courtship—like hambone-flavored pot liquor (with hot biscuits for dipping) or navy beans tunneled with diced onion and bacon, then laced with molasses and slow-cooked in the coals of a day-long campfire. Tiny slivers of uncooked vegetables don't do anything but clutter up the pot. I chunk my carrots and celery, quarter or halve the onions, depending on size, and whack potatoes or turnips into forkable slabs so they can release their juices and sop up the others. When a big carrot has soaked in an elk stew for three or four days, it may not be the nutritious root urban food mavens have in mind, but by that time the carrot and elk are no longer a gastronomic cliché.

The prolific number of stew recipes is more illusory than real. By adding a carrot, subtracting the celery, or splashing the pot with sherry, the chef might claim an original version. It's an innocent practice (and one not perpetuated here, where only the classic Brunswick Stew is presented). There are very few stews that follow a strict ingredient formula. In a spike-camp you may lack an ingredient or two, but game is the name.

BRUNSWICK STEW

SERVES 6

2   large squirrels *or* 3 small
    ones, dressed and cut
    into serving pieces
2   quarts chicken broth
¼   cup diced bacon
1   cup chopped onion
2   cups diced potatoes
2   cups baby lima or butter
    beans
2   cups fresh corn kernels
2   cups drained canned
    plum tomatoes
½   teaspoon freshly ground
    black pepper
2   teaspoons Worcestershire
    sauce

2   teaspoons sugar
2   tablespoons butter or
    margarine

Put the squirrel pieces and chicken broth in a large kettle and simmer until the meat is tender—about 1¼ hours. Skim to remove fat and foam. Remove the squirrel from the broth and, when cool, remove the meat from the bones. Return the meat to the kettle along with the bacon, onion, potatoes, and beans. Continue to simmer until the vegetables are just tender—about 30 minutes. Add corn and all remaining ingredients except butter. Cook for 10 minutes longer, stirring to prevent sticking. Serve in bowls with a lump of butter whisked through.

Note:

Rabbit or pheasant may be substituted for squirrel.

20. BARBECUE METHODS

Barbecuing probably began when the first troglodyte man threw a dinosaur chop on the fire; in fact that very primitive method still exists in remote places. I have made a half dozen trips up the Orinoco, once as far as the Jasubueteri Indian Region of Venezuela, and at that time these members of the Waikas were still preparing monkey, parrot, tapir, capybara, ocelot, anteater, and various other game by placing them directly on the coals without skinning or even drawing the entrails. This resulted in a peculiar homogeneity in the end products. The meats, seasoned with wood ash, obviously not a salt surrogate as ash contains no sodium chloride, were, to say the least, well-done, if not incinerated. But the tribal practice of "a barbecue," whether in the jungles of South America or in Westport, Connecticut, is probably the most versatile form of feeding a small or large group of people.

My wife, Patti, and I once hosted a sit-down buffet at our home for participants in the Gold Cup Fishing Tournament, an annual event in Palm Beach. Although the original projection was for 200 guests, the number swelled to 300 a week before the opening gun, and at dinnertime well over that number attended. Fortunately we have a spacious lawn, and under a tent rented for the occasion that would almost qualify at Barnum and Bailey we delivered twenty-six fish and game dishes. There were a number of preprepared foods such as smoked salmon, smoked goldeye, and smoked pheasant, but others— such as the venison, wild pigs, snow geese, and buffalo steaks and roasts—required cooking until, or at, zero hour. Despite chaos and premonitions of catastrophe, everything came out *à point*, thanks to a variety of grills and that magical instrument, the Meat

Lou Gainey at the barbecue.

Thermicator. Without it, eyeballing for doneness while dashing from fire to fire would have been beyond our capacity to cope.

Americans spent $5 billion for outdoor cooking equipment last year. This figure encompasses grills, wire baskets, tongs, skewers, spatulas, basting brushes, and all the other pyrotechnic paraphernalia familiar to brothers of the singed eyebrow. Today there are nearly ninety million grills in home operation consuming charcoal briquets at the rate of more than 740 million tons annually. This doesn't reflect the "true effort" figure in this age of lava rock and ceramic briquets. There was an era, shortly after Henry Ford invented the briquet, when the chef often got marinated along with the venison chops and guests took bets on whether they would dine or call the fire department. No longer a macho sport, barbecuing has become an art form with somewhat more sophisticated equipment, including gas and electric grills.

Basically, there are four types of charcoal grills: (1) the small portable outdoor tabletop with or without a lid; (2) the open brazier, which is an uncovered grill, although some have hoods and rotisseries; (3) the covered cooker, which has a lid; and (4) the water smoker, which is a tall cylindrical cooker featuring a water pan. I own all four types as well as a large cement barbecue "pit," which is a permanent lawn fixture. However, the two that get the most use are the covered cooker and the water smoker. The latter differs from the other grills in that water pan over the fire bed. Presoaked wood chips or chunks are added to the coals, creating a moist smoke that prevents the product from dehydrating. Some of the meat juices will drop into the pan, but these drippings are collected ambrosia. An herbed marinade, or wine, beer, or cider can be added to the pan before cooking, which not only imparts flavor to the food as the liquid simmers but also results in a savory base for a sauce or gravy. This method of cooking is an ideal substitute for the sportsman who doesn't have a smokehouse. A water smoker is also versatile: if you remove the pan, the unit can be used as a regular barbecue grill; if you eliminate the wood and don't fill the pan, it can be used for roasting; and if you eliminate the wood and fill the water pan, it operates as a steamer.

The following recipe is for a festive game cookout for twelve. For specific information on smoking wild turkey and roasting a whole pig, see Chapters 10 and 14, respectively.

Overleaf: Venison and vegetable brochettes on the grill.

Grand Lake Stream
Venison Cookout

SERVES 12

6   pounds venison top
    round, outside round,
    or rump, cut into 1½-
    to 2-inch cubes

MARINADE

1½ cups olive oil	1 tablespoon seasoned salt	4 garlic cloves, peeled and minced fine, or more to taste
1 cup vegetable oil	3 tablespoons sweet Hungarian paprika	2 tablespoons dried tarragon *or* 1 tablespoon chopped fresh
¼ cup soy sauce		
juice of 1 large lemon		

SAUCE

1 cup (½ pound) unsalted butter or margarine	4 garlic cloves, peeled and minced fine	1 teaspoon dried tarragon
		1 tablespoon lemon juice

GARNISHES

6 yellow or Spanish onions (1½ pounds total)	24 large white mushrooms	Place the venison in a non-metallic bowl. Combine the marinade ingredients and stir until well blended. Pour the marinade over the meat and marinate for 6 hours or more,
6 tomatoes (2¼ pounds total)	1 pound white rice, cooked	
6 green bell peppers (2¼ pounds total)	¼ cup finely chopped fresh parsley	

rotating the meat at least twice.

Combine the sauce ingredients in a saucepan and simmer until the garlic is soft and the ingredients are blended. You won't need this until serving time; set aside.

Leave the onions unskinned. Wash the tomatoes and cut in half crosswise. Trim the peppers, discarding stems, ribs, and seeds, and cut into quarters. Pluck the stems from the mushrooms and reserve for another use. Place these vegetables in a shallow roasting pan and deliver to the grill.

When the briquets are glowing, throw on a handful of wet hickory chips. Place the unpeeled onions on the grill and cook with the lid on for about 20 minutes or until fork-tender. Use tongs to roll the onions around so they cook evenly. The outer skin will burn. When you remove the onions from the fire, if your grill is adjustable, elevate to about 10 inches above the fire bed and add more hickory chips. Arrange the tomato halves, pepper quarters, and mushrooms on the grill. Cook these for about 15 to 20 minutes, turning the tomatoes with tongs; their skins will

crack, turn golden, and blister. Flip the pepper pieces over once or twice. The peppers will blister and blacken in spots. The mushrooms will shrivel a bit, gaining a crunchy texture, but they will moisten in the marinade bath to come.

By this time the onions will be cool enough to handle. Hold each onion with a paper towel and gently press downward (toward stem end) and inward. The steamy globes will pop out of their skins. Cut the onions crosswise into halves and place in the roasting pan. Peel any extensive black skin patches off the peppers with your fingers and combine in the pan with the tomatoes and mushrooms.

Remove the venison from the bowl and, after laying it flat on the grill, drizzle the marinade over the vegetables and place the pan in a warm oven.

Cooking the venison is also an eyeballing process. If your fire is fading, you may want to lower the grill or add more briquets. Initially the residual marinade will drip onto the coals and flare, but don't be concerned as it only sears the meat. Brown the venison on all sides, add more hickory chips, and put the cover on

again. I like my venison medium-rare, cooked crusty on the outside but mostly pink on the inside, which is an internal temperature of 140°F at the center.

When you are ready to serve, line up 12 warmed plates on your work counter and spoon a small bed of cooked white rice in the center of each. Fan venison cubes over the rice. From the roasting pan, spoon out individual vegetables, artfully arranging pieces of pepper, onions, tomatoes, and mushrooms around the perimeter of each dish. It can be very decorative—a red, green, and golden border. Pour the remaining marinade into that standby saucepan of melted butter, heat quickly to a sizzle, and splash over the venison. Shower each serving with very finely chopped parsley and deliver to the table.

Obviously, this is no dish for a big grand cru wine as it would be lost in the diversity of pungent flavors. I heartily endorse a dry rosé from the Loire Valley such as a Cabernet d'Anjou Rosé or, to add sparkle to a festive occasion, a Perrier Jouet Fleur de Champagne Rosé. A mint or lemon sorbet is the perfect curtain call.

BIBLIOGRAPHY AND
SUPPLEMENTAL READING

Ali-Bab (Henry Babinsky). *Gastronomique pratique*. Paris: Flammarion, 1907.

Apicius. *De Re Coquinaria* (as *The Roman Cookery Book*). Edited by Barbara Flower and Elisabeth Rosenbaum. London: Harrap, 1958.

Aresty, Esther B. *The Delectable Past*. London: George Allen and Unwin, 1965.

Ashbrook, Frank G., and Edna State. *Cooking Wild Game*. New York: Orange Judd Publishing Co., 1945.

Beeton, Isabella. *Beeton's Book of Household Management*. London: Beeton, 1861.

Belden, Robert C., and William B. Frankenberger. *Management of Feral Hogs in Florida—Past, Present and Future*. Gainesville, Florida:

Florida Game and Fresh Water Fish Commission, Wildlife Research Laboratory, 1977.

Belden, Robert C., and Michael R. Pelton. "Wallows of the European Wild Hog in the Mountains of East Tennessee." *Journal of the Tennessee Academy of Science*. Volume 51, Number 3, 1976.

Bennett, Logan Johnson. *The Blue-winged Teal, Its Ecology and Management*. Ames, Iowa: Collegiate Press Inc., 1938.

Brillat-Savarin, J. A. *La Physiologie du goût*. Paris: A. Sautelet, 1826.

Camp, Raymond R. *Game Cookery in America and Europe*. New York: Coward-McCann, 1958.

Cosman, Madeleine Pelner. *Fabulous Feasts, Medieval Cookery and Ceremony*. New York: George Braziller, 1976.

de la Valdene, Guy. *Making Game: An Essay on Woodcock*. Oshkosh, Wisconsin: Willow Creek Press, 1985.

Elias, Norbert. *The Court Society*. Oxford: Basil Blackwell, 1969.

Fernow, Berthold, ed. *The Records of New Amsterdam from 1653 to 1674*. 7 vols. New York: New York Historical Society, 1897.

Forrester, Rex. *The Chopper Boys*. Christchurch, New Zealand: Whitcoulls Publishers, 1983.

Francatelli, Charles Elmé. *The Modern Cook*. London: Richard Bentley, 1846.

Harbour, Dave. *Advanced Wild Turkey Hunting & World Records.* Piscataway, New Jersey: New Century Publishers, 1985.

Herbert, Henry William (Frank Forester). *American Game in Its Season.* New York: Charles Scribner, 1853.

Hyde, Daton O., ed. *Raising Wild Ducks in Captivity.* New York: E. P. Dutton, 1947.

Josephson, Matthew. *The Robber Barons.* New York: Harcourt Brace, 1934.

Kalchreuter, Heribert. *The Woodcock (Die Waldschnepfe).* Mainz, Germany: Verlag Dieter Hoffmann, 1982.

Louthridge, Rev. R. M. *Dictionary of the Muskokee or Creek Language in Creek and English.* Elder David M. Hodge, Interpreter; Red Ford, Indian Territory, 1853.

Montagné, Prosper. *Larousse Gastronomique,* edited by Charlotte Turgeon and Nina Froud. New York: Crown Publishers, 1961.

Morrell, Parker. *Diamond Jim.* New York: Simon & Schuster, 1934.

O'Connor, Richard. *The Scandalous Mr. Bennett.* New York: Doubleday, 1962.

Reiger, George. *The Wings of Dawn.* New York: Stein and Day, 1980.

Silver, H., and N. F. Colovos. *Nutritive evaluation of some forage rations of deer.* New Hampshire Fish and Game Department: Technical Circular 15, 1957.

Soyer, Alexis. *The Pantropheon, A History of Food and Its Preparation in Ancient Times.* A reprint of the 1853 edition. London: Paddington Press, 1977.

Thomas, Davis, and Karin Ronnefeldt, eds. *People of the First Man, Life Among the Plains Indians in Their Final Days of Glory: The Firsthand Account of Prince Maximilian's Expedition up the Missouri River 1833–34.* New York: E. P. Dutton, 1976.

Tome, Philip. *Pioneer Life or Thirty Years a Hunter.* A reprint of the 1854 edition. Harrisburg, Pennsylvania: privately printed by The Aurand Press, 1928.

Walsh, Roy E. *Gunning the Chesapeake, Duck and Goose Shooting on the Eastern Shore.* Cambridge, Maryland: Tidewater Publishers, 1960.

Wildlife Management Institute. *Big Game of North America, Ecology and Management,* compiled and edited by John L. Schmidt and Douglas L. Gilbert. Harrisburg, Pennsylvania: Stackpole Books, 1978.

Winston, Frank A. *Status, Movement and Management of the Mourning Dove in Florida.* Florida Game and Fresh Water Fish Commission, Technical Bulletin No. 2, Pittman-Robertson Projects, 1954.

Game Suppliers— Mail Order

Cavin's Game Bird Farm
9215 Sylvan Hills Road
Sherwood, AR 71226
Quail

Czimer Foods
Route 1, Box 285
Lockport, IL 60441
Venison, antelope, beaver, mountain sheep, bear, elk, buffalo, other game

Durham Meat Company
160 Sunol Street
P.O. Box 16158
San Jose, CA 95159
Buffalo

Enzed Traders
P.O. Box 7108
Ann Arbor, MI 48107
Venison

Fare Game Food Unlimited
P.O. Box 18431
Rochester, NY 14618
Buffalo, venison, all kinds of game birds

Highland Game Birds
Box 54
Franktown, CO 80116
Quail, mallard duck, wild turkey, pheasant, chukar partridge

Iron Gate Products
424 W. 54th Street
New York, NY 10019
Venison, wild boar, bear, elk, beaver, hare, chukar partridge, woodcock, quail, mallard duck

Jackson Cold Storage & Distributors
Box A
Jackson, WY 83001
Buffalo

Jugtown Mountain Smokehouse
77 Park Avenue
Flemington, NJ 08822
Pheasant, mallard duck

L & L Pheasantry
East Mountain Road
Hegins, RD 2, PA 17938
Pheasants, wild turkey, chukar partridge

Lobel Brothers Prime Meats
1096 Madison Avenue
New York, NY 10028
Pheasant, squab, quail, rabbit, venison

Manchester Farms
G.P.O. 97
Dalzell, SC 29040
Quail

The Native Game Company
1105 W. Oliver
P.O. Box 1046
Spearfish, SD 57783

Buffalo, wild boar, bear, all kinds of venison and game birds

Palmetto Pigeon Plant
333 Broad Street
Sumter, SC 29150
Squab

George H. Shaffer
1174 Lexington Avenue
New York, NY 10028
Pheasant, venison, wild boar, snow grouse, woodcock

Squab Producers of California
409 Primo Way
Modesto, CA 95351
Squab, pheasant, chukar partridge, quail

INDEX

Page numbers referring to illustrations are set in **boldface**.

Photo Credits

Page iii: The Image Bank
Pages x–xi, 20–21: The Image Bank
Page xiv: George Reiger
Pages 2–3: George Reiger
Page 12: George Reiger
Page 32: George Reiger
Pages 36–37: Arie deZanger
Page 42: Arthur Oglesby
Pages 44–45: Arthur Oglesby
Page 58: Arie deZanger
Page 68: George Reiger
Page 80: Arthur Oglesby
Page 88: Arie deZanger
Page 100: Arie deZanger
Pages 122–123: Arie deZanger
Page 126: Arie deZanger
Page 129: George Reiger
Pages 148–149: George Reiger
Page 152: George Reiger
Page 158: Thomas Kitchin/Tom Stack & Associates
Pages 168–169: Arie deZanger
Pages 186–187: The Explorers
Page 200: Jake Eiesenmann
Page 220: The Thomas Gilcrease Institute of American History and Art, Tulsa, Oklahoma
Page 232: Robert Reed
Page 238: © Stock Imagery, 1991
Page 266: Arie deZanger
Page 274: Arie deZanger
Pages 276–277: Arie deZanger
Page 280: Arie deZanger
Page 288: Arie deZanger

(All other photos by Donna Turner)

CONVERSION TABLES

The conversions that follow are not precise; rather they have been rounded for convenience. To get more accurate conversions, use the following equivalents:

1 teaspoon = 5 milliliters
1 tablespoon = 15 milliliters
1 fluid ounce = 30 milliliters
1 cup = 240 milliliters
1 pint = 440 milliliters
1 quart = 0.95 liter

1 ounce = 28.35 grams
1 pound = 454 grams

1 inch = 2.54 centimeters

QUARTS (qt) TO LITERS (L)

Quarts		Liters
1 qt	=	1 L
1½ qt	=	1½ L
2 qt	=	2 L
2½ qt	=	2⅓ L
3 qt	=	2¾ L
4 qt	=	3¼ L
5 qt	=	4¼ L
6 qt	=	5½ L
7 qt	=	6½ L
8 qt	=	7½ L
9 qt	=	8½ L
10 qt	=	9½ L

OUNCES (oz) TO GRAMS (g)

Ounces		Grams
1 oz	=	30 g
2 oz	=	60 g
3 oz	=	85 g
4 oz	=	115 g
5 oz	=	140 g
6 oz	=	180 g
7 oz	=	200 g
8 oz	=	225 g
9 oz	=	250 g
10 oz	=	285 g
11 oz	=	300 g
12 oz	=	340 g
13 oz	=	370 g
14 oz	=	400 g
15 oz	=	425 g
16 oz	=	450 g
20 oz	=	570 g
24 oz	=	680 g
28 oz	=	700 f
32 oz	=	900 g

FAHRENHEIT TO CELSIUS

Fahrenheit		Celsius	Gas Settings
170°F	=	77°C	
180°F	=	82°C	
190°F	=	88°C	
200°F	=	95°C	
225°F	=	110°C	¼
250°F	=	120°C	½
275°F	=	140°C	1
300°F	=	150°C	2
325°F	=	165°C	3
350°F	=	180°C	4
375°F	=	190°C	5
400°F	=	205°C	6
425°F	=	220°C	7
450°F	=	230°C	8
475°F	=	245°C	9
500°F	=	260°C	
525°F	=	275°C	
550°F	=	290°C	

POUNDS (lb) TO GRAMS (g) AND KILOGRAMS (kg)

Pounds		Grams Kilograms	Pounds		Grams Kilograms
1 lb	=	450 g	5 lb	=	2¼ kg
1¼ lb	=	565 g	5½ lb	=	2½ kg
1½ lb	=	675 g	6 lb	=	2¾ kg
1¾ lb	=	800 g	6½ lb	=	3 kg
2 lb	=	900 g	7 lb	=	3¼ kg
2½ lb	=	1,125 g; 1¼ kg	7½ lb	=	3½ lb
3 lb	=	1,350 g	8 lb	=	3¾ kg
3½ lb	=	1,500 g; 1½ kg	9 lb	=	4 kg
4 lb	=	1,800 g	10 lb	=	4½ kg
4½ lb	=	2 kg			

INCHES (in) TO CENTIMETERS (cm)

Inches		Centimeters	Inches		Centimeters
1/16 in	=	1/4 cm	10 in	=	25 cm
1/8 in	=	1/2 cm	11 in	=	28 cm
1/2 in	=	1 1/2 cm	12 in	=	30 cm
3/4 in	=	2 cm	13 in	=	33 cm
1 in	=	2 1/2 cm	14 in	=	35 cm
1 1/2 in	=	4 cm	15 in	=	38 cm
2 in	=	5 cm	16 in	=	41 cm
2 1/2 in	=	6 1/2 cm	17 in	=	43 cm
3 in	=	8 cm	18 in	=	46 cm
3 1/2 in	=	9 cm	19 in	=	48 cm
4 in	=	10 cm	20 in	=	51 cm
4 1/2 in	=	11 1/2 cm	21 in	=	53 cm
5 in	=	13 cm	22 in	=	56 cm
5 1/2 in	=	14 cm	23 in	=	58 cm
6 in	=	15 cm	24 in	=	61 cm
6 1/2 in	=	16 1/2 cm	25 in	=	63 1/2 cm
7 in	=	18 cm	30 in	=	76 cm
7 1/2 in	=	19 cm	35 in	=	89 cm
8 in	=	20 cm	40 in	=	102 cm
8 1/2	=	21 1/2 cm	45 in	=	114 cm
9 in	=	23 cm	50 in	=	127 cm
9 1/2 in	=	24 cm			

Special thanks to Christine Benton, Stanley Drate, Len Fleischman, Lynda Klich, Madeleine Morel and Dave Zable.